Henry Morley

A Miscellany containing Richard of Bury's Philobiblon and the the

Basilikon Doron of King James I

Henry Morley

A Miscellany containing Richard of Bury's Philobiblon and the the Basilikon Doron of King James I

ISBN/EAN: 9783743397590

Manufactured in Europe, USA, Canada, Australia, Japa

Cover: Foto ©Thomas Meinert / pixelio.de

Manufactured and distributed by brebook publishing software (www.brebook.com)

Henry Morley

A Miscellany containing Richard of Bury's Philobiblon and the the

Basilikon Doron of King James I

SOUTHEY'S LIFE OF NELSON

SCOTT'S

DEMONOLOGY AND WITCHCRAFT

COLERIDGE'S TABLE TALK

[A.D. 1813 TO A.D. 1834]

WITH INTRODUCTIONS BY HENRY MORLEY

LL.D., PROFESSOR OF ENGLISH LITERATURE AT
UNIVERSITY COLLEGE, LONDON

LONDON
GEORGE ROUTLEDGE AND SONS
BROADWAY, LUDGATE HILL
GLASGOW AND NEW YORK
1888

TALES AND SONGS OF IRELAND

AND THE

NORTH OF ENGLAND

MARIA EDGEWORTH

THOMAS CROFTON CROKER

ALLAN CUNNINGHAM

[A.D. 1800 TO A.D. 1839]

WITH INTRODUCTIONS BY HENRY MORLEY

LL.D., PROFESSOR OF ENGLISH LITERATURE AT
UNIVERSITY COLLEGE, LONDON

LONDON
GEORGE ROUTLEDGE AND SONS
BROADWAY, LUDGATE HILL
GLASGOW AND NEW YORK
1888

PRAED'S ESSAYS

WALKER'S ORIGINAL

COBBETT'S
ADVICE TO YOUNG MEN

[A.D. 1821 TO A.D. 1835]

WITH INTRODUCTIONS BY HENRY MORLEY

LL D , PROFESSOR OF ENGLISH LITERATURE AT
UNIVERSITY COLLEGE, LONDON

LONDON
GEORGE ROUTLEDGE AND SONS
BROADWAY, LUDGATE HILL
GLASGOW AND NEW YORK
1888

PRAED'S ESSAYS.

CONTENTS.

CONTENTS.

VESTIGES

OF THE

NATURAL HISTORY OF CREATION

EMERSON'S ESSAYS

[A.D. 1844 TO A.D. 1870]

APPENDIX
A MISCELLANY

WITH INTRODUCTIONS BY HENRY MORLEY

I.L.D., PROFESSOR OF ENGLISH LITERATURE AT
UNIVERSITY COLLEGE, LONDON

LONDON
GEORGE ROUTLEDGE AND SONS
BROADWAY, LUDGATE HILL
GLASGOW AND NEW YORK
1888

PLAYS AND POEMS

BY

GEORGE PEELE

DRAYTON'S BARONS' WARS

HOOKER'S ECCLESIASTICAL POLITY

BOOKS I.-IV.

[A.D. 1584 TO A.D. 1603]

WITH INTRODUCTIONS BY HENRY MORLEY

LL.D., PROFESSOR OF ENGLISH LITERATURE AT
UNIVERSITY COLLEGE, LONDON

LONDON
GEORGE ROUTLEDGE AND SONS
BROADWAY, LUDGATE HILL
GLASGOW AND NEW YORK
1888

BACON'S ESSAYS

PLAYS AND POEMS
BY
BEN JONSON,

HERRICK'S HESPERIDES

[A.D. 1597 TO A.D. 1648]

WITH INTRODUCTIONS BY HENRY MORLEY
LL.D., PROFESSOR OF ENGLISH LITERATURE AT
UNIVERSITY COLLEGE, LONDON

LONDON
GEORGE ROUTLEDGE AND SONS
BROADWAY, LUDGATE HILL
GLASGOW AND NEW YORK
1888

DON QUIXOTE

BURLESQUE PLAYS AND POEMS

[A.D. 1605 TO A.D. 1825]

WITH INTRODUCTIONS BY HENRY MORLEY

LL.D., PROFESSOR OF ENGLISH LITERATURE AT
UNIVERSITY COLLEGE, LONDON

LONDON
GEORGE ROUTLEDGE AND SONS
BROADWAY, LUDGATE HILL
GLASGOW AND NEW YORK
1888

HOBBES'S LEVIATHAN

HARRINGTON'S OCEANA

FAMOUS PAMPHLETS

[A.D. 1644 TO A.D. 1795]

WITH INTRODUCTIONS BY HENRY MORLEY

LL.D., PROFESSOR OF ENGLISH LITERATURE AT
UNIVERSITY COLLEGE, LONDON

LONDON
GEORGE ROUTLEDGE AND SONS
BROADWAY, LUDGATE HILL
GLASGOW AND NEW YORK
1888

BUTLER'S HUDIBRAS

IZAAK WALTON'S LIVES

PLAYS FROM MOLIÈRE

[A.D. 1663 TO A.D. 1733]

WITH INTRODUCTIONS BY HENRY MORLEY

LL.D., PROFESSOR OF ENGLISH LITERATURE AT
UNIVERSITY COLLEGE, LONDON

LONDON
GEORGE ROUTLEDGE AND SONS
BROADWAY, LUDGATE HILL
GLASGOW AND NEW YORK
1888

LOCKE ON CIVIL GOVERNMENT

FILMER'S PATRIARCHA

LIFE OF THOMAS ELLWOOD

AND

DEFOE'S

HISTORY OF THE PLAGUE YEAR

[A.D. 1680 TO A.D. 1722]

WITH INTRODUCTIONS BY HENRY MORLEY

LL.D., PROFESSOR OF ENGLISH LITERATURE AT
UNIVERSITY COLLEGE, LONDON

LONDON

GEORGE ROUTLEDGE AND SONS

BROADWAY, LUDGATE HILL

GLASGOW AND NEW YORK

1888

BUTLER'S ANALOGY

JOHNSON'S RASSELAS

VOLTAIRE'S CANDIDE

AND

GOLDSMITH'S

VICAR OF WAKEFIELD

[A.D. 1736 TO A.D. 1766]

WITH INTRODUCTIONS BY HENRY MORLEY

LL.D., PROFESSOR OF ENGLISH LITERATURE AT
UNIVERSITY COLLEGE, LONDON

LONDON
GEORGE ROUTLEDGE AND SONS
BROADWAY, LUDGATE HILL
GLASGOW AND NEW YORK
1888

STERNE'S TRISTRAM SHANDY

SPEECHES AND LETTERS

OF

BURKE

SHERIDAN'S PLAYS

[A.D. 1759 TO A.D. 1779]

WITH INTRODUCTIONS BY HENRY MORLEY

LL.D., PROFESSOR OF ENGLISH LITERATURE AT
UNIVERSITY COLLEGE, LONDON

LONDON

GEORGE ROUTLEDGE AND SONS

BROADWAY, LUDGATE HILL

GLASGOW AND NEW YORK

1888

www.ingramcontent.com/pod-product-compliance
Lightning Source LLC
Chambersburg PA
CBHW031403270326
41929CB00010BA/1306

A MISCELLANY

CONTAINING

RICHARD OF BURY'S PHILOBIBLON

THE BASILIKON DŌRON OF KING JAMES I.

MONKS AND GIANTS
BY JOHN HOOKHAM FRERE

THE CYPRESS CROWN
BY DE LA MOTTE FOUQUÉ
Translated out of German into English by a Dutchman

AND

THE LIBRARY
A POEM BY GEORGE CRABBE

WITH AN INTRODUCTION BY HENRY MORLEY

LL.D., PROFESSOR OF ENGLISH LITERATURE AT
UNIVERSITY COLLEGE, LONDON

LONDON
GEORGE ROUTLEDGE AND SONS
BROADWAY, LUDGATE HILL
GLASGOW AND NEW YORK
1888

MORLEY'S UNIVERSAL LIBRARY

IS NOW COMPLETED WITH

A MISCELLANY.

This Volume contains a Series of Title-pages for the use of Subscribers who may wish to bind their sets in the form in which they are to be re-issued.

The Re-issue will be in Twenty-one Monthly Volumes, which will reproduce the sixty-three volumes of the Library grouped and arranged in Historical Order.

Now published, price 3s. 6d., the first volume of the Re-issue :

HOMER'S ILIAD

WITH THE PLAYS OF

ÆSCHYLUS AND SOPHOCLES.

[B C. . . . 800 TO B.C. 405.]

THE CARISBROOKE LIBRARY.

No. 1 of THE CARISBROOKE LIBRARY, price 2s. 6d.

will be published next October.

THE CARISBROOKE LIBRARY will continue the work of MORLEY'S UNIVERSAL LIBRARY without change of Plan or Editor. Its volumes will be considerably larger, and they will be published in alternate months, price 2s. 6d. each.

They will be produced as Library Editions on good paper and without use of small print. There will be space also for full Introductions and for any necessary Notes.

May 1888.

GEORGE ROUTLEDGE & SONS.

INTRODUCTION.

THIS closing volume of the UNIVERSAL LIBRARY begins and ends with notes of pleasure in the gathering of books.

Richard Aungervile was born at Bury St. Edmunds in Suffolk in the year 1281, and is therefore known as Richard de Bury. His father, a Norman knight, died young and left him to the care of uncles on the mother's side. He was sent to Oxford, where he acquired such credit for his scholarship that Edward the Second chose him for tutor to Prince Edward, afterwards Edward the Third. Through the troubles of the reign of Edward the Second, Richard Aungervile remained quiet until the time was ripe for a revolt from the service of the King, in favour of Queen Isabel and Prince Edward. He thus obtained unbounded confidence and favour from Edward the Third ; and in December 1333 Richard of Bury was consecrated Bishop of Durham. He was already Treasurer of the Kingdom, and within a year of his consecration to the Bishopric he was made also Lord Chancellor. Money flowed in on him, and out from him. He was liberal to the poor, and especially he was a good father to poor students. He loved books, and gathered them from all quarters into a Library which he valued, not as a collection of rarities to be wondered at, but as a company of friends and teachers to be used. Any real student who desired to consult books might knock at the door of his palace at Bishop's Auckland, and be lodged and boarded while he stayed to make his references.

As Richard Aungervile's life drew to a close, he made arrangements for the continuous use of his books after his

death.   He provided for the maintenance of his Library at
Durham College in the University of Oxford, under
provisions that set no check on its free general use beyond
the conditions necessary for safe custody.   And then he
wrote the famous little book called "Philobiblon," to show
why he had loved the collection of books; why books were
to be loved, and why and how they were to be used; while
setting forth his plan for the placing of his library for
ever at the service of all seekers after knowledge.   The
writing of this treatise was completed a little while before
Richard de Bury's death.   He died on the 14th of April
1345.
    The Library so founded was scattered when Durham
College was dissolved by Henry the Eighth.   Some of the
books were in Duke Humphrey's Library until the reign of
Edward VI.; others went to Balliol College; others went
into the possession of Dr. George Owen of Godstow, the
King's physician, who, with William Martyn, obtained a
grant of the site of Durham College.
    There was an English translation of Richard of Bury's
"Philobiblon" by J. B. Inglis, published in 1832 by Thomas
Rodd the bookseller, in a limited edition, of which a second-
hand copy now costs a guinea.   This translation, which was
made from the first printed edition of 1473, is the first
piece in our Miscellany.
    The next piece in the little collection is the "Basilikon
Dōron," or Royal Gift of James the Sixth of Scotland to his
son Prince Henry; a king's counsel to his son and heir.
This book was at first printed for the King of Scotland in
1599, by Robert Waldegrave of Edinburgh, who was sworn
to secrecy.   The impression was of only seven copies, printed
in a large italic letter, being three or four copies beyond
those required by the King and his son Henry, which were
"dispersed among some of the trustiest of his servants, to
be kept close by them."   When James the Sixth of Scotland became James the First of England, in 1603, he

desired to check comments that had been founded upon many reports as to his view of a king's office, and the duties of his successor. Such reports were scattered about as statements of what he had written in this private communication between himself and his son, which only particular friends had been allowed to see, and open again to the view of their particular friends, who told their friends generally, who retailed what they heard to talkers and writers. King James was credited with hostility to the Puritans, and his notions about the office of a king were put into ferms not always friendly. To meet these rumours the new King of England, in the first year of his reign, had a public edition of his "Basilikon Dōron" issued both in Edinburgh and London. From one of the London copies of that edition of 1603, still in its old parchment binding with its leather ties, the work has been directly reprinted for this Miscellany. The eldest son to whom it was addressed died in the year 1612. Had he lived to be Henry the Ninth, he would probably have avoided the mistakes of policy which brought on the Civil War of the reign of his brother, Charles the First.

The next piece in the Miscellany is the playful mock heroic by John Hookham Frere, which in a later edition was entitled "Monks and Giants." It is here printed directly from a copy of the first edition of 1817. Some account of Frere has been given in the Introduction to a volume of our Library which contained his translations from Aristophanes. The playful versification of this piece comes by lineal descent from Pulci's "Morgante Maggiore" of the fifteenth century, and it has also an ancestor in Wieland's "Oberon" of the eighteenth, but in Frere there was enlargement of its freedom, and it was own father to "Beppo" and "Don Juan." Byron avowed that when he wrote "Beppo" he was imitating this poem of Frere's, which has been for the last fifty years almost unknown to the great body of English readers.

The next piece in the Miscellany is amusing in an unintended way, and is certainly new to most readers. It is a serious translation of "The Cypress Crown," a sentimental story by La Motte Fouqué made into English from the German by a conscientious Dutchman, who breaks into the sentiment with small oddities of translation that indicate good dictionary knowledge of the language, by one who is not familiar with the kind of context for which words are fit. We do not say when we are sentimental that a flower waggles on its stalk, or that a soldier winks at an angelic child. So we have a clever tale told in a way that adds much to its power of giving amusement.

Lastly, the book ends as it begins, with praise of books collected in a Library. Crabbe's poem of "The Library" was his first bid for fame. When he had been rescued from starvation and ruin by the kindness of Edmund Burke, Burke and Samuel Johnson put their heads together, looked over the poor poet's papers, and selected for first publication the poem of "The Library," in which there are touches from the pens of both Johnson and Burke. Crabbe's verse dwelt rather upon men than upon books, and his credit was established a little later by his poem of "The Village." Every human being is a book, and villages and towns are in their own way smaller and greater libraries. So also what we call our smaller and greater libraries are villages and cities of men's minds and souls.

And now we pass out of the township of the UNIVERSAL LIBRARY, where every inhabitant is sound in health and lives to the world's end. A short path leads us to the site of a new City of the Living. The first volume of THE CARISBROOKE LIBRARY will be published on the 25th of next September.

H. M.

June 1888.

PHILOBIBLON,

A TREATISE ON THE LOVE OF BOOKS.

BY

RICHARD DE BURY,

Bishop of Durham
from A.D. 1333 *to* A.D. 1345.

CONTENTS.

PHILOBIBLON.

———•◦•———

PROLOGUE.

To all the faithful in Christ, to whom the tenor of this present writing may descend, Richard de Bury, by divine commiseration Bishop of Durham, wisheth eternal health in the Lord, as also to present a pious memorial of himself before God, while he yet liveth, and likewise after his decease.

The invincible king, psalmist, and greatest of prophets, most devoutly asks, "What can I render to the Lord for all that He hath conferred upon me?" In which most grateful question he recognizeth in himself the willing retributer, the multifarious debtor, and the most soundly discerning counsellor; agreeing with Aristotle, the prince of philosophers, who proves the whole question about things practicable, to be deliberate choice (Ethics, B. 3 and 6). Truly, if so admirable a prophet, having a foreknowledge of divine secrets, was willing thus earnestly to premeditate upon the manner in which he might acceptably return gifts by thanks, what more worthily shall we, who are rude thankers and most eager receivers, laden with infinite divine benefactions, be able to resolve upon? Without doubt, in anxious deliberation and increased circumspection, the septiform Spirit being first invoked, so that an illuminating fire may burn in our meditation, we ought most attentively to

look forward to the unbeaten way in which the Dispenser
of all things would willingly be reciprocally venerated on
account of His gifts conferred upon us.   Let our neighbour
be relieved of his burthen, and the guilt daily contracted by
our sins be redeemed by the remedy of alms.

Forewarned, therefore, by admonition of this devotion, by
Him who alone anticipates and perfects the goodwill of man
(without whom no sufficiency of thinking in any way
suggests itself ; of whom we doubt not is the reward for
whatever good we shall have done), we have diligently discussed within ourselves, and also inquired of others, which
amongst the duties of the various kinds of piety might be
in the first degree pleasing to the Most High, and best
promote the Church militant.   And behold a hera of
outcast rather than of elect scholars meets the views of our
contemplation, in whom God the artificer, and Nature his
handmaid, have planted the roots of the best morals and
most celebrated sciences.   But the penury of their private
affairs so oppresses them, being opposed by adverse fortune,
that the fruitful seeds of virtue, so productive in the unex-
hausted field of youth, unmoistened by their wonted dews,
are compelled to wither.   Whence it happens, as Boethius
says, that bright virtue lies hid in obscurity, and the burning lamp is not put under a bushel, but is utterly extin-
guished for want of oil.   Thus the flowery field in spring is
ploughed up before harvest ; thus wheat gives way to tares,
the vine degenerates to woodbine, and the olive grows wild
and unproductive.   The slender beams which might have
grown into strong pillars of the Church entirely decay.
Men, endowed with the capacity of a subtle wit, relinquish
the schools of learning, violently repelled by the sole envy
of a stepmother from the nectareous cup of philosophy,
having first tasted of it, and by the very taste become more
fervently thirsty.   Fitted for the liberal arts, and equally
disposed to the contemplation of Scripture, but destitute of
the needful aid, they revert, as it were, by a sort of apostasy

to mechanical arts solely for the sake of food, to the impoverishment of the Church, and the degradation of the whole clerical profession. Thus the mother Church conceiving sons, is compelled to miscarry, if indeed some monstrous misshapen abortion is not torn from her womb; and instead of the few and the smallest with which she is by nature contented, she sends forth egregious bantlings, and finally promotes them as the athletæ and champions of the faith. Alas, how quickly the web is cut up, while the hand of the weaver is yet at work ! How soon the sun is eclipsed in the clearest sky, and the progressing planet becomes retrograde! How suddenly the meteor, exhibiting the nature and appearance of a real star, falls down ; for it is formed from below. What can the pious man more pitifully behold? What can more keenly penetrate the bowels of compassion? What more readily dissolve a heart, though hard as an anvil, into the warmest tears?

Arguing further on the contrary side, let us call to mind from the events of former times, how greatly it profited the whole Christian republic, not indeed to enervate students by the luxuries of Sardanapalus, nor yet by the riches of Crœsus, but rather to support the poor in scholastic mediocrity. How many have we seen, how many have we collected from writings, who, not being distinguished by brilliancy of birth, nor boasting of hereditary succession, but supported alone by the piety of just men, have deserved the Apostolical Chair, and most honourably presided over its faithful subjects, have subjected the necks of the proud and exalted to the ecclesiastical yoke, and easily procured the liberty of the Church !

Wherefore, taking a thorough survey of human wants, with a view of charitable consideration for this obscure class of men, in whom, however, such great hopes of advantage to the Church are felt, the bent of our compassion has peculiarly predisposed us to offer our pious aid ; and not only to provide them with necessary food, but, what is more, with the most useful books for study. For this purpose, most acceptable to the Lord, our unwearied attention hath already been long upon the watch. This ecstatic love hath indeed so powerfully seized upon us, that, discharging all other earthly pursuits from our mind, we have alone ardently desired the acquisition of books. That the motive of our object, therefore, may be manifest as well to posterity as to our contemporaries, and that we may, in so far as it concerns ourselves, for ever close the perverse mouths of talkers, we have drawn up a little treatise, in the lightest style indeed of the moderns (for it is ridiculous in rhetoricians to write pompously when the subject is trifling), which treatise will purge the love we have had for books from excess, will advance the purpose of our intense devotion, and will narrate in the clearest manner all the circumstances of our undertaking, dividing them into twenty chapters. But because it principally treats of the Love of Books, it hath pleased us, after the fashion of the ancient Latins, fondly to name it by a Greek word—PHILOBIBLON.

CHAPTER I.

On the Commendation of Wisdom, and of Books in which Wisdom dwelleth.

THE desirable treasure of wisdom and knowledge, which all men covet from the impulse of nature, infinitely surpasses all the riches of the world; in comparison with which, precious stones are vile, silver is clay, and purified gold grains of sand; in the splendour of which, the sun and moon grow dim to the sight; in the admirable sweetness of which, honey and manna are bitter to the taste. The value of wisdom decreaseth not with time; it hath an ever-flourishing virtue that cleanseth its possessor from every venom. O celestial gift of divine liberality, descending from the Father of Light to raise up the rational soul even to heaven! Thou art the celestial alimony of intellect, of which whosoever eateth shall yet hunger, and whoso drinketh shall yet thirst; a harmony rejoicing the soul of the sorrowful, and never in any way discomposing the hearer. Thou art the moderator and the rule of morals, operating according to which none will err. By thee kings reign, and lawgivers decree justly. Through thee, the rusticity of nature being cast off, wits and tongues being polished, and the thorns of vice utterly eradicated, the summit of honour is reached; and they become fathers of their country and companions of princes, who, without thee, might have forged their lances into spades and plough-shares, or perhaps have fed swine with the prodigal son. Where then, most potent, most longed-for treasure, art thou concealed? and where shall the thirsty soul find thee? Undoubtedly, indeed, thou hast placed thy desirable taber-nacle in books, where the Most High, the Light of light, the Book of Life hath established thee. There then all who ask receive, all who seek find thee, to those who knock thou openest quickly. In books cherubim expand their wings, that the soul of the student may ascend and look around from pole to pole, from the rising to the setting sun, from the north and from the sea. In them the Most High incomprehensible God himself is contained and worshipped. In them the nature of celestial, terrestrial and infernal beings is laid open. In them the laws by which every polity is governed are decreed, the offices of the celestial hierarchy are distinguished, and tyrannies of such demons are described as the ideas of Plato never surpassed, and the chair of Crato never contained.

In books we find the dead as it were living; in books we foresee things to come; in books warlike affairs are metho-dized; the rights of peace proceed from books. All things are corrupted and decay with time. Saturn never ceases to devour those whom he generates; insomuch that the glory of the world would be lost in oblivion if God had not provided mortals with a remedy in books. Alexander the ruler of the world; Julius the invader of the world and of the city, the first who in unity of person assumed the empire in arms and arts; the faithful Fabricius, the rigid Cato, would at this day have been without a memorial if the aid of books had failed them. Towers are razed to the earth, cities overthrown, triumphal arches mouldered to dust; nor can the King or Pope be found upon whom the privilege of a lasting name can be conferred more easily than by books. A book made, renders succession to the author: for as long as the book exists, the author remaining ἀθάνατος, immortal, cannot perish; as Ptolemy witnesseth in the Prologue of his Almagest, he (he says) is not dead who gave life to science.

What learned scribe, therefore, who draws out things new and old from an infinite treasury of books, will limit their price by any other thing whatever of another kind? Truth overcoming all things, which ranks above kings, wine and women, to honour which above friends obtains the benefit of sanctity, which is the way that deviates not, and the life without end; to which the holy Boethius attributes a threefold existence, in the mind, in the voice, and in writing, appears to abide most usefully and fructify most productively of advantage in books. For the truth of the voice perishes with the sound. Truth latent in the mind is hidden wisdom and invisible treasure; but the truth which illuminates books desires to manifest itself to every disciplinable sense, to the sight when read, to the hearing when heard; it, moreover, in a manner commends itself to the touch, when submitting to be transcribed, collated, corrected and preserved. Truth confined to the mind, though it may be the possession of a noble soul, while it wants a companion and is not judged of, either by the sight or the hearing, appears to be inconsistent with pleasure. But the truth of the voice is open to the hearing only, and latent to the sight (which shows us many differences of things fixed upon by a most subtle motion, beginning and ending as it were simultaneously). But the truth written in a book, being not fluctuating, but permanent, shows itself openly to the sight, passing through the spiritual ways of the eyes, as the porches and halls of common sense and imagination; it enters the chamber of intellect, reposes itself upon the couch of memory, and there congenerates the eternal truth of the mind.

Lastly, let us consider how great a commodity of doctrine exists in books, how easily, how secretly, how safely they expose the nakedness of human ignorance without putting it to shame. These are the masters who instruct us without rods and ferules, without hard words and anger, without clothes or money. If you approach them, they are not asleep; if investigating you interrogate them, they conceal nothing: if you mistake them, they never grumble; if you are ignorant, they cannot laugh at you.

You only, O Books, are liberal and independent. You give to all who ask, and enfranchise all who serve you assiduously. How many thousands of things do you typically recommend to learned men, in writing after a divinely inspired manner; for you are the deepest mines of wisdom, to which the wise man sent his son that he might thence dig up treasure (Prov. ii.). You are the wells of living water, which the patriarch Abraham first dug, and Isaac again cleared out after the Philistines had endeavoured to fill them up (Gen. xxvi.). Truly you are the ears filled with most palatable grains, to be rubbed out by apostolical hands alone, that the most grateful food for hungry souls may come out of them (Matt. xii.). You are golden urns in which manna is laid up, rocks flowing with honey, or rather indeed honey-combs; udders most copiously yielding the milk of life; store-rooms ever full; the tree of life, the four-streamed river of Paradise, where the human mind is fed, and the arid intellect moistened and watered; the ark of Noah, the ladder of Jacob, the troughs by which the fœtus in those who look upon them is coloured, the stones of the covenant, and the pitchers preserving the lamps of Gideon; the bag of David from which polished stones are taken that Goliath may be prostrated. You, O Books, are the golden vessels of the temple, the arms of the clerical militia, with which the missiles of the most wicked are destroyed, fruitful olives, vines of Engedi, fig-trees knowing no sterility; burning lamps to be ever held in the hand. And, if it please us to speak figuratively, we shall be able to adapt the best sayings of every writing whatever to books.

CHAPTER II.

Showeth that Books are to be preferred to Riches and Corporal Pleasures.

IF anything whatever, according to a degree of value deserves a degree of love, the present chapter truly proves the ineffable value of books, though its conclusions may probably not appear clear to the reader; for we do not make use of demonstration in moral subjects, seeing that it is the business of a moral man to seek for certainty accordingly as he may have perceived the nature of the subject to bear it, as the arch-philosopher witnesseth (1. Ethic, 2. Metaph.); for Tully neither requires Euclid, nor does Euclid put faith in Tully. But this indeed we endeavour either logically or rhetorically to inculcate, that riches and pleasures of every kind ought to give way to books in a spiritual mind, where the spirit, which is charity, ordaineth charity.

' In the first place indeed, because more wisdom is contained in books than all mortals comprehend; and wisdom holds riches in no esteem, as alleged in the preceding chapter. Moreover, Aristotle (Problems, Sect. 30, Dis. 11) determines this question—viz., upon what account did the ancients chiefly appoint prizes for gymnastic and corporal exertions, and never decree any reward for wisdom? Which question he thus solves. In gymnastic exercises, the reward is better and more eligible than that for which it is given; but it is evident nothing is better than wisdom, wherefore no reward could have been assigned to wisdom; therefore neither riches nor pleasures are more excellent than wisdom. Again, that friendship is to be preferred to riches none but a fool will deny; to this the wisest of men bears witness. But the arch-philosopher honours truth above friendship, and the ancient Zorobabel gives it precedence over all things; therefore pleasures are inferior to truth. But the Sacred Books most powerfully preserve and contain the truth; they are assuredly the written truth itself; for upon this occasion we do not assert the main beams of the books to be parts of books, wherefore riches are inferior to books, more especially as the most precious of all kinds of riches are friends (witness Boethius, De Consolatione, B. 2), to which, however, the truth of books is preferred by Aristotle. But, further, as riches are primarily and principally acknowledged to pertain to the aid of the body only, and as the truth of books is the perfection of reason, which is properly named the good of mankind, so it appears that books to a man using them with reason are dearer than riches. Again, that by which the faith is most conveniently defended, most widely diffused, and most clearly preached, ought to be most beloved by a faithful man; and that is the truth of books, inscribed in books; which our Saviour most evidently figured when, manfully fighting against temptation, He covered himself with the shield of truth, not indeed of writing of any sort; but premising, that what He was about to declare by the sound of His living voice, was also written (Matt. iv.).

Again, therefore, nobody doubts that happiness is to be preferred to riches, for happiness is consistent with the operation of the most noble and divine power we possess—namely, when the intellect is entirely at leisure for the contemplation of the truth of knowledge, which is the most delectable of all operations according to virtue, as the prince of philosophers determines in the Nicomachian Ethics, B. 10 ; on which account philosophy also appears to possess admirable delights from its purity and stability, as the same author states in the sequel. But the contemplation of truth is never more perfect than in books, as the active imagination, kept up by a book, does not permit the operation of the intellect upon visible truths to be interrupted. For which reason books appear to be the most immediate instruments of speculative happiness; whence Aristotle, the sun of physical truth, where he unfolds the doctrine of objects of choice, teaches that to philosophise is in itself more eligible than to grow rich, although from necessary circumstances in the case, it may be thought more eligible for an indigent man to grow rich than to philosophise (Topics 3). Inasmuch, then, as books are our most convenient masters, as the preceding chapter assumes, it becomes us not undeservedly to bestow upon them, not only love, but magisterial honour.

Finally, as all men by nature are desirous of knowledge, and as we are able by books to obtain the knowledge of truth, to be chosen before all riches, what man, living according to nature, can be without an appetite for books? But although we may see hogs despise pearls, the opinion of a prudent man is in no way injured by that; he will not the less purchase proffered pearls. The library, therefore, of wisdom is more precious than all riches, and nothing that can be wished for is worthy to be compared with it (Prov. iii.). Whosoever, therefore, acknowledges himself to be a zealous follower of truth, of happiness, of wisdom, of science, or even of the faith, must of necessity make himself a lover of books.

―――――

CHAPTER III.

Books ought always to be Bought, except in two Cases.

WE draw this corollary satisfactory to ourselves from what has been said, although, as we believe, but few will receive it—namely, that no expense ought to prevent men from buying books when what is demanded for them is at their command, unless the knavery of the seller is to be withstood or a better opportunity of purchasing is expected. Because if wisdom alone, which is an infinite treasure to man, determines the price of books, and if the value of books is ineffable, as the premisses suppose, how can a bargain be proved to be dear which purchases an infinite benefit. For this reason Solomon, the sun of mankind (Prov. xxiii.), exhorts us to buy books freely and sell sparingly. He says: "Buy truth, and sell not wisdom." But what we now rhetorically and logically inculcate, we can support by histories of past events. The arch-philosopher Aristotle, of whom Averroes thinks that he was given as it were for a rule in nature, bought a few of Speusippus's books immediately after his death for 72,000 sesterces. Plato, prior to him as to time, but his inferior as to doctrine, bought the library of Philolaus the Pythagorean for 10,000 denarii; from which he is said to have extracted the dialogue of Timæus, as Aulus Gellius relates (Noct. Attic., lib. 3, c. 16). But Aulus Gellius relates these things, that the ignorant may consider how greatly the wise undervalue money in comparison with books; and, on the contrary, that we may all know the folly attached to pride, let us here review the folly of Tarquin the Proud in undervaluing books, as the same Aulus Gellius relates it (Noct. Attic., lib. I, c. 19). "A certain old woman, quite unknown, is said to have come into the presence of Tarquin the Proud, the seventh king of the Romans, and offered him nine books for sale, in which, as she asserted, the Divine oracles were contained; but she demanded such an immense sum of money for them, that the king said she was mad. Taking offence at this, she threw three of the books into the fire, and demanded the sum first asked for the rest. The king refusing, she threw three more of the books into the fire, and still demanded the same sum for the remaining three. At length Tarquin, being astonished beyond measure, was glad to pay the sum for three books for which he could have bought the whole nine. The old woman, who was never seen before nor afterwards, immediately disappeared." These are the Sibylline books which the Romans consult as Divine oracles, through one of the quindecemvirs, and from them the quindecemvirate office is supposed to have had its origin. What else did this Sibylline prophetess teach the proud king by so subtle a device, but that the vases of wisdom, the sacred books, surpass all human estimation; and as Gregory says of the kingdom of heaven, "Whatsoever you may possess, that is its value!"

CHAPTER IV.

How much Good arises from Books; and that the corrupt Clergy are for the most part ungrateful to Books.

A PROGENY of vipers destroying its own parents, and the cruel offspring of the most ungrateful cuckoo, which, when it hath acquired strength, slays its little nurse, the liberal donor of its power—such are the degenerate clergy with respect to books. Turn to your hearts, ye prevaricators, and faithfully compute how much you have received from books, and you will find books to have been in a manner the creators of your entire noble estate ; without them it would certainly have been deficient of promoters. Hear them speak for themselves. Well then,—" When you were altogether ignorant and helpless, you spoke like children, you knew like children ; and crying like children you crept towards us, and begged to be participators of our milk. We indeed, moved by your tears, instantly tendered you the paps of grammar to suck, which you firmly adhered to with tooth and tongue, till your babbling accents were over-come, and you began to utter the mighty acts of God in our own language. After that we clothed you with the right comely garments of philosophy, dialectics, and rhetoric, which we had and keep by us ; as you were naked, and like tablets for painting upon : for all the inmates of philosophy are doubly clothed, that the nakedness as well as the rude-ness of their understandings may be concealed. Lastly, affixing to you the four wings of the four converging ways, that being winged in a seraphic manner you might soar above the cherubim, we transmitted you to a friend, at whose door, while you yet knocked earnestly, the three loaves of the intelligence of the Trinity, upon which the final happiness of every wayfaring man whatever depends, would be prepared for you. What if you should say, ' You have no such gifts ;' we confidently assert that you either lost them, when conferred upon you, through carelessness, or rejected them from the beginning, when offered to you, through indolence. If trifles of this kind are found dis-agreeable, we will add something more important. You are the elect race, the royal priesthood, the holy tribe and people of the acquisition ; you are held to be in the peculiar lot of the Lord, the priests and ministers of God ; indeed, you may be called by antonomasia the Church itself, inasmuch as laymen cannot be called Churchmen. You chant psalms and hymns in the chancel, and serve at the altar of God, participating with the altar, while the laity are placed behind you. You concoct the true body of Christ, in which God himself hath honoured you, not only above laymen, but even somewhat above His angels; for to which of the angels hath He ever said, 'Thou art a priest for ever after the order of Melchisedech?' You dispense the testimony of Christ crucified, to the poor. Where is it now sought for amongst the dispensers, so that any faithful man can find it? You are the pastors of the flock of the Lord, as well by the example of your lives as by the words of your doctrine, which is kept by you to distribute the milk and the wool. Who, O clergy, are the liberal bestowers of these gifts? Are they not books? We beg it may please you to remember how many excellent privileges of exemption and freedom have been conceded to the clergy through us. Qualified indeed by us alone, the vessels of wisdom and intellect, you ascend the magisterial chair, and men call you Rabbi. Through us you are admirable in the sight of the laity, as the great luminaries of the world; and you possess the dignities of the Church according to your various destinies. Constituted by us at a tender age, while you yet wanted the down upon your chins, you bore the tonsure upon your crowns, bespeaking the formidable state of the Church, in the decree, 'Touch not my anointed, and do my prophets no harm; and whoever rashly toucheth them, his own blow shall instantly recoil upon him with the wound of an anathema.'

"At length, falling into the age of wickedness, arriving at the double way of the Pythagoric symbol Y, you choose the left-hand branch, and turning aside cast off the pre-assumed destination of the Lord, and become companions of thieves; and thus ever progressing to worse, you are defiled by robberies, homicide, and various shameful crimes, your character and conscience being equally corrupted by wickedness. Being called to justice, you are kept bound in manacles and fetters, to be punished by a most ignominious death. Then your friend and neighbour is absent, nor is there any one to pity your fate. Peter swears he never knew the man: the mob cry out to the judge, 'Crucify him! crucify him! for if you discharge this man you will not be the friend of Cæsar.' It is now too late to fly; you must stand before the tribunal; no place of appeal offers itself; nothing but hanging is to be expected. When sorrow and the broken song of lamentation alone shall have thus filled the heart of a wretched man; when his cheeks are watered with tears, and he becomes surrounded with anguish on every side, let him remember us; and that he may avoid the peril of approaching death, let him display the little token of the antiquated tonsure which we gave him, begging that we may be called in on his behalf, and bear witness to the benefit conferred.

"Then moved by pity we instantly run to meet the prodigal son, and snatch the fugitive servant from the gates of death; the well-known book is tendered to be read, and after a slight reading by the criminal, stammering from fear, the power of the judge is dissolved, the accuser is withdrawn, death is put to flight. O wonderful virtue of an empiric verse! O salutary antidote to dire calamity! O precious reading of the psalter, which deserves henceforth from this itself to be called the Book of Life! Laymen must undergo secular punishment; either being sewn up in sacks they may be consigned to Neptune; or planted in the ground may fructify for Pluto; or may offer themselves up by fire, as fattened holocausts to Vulcan; or at all events, being hanged they may be victims to Juno, while our pupil, by a single reading of the Book of Life, is commended to the custody of the pontiff, and rigour is converted into favour. And while the bench is transferred from the layman, death is averted from the clerical nursling of books.

" Let us now speak of those clergy who are the vessels of virtue. Which of you ascends the pulpit or desk to preach without first consulting us? Which enters the schools either to lecture, dispute or preach, who is not enlightened by our rays?

" You must first eat the volume with Ezekiel, that the stomach of your memory may be internally sweetened; and thus after the manner of the perfumed panther (to the breath of which men, beasts, and cattle draw near that they may inhale it), the sweet odour of your aromatic conceptions will be externally redolent. Thus our nature, secretly and most intimately working within you, benevolent auditors flock about you, as the magnet attracts iron, by no means unwillingly. What though an infinite multitude of books be deposited in Paris or Athens, do they not likewise speak aloud in Britain and in Rome—for even being at rest they are moved : while confining themselves to their proper places, they are everywhere carried about to the understandings of hearers.

" Finally, we establish priests, pontiffs, cardinals, and the pope, that all things in the ecclesiastical hierarchy may be set in order by the knowledge of letters; for every benefit that arises out of the clerical state has its origin in books. But even now it grieves us to reflect upon what we have given to the degenerate race of clergy, because gifts bestowed upon the ungrateful appear to be rather lost than conferred.

" In the next place, let us stop a little to recite the injuries, indignities and reproaches they repay us with, of which we are not competent to recount all of every kind— scarcely indeed the first kinds of them all.

" In the first place, we are expelled with heart and hand from the domiciles of the clergy, apportioned to us by hereditary right, in some interior chamber of which we had our peaceful cells; but, to their shame, in these nefarious times we are altogether banished to suffer opprobrium out of doors; our places, moreover, are occupied by hounds and hawks, and sometimes by a biped beast: woman, to wit, whose cohabitation was formerly shunned by the clergy, from whom we have ever taught our pupils to fly, more than from the asp and the basilisk; wherefore this beast, ever jealous of our studies, and at all times implacable, spying us at last in a corner, protected only by the web of some long-deceased spider, drawing her forehead into wrinkles, laughs us to scorn, abuses us in virulent speeches, points us out as the only superfluous furniture lodged in the whole house, complains that we are useless for any purpose of domestic economy whatever, and recommends our being bartered away forthwith for costly head-dresses, cambric, silk, twice-dipped purple garments, woollen, linen, and furs: and indeed with reason, if she could see the interior of our hearts, or be present at our secret councils, or could read the volumes of Theophrastus and Valerius, or at least hear the twenty-fifth chapter of Ecclesiasticus with the ears of understanding.

"We complain, therefore, because our domiciles are unjustly taken from us, not that garments are not given to us, but that those which were formerly given are torn off by violent hands, insomuch that our souls adhere to the pavement, our belly is agglutinated to the earth, and our glory is reduced to dust (Ps. xliv. and cxix.). We labour under various diseases; our back and sides ache, we lie down disabled and paralyzed in every limb, nobody thinks of us, nor is there any one who will benignly apply an emollient to our sores. Our native whiteness, perspicuous with light, is now turned tawny and yellow; so that no medical man who may find us out, can doubt that we are infected with jaundice. Some of us are gouty, as our distorted extremities evidently indicate. The damp, smoke, and dust with which we are constantly infested, dim the field of our visual rays, and superinduce ophthalmia upon our already bleared eyes.

" Our stomachs are destroyed by the severe griping of our bowels, which greedy worms never cease to gnaw. We suffer corruption inside and out, and nobody is found to anoint us with turpentine; or who, calling to us on the fourth day of putrefaction, will say, ' Lazarus, come forth ! ' The cruel wounds atrociously inflicted upon us who are harmless, are not bound up with any bandage, nor does any one apply a plaster to our ulcers. But we are thrown into dark corners, ragged, shivering, and weeping, or with holy Job seated on a dunghill, or (what appears too indecent to be told) we are buried in the abysses of the common sewer. The supporting cushion is drawn from under our evangelical sides, from whose oracles the subsidies of the clergy ought first of all to come, they being deputed to us for their service, and thus the common provision for their maintenance ought for ever to be derived from us.

" Again : we complain of another kind of calamity that is very often unjustly imposed upon our persons; for we are sold like slaves and female captives, or left as pledges in taverns without redemption. We are given to cruel butchers to be cut up like sheep and cattle ; we do not behold this without pious tears, and where there is death in a thousand forms, we die of fear itself, which is able to overthrow irresolute man. We are turned over to Jews, Saracens, heretics and pagans, whose poison we dread above all things, and by whose pestiferous venom it is evident some of our forefathers have been corrupted.

" Truly, we who ought to be considered as the master builders in science, who give orders to our subject mechanics, are, on the contrary, subjected to the government of subalterns : as if a most noble monarch should be trampled upon by rustic heels. Every botcher, cobbler, and tailor whatever, or any artificer of whatever trade, keeps us shut up in prison, for the superfluous and lascivious pleasures of the clergy.

" We will now proceed to a new sort of insult by which we

are injured both in our persons and in our fame, than which
we possess nothing dearer to us. Our genuineness is every
day detracted from, for new names of authors are imposed
upon us by worthless compilers, translators, and transformers,
being reproduced in multiplied regeneration; our ancient
nobility is changed, and we become altogether degenerate;
and thus the names of vile authors are fixed upon us against
our will, and the words of the true fathers are filched from
them by the sons. A certain pseudo-versifier usurped the
verses of Virgil while he was yet living; and one Fidentinus
falsely arrogated to himself the books of Martial the poet,
upon whom the said Martial justly retorted in these
words—

> Quem recitas meus est, o Fidentine, libellus,
> Sed male dum recitas incipit esse tuus.

> The book thou recitest, Fidentinus, is mine,
> Though from vile recitation it passeth for thine.

"What wonder is it then if clerical apes magnify their
margins from the works of authors who are dead, as while
they are yet living they endeavour to seize upon their
recent editions? Ah, how often do you pretend that we
who are old are but just born, and attempt to call us sons,
who are fathers? and to call that which brought you into
clerical existence the fabric of your own studies? In truth,
we who now pretend to be Romans, are evidently sprung
from the Athenians; for Carmentis was ever a pillager of
Cadmus: and we who are just born in England shall be
born again to-morrow in Paris, and being thence carried on
to Bologna, shall be allotted an Italian origin, unsupported
by any consanguinity.

"Alas! to how many false transcribers have you committed us to be copied; how corruptly do you read us, and
by amending, destroy what in pious zeal you intend to
correct. In how many ways do we suffer from barbarous
interpreters, who presume to translate us from one language
to another, though ignorant of the idioms of either! The

propriety of speech being thus taken away, its sense is basely mutilated, and contrary to the meaning of the author. The condition of books would have been right genuine, if the presumption of the Tower of Babel had not come in its way, and the only preserved form of speech of the whole human race had descended to us.

" We will now subjoin the last of our prolix complaints, but most briefly, in proportion to the matter we have to complain of ; for indeed natural use in us is converted into that which is contrary to Nature : as, for instance, we are given up to painters ignorant of letters ; and we who are the light of faithful souls are shamefully consigned to goldsmiths, that we may become repositories for gold-leaf, as if we were not the sacred vessels of science. We fall unduly into the power of laymen, which to us is more bitter than any death ; for they sell our people without a price, and our enemies become our judges. It is clear from all these premisses, what infinite invectives we could have thrown out against the clergy if we had not spared them for our own credit. For the pensioned soldier venerates his shield and arms. Carts, harrows, flails, and spades are grateful to the worn-out ploughman Coridon ; and every manual artificer exhibits extraordinary care for his own tools. The ungrateful clerk alone undervalues and neglects those things from which he must ever take the prognostics of his future honour."

CHAPTER V.

Good Professors of Religion write Books; bad ones are occupied with other things.

THERE used to be an anxious and reverential devotion in the culture of books of religious offices, and the clergy delighted in communing with them as their whole wealth ; for many wrote them out with their own hands in the intervals of the canonical hours, and gave up the time appointed for bodily rest to the fabrication of volumes: those sacred treasuries of whose labours, filled with cherubic letters, are at this day resplendent in most monasteries, to give the knowledge of salvation to students, and a delectable light to the paths of the laity. O happy manual labour above all agricultural cares! O devout solicitude, from which neither Martha nor Mary would have earned the wages of corruption! O joyful house, in which the fair Rachel envieth not the prolific Lya, but where contemplation mingles with its own active pleasures! Happy provision for the future, available to infinite posterity; to which no planting of trees, no sowing of seeds, no pastoral curiosity about any sort of cattle, no building of fortified castles is to be compared! Wherefore the memory of those Fathers ought to be immortal, whom the treasure of wisdom alone delighted, who most artificially provided luminous lanterns against future darkness, and prepared, against a dearth of hearing the Word of God, bread not baked in ashes, nor musty, nor of barley, but un- leavened loaves most carefully composed of the purest flour of holy wisdom, with which they fed the souls of the hungry. But these were the most virtuous combatants of the Christian militia, who fortified our infirmity with most powerful arms. They were the most cunning fox-hunters of their times, who have yet left us their snares, that we may catch the little foxes which never cease to demolish the flourishing vines. Truly these mighty Fathers are to be remembered with perpetual benedictions. Deservedly happy would you be, if a similar progeny were begotten by you, if it were permitted to you to leave an heir neither degenerate nor doubtful, to be a help in times to come. But now (we say it with sorrow) base Thersites handles the arms of Achilles; the choicest trappings are thrown away upon lazy asses; blinking night-birds lord it in the nests of eagles, and the silly kite sits on the perch of the hawk. Liber Bacchus is respected, and passes daily and nightly into the belly; Liber Codex is rejected far and wide out of reach; so that the simple modern people are deceived by a multiplicity of equivocations of every kind; Liber Patera takes precedence of Liber Patrum (libations of the Lives of the Fathers). The study of the monks nowadays dispenses with emptying bowls, not emending books, to which they neither scruple to add the lascivious music of Timotheus, nor to emulate his shameless manners; and thus the song of merriment, not the plaint of mournfulness, is become the monasterial duty. Flocks and fleeces, crops and barns, gardens and olive-yards, drink and cups, are now the lessons and studies of monks; excepting, of some chosen few, in whom not the image but a slight vestige of their forefathers remains.

Again: none whatever of that matter is administered to us touching our culture and study, for which the Regular Canons can at this day be commended; who, though they bear the great name of Augustine from the double rule, yet neglect the notable little verse by which we are recommended to his clergy in these words: "Books are to be asked for at certain hours every day; he who demands them out of hours, shall not receive them." This devout canon of study scarcely any one observes after repeating the Church service or Horæ; but to be knowing in secular affairs, and to look after the neglected plough, is held to be the height of prudence. They carry bows and arrows; assume arms and bucklers; distribute the tribute of alms amongst their dogs, not amongst the necessitous; use dice and draughts, and such things as we are accustomed to forbid to secular men; so that indeed we wonder not that they never deign to look upon us, whom they thus perceive to oppose their immoral practices.

Condescend therefore, reverend Fathers, to remember your predecessors, and to indulge more freely in the study of the Sacred Books; without which all religion whatever

will vacillate; without which, as a watering-pot, the virtue
of devotion will dry up; and without which no light will
be held up to the world.

***

CHAPTER VI.

*In Praise of the Ancient, and Reprehension of the Modern,
Religious Mendicants.*

POOR in spirit, but most rich in faith, the offscourings of
the world, the salt of the earth, despisers of worldly affairs,
and fishers of men, how happy are you if, suffering penury
for Christ, you know you possess your souls in suffering!
For thus neither the revenger, from lack of injury, nor the
adverse fortune of relations, nor any violent necessity, nor
hunger oppresses you; if the will is devout and the election
Christiform, by which you have chosen that best life which
God Almighty made man set forth both by word and
example. Truly you are the new birth of the ever pro-
creating Church, recently and divinely substituted for the
Fathers and Prophets, that the sound of your voice may go
forth over all the earth; for being instructed in our salutary doctrines, you can promulgate the unassailable doctrine
of the faith of Christ to all kings and people. Moreover,
our second chapter superabundantly proves the faith of the
Fathers to be most amply contained in books; wherefore it
most clearly appears that you ought to be zealous lovers of
books, who, above all other Christians, are commanded to
sow upon all waters. For the Most High is no respecter of
persons; nor doth the most pious, who was willing to be
slain for sinners, wish for the death of sinners, but He
desires the broken-hearted to be healed, the fallen to be
raised up, and the perverse to be corrected in the spirit of
lenity. For which most salutary purpose, our fostering

B

mother Church gratuitously planted you; being planted, she watered you with favours; and being watered, propped you with privileges that you might be coadjutors to pastors and curates in procuring the salvation of faithful souls. Whence also, as their constitutions declare, the order of preachers was principally instituted for the study of Holy Writ and for the salvation of their neighbours; as not only from the rule of their founder, Augustine, who ordered books to be sought for every day, but immediately upon reading the preface of the said constitutions, at the beginning of his own volume, they know the love of books to be an obligation imposed upon them. But, to their shame, both these and others following their example are withdrawn from the study and paternal care of books by a threefold superfluous care; namely, of their bellies, clothing, and houses. For, neglecting the providence of our Saviour, whom the Psalmist premises to be solicitous about the poor and mendicant, they are occupied about the wants of their perishable bodies, such as splendid banquets, delicate garments contrary to their rule, and even piles of buildings like the bulwarks of fortifications, raised to a height little consistent with the profession of poverty. For the sake of these three things, We, their books, who have ever advanced them to preferment and conceded the seat of honour to them amongst the powerful and noble, are estranged from the affections of their hearts and looked upon as useless lumber, excepting that they make some account of certain tracts of little value, from which they produce mongrel trifles and apocryphal ravings, not for the refreshment of hungry souls, but rather to tickle the ears of their auditors.

The Holy Scriptures are not expounded, but exploded as trite sayings supposed to be already divulged in the streets and to all men, whose margins, however, very few have touched, whose profundity is even so great that it cannot be comprehended by human intellect, however vigilant it may be, at its utmost leisure and with the greatest study. He who constantly studies these, will be able to pick out the thousand maxims of moral discipline which they enforce with the most perfect novelty, refreshing the understandings of their hearers with the most soothing suavity, if He who founded the spirit of piety will only deign to open the door. For which reason the first professors of evangelical poverty, taking leave of every secular science whatever, gathering together the whole force of their minds, devoted themselves to the labours of these holy writings, meditating daily and nightly on the law of the Lord. Whatsoever they could steal from their famishing stomachs, or tear from their half-covered bodies, they applied to emending or editing books, esteeming them their greatest gain ; their secular contemporaries, holding both their office and studies in respect, having conferred such books upon them as they had collected at great cost, here and there in divers parts of the world, to the edification of the whole Church.

Truly in these days, when with all diligence you are intent upon lucre, it might be believed with probable presumption, according to anthropospathos (if the word may be allowed) or human feeling, that God entertains little anxiety about those whom He considers to distrust His promises, placing their hopes upon human foresight, neither considering the crow nor the lily which the Most High feeds and clothes. You ponder not upon Daniel, nor Abacuc the bearer of the dish of boiled pottage, nor remember Elijah fed by angels in the desert, again by crows at the brook, and, lastly, by the widow at Sarepta, relieved from the cravings of hunger by the divine bounty, which gives food to all flesh in due season. You are descending, we fear, by a wretched ladder, while a reliance upon self-sufficiency produces distrust of divine piety, but reliance upon self-sufficiency begets solicitude about worldly affairs, and too much solicitude about worldly affairs takes away the love of books and study, and thus poverty now gives way

through abuse, at the expense of the Word of God, though
you chose it only for its support. You draw boys into your
religion with hooks of apples, as the people commonly report,
whom having professed, you do not instruct in doctrines by
compulsion and fear as their age requires, but maintain
them to go upon beggarly excursions, and suffer them to
consume the time in which they might learn, in catching at
the favours of their friends, to the offence of their parents,
the danger of the boys, and the detriment of the Order.
And thus without doubt it happens that unwilling boys, in
no way compelled to learn, when grown up presume to
teach, being altogether worthless and ignorant. A small
error in the beginning becomes a very great one in the end;
for thus also a certain and generally burthensome multitude
of laymen grows up in your promiscuous flock, who, however,
thrust themselves into the office of preaching the more
impudently the less they understand what they talk about, in
contempt of the Word of the Lord, and to the ruin of souls.
Verily you plough with the ox and the ass contrary to the
law, when you commit the culture of the Lord's field to the
learned and unlearned without distinction. It is written,
oxen plough, and asses feed by them; because it is the business of the discreet to preach, but of the simple to feed themselves in silence by hearing sacred eloquence. How many
stones do you throw upon the heap of Mercury in these
days? How many marriages do you procure for the eunuchs
of wisdom? How many blind speculators do you teach to go
about upon the walls of the church?

O slothful fishermen, who only use other men's nets,
which you have hardly skill to mend if broken, and none
whatever to weave anew! You intrude upon the labours of
others, recite their compositions, repeat their wisdom by
rote, and mouth it with theatrical rant. As the stupid
parrot imitates the words it hears, so such as you become
reciters of everything, authors of nothing, imitating
Balaam's ass, which, though naturally insensible of lan-

guage, yet by her eloquent tongue was made the school-mistress both of a master and a prophet.

Repent, ye paupers of Christ, and studiously revert to us your books, without whom you will never be able to put on your shoes in advancement of the Gospel of peace. Paul the apostle, preacher of the truth and first teacher of the Gentiles, ordered these three things to be brought to him by Timothy instead of all his furniture—his cloak, books, and parchment (2 Tim.); exhibiting a formulary to evangelical men that they may wear the habit ordained, have books to aid them in studying, and parchment for writing, which the apostle lays most stress upon, saying, "but especially the parchments." Truly that clergyman is maimed, and indeed basely mutilated, to the wreck of many things, who is totally ignorant of the art of writing; he beats the air with his voice; he edifies only the present, and provides nothing for the absent or for posterity. "A man carried the inkhorn of a writer at his loins, who set the mark T upon the foreheads of those who sighed," figuratively insinuating that if any man is deficient in the skill of writing he must not take upon himself the office of preaching penitence.

Finally, in closing the present chapter, your books, administering the needful, supplicate you to turn the attention of ignorant youths of apt wit to their studies, that you may not only truly teach them truth, discipline and knowledge, but terrify them with the rod, attract them with blandishments, soothe them with presents, and urge them with penal severities, that they may at once be made Socratics in morals and Peripatetics in doctrine.

Yesterday, as it were at the eleventh hour, the discreet landlord introduced you into the vineyard; repent, therefore, of being idle before it is altogether too late. Would that with the prudent steward you would be ashamed of begging so dishonourably; for then without doubt you would have leisure for us your books, and for study.

CHAPTER VII.

Deploring the Destruction of Books by Wars and Fire.

O most high author and lover of peace ! scatter the nations that are desirous of war, more injurious to books than all other plagues ; for war, wanting the discretion of reason, furiously attacks whatever falls in its way, and, not being under the guidance of reason, it destroys the vessels of reason, having no scale of discretion. Then the wise Apollo is subjected to Pluto, the prolific mother Phronesis becomes Phrenesis, and is submitted to the power of Frenzy. Then the winged Pegasus is shut up in the stable of Corydon, and the eloquent Mercury is choked. The prudent Pallas is pierced by the dart of error, and the jocund Pierides are suppressed by the truculent tyranny of Fury. O cruel sight! where Aristotle, the Phœbus of philosophers, to whom the lord of the domain himself committed the dominion over all things, is seen bound by impious hands, fettered with infamous chains, and carried off from the house of Socrates upon the shoulders of gladiators ; and him who deserved to obtain the magistracy in the government of the world, and the empire over its emperor, you may see subjected to a vile scoffer, by the most unjust rights of war.

O most iniquitous power of darkness ! that feared not to trample upon the approved divinity of Plato, who alone in the sight of the Creator was worthy to interpose ideal forms, before he could appease the strife of jarring chaos, and before he could invest matter with permanent form ; that he might demonstrate the archetype world from its author, and that the sensible world might be deduced from its supernal prototype.

O sorrowful sight ! where the moral Socrates, whose acts are virtue, and whose words are doctrine, who produced justness of policy from the principles of Nature, is seen devoted to the service of a depraved undertaker! We lament Pythagoras, the parent of harmony, atrociously scourged by furious female singers, uttering plaintive groans instead of songs. We pity Zeno, the chief of the Stoics, who, rather than divulge a secret, bit off his tongue, and boldly spat it in the face of a tyrant. Alas, now again, for the bruised Anaxarchus pounded in a mortar by Nicrocreon! Certainly, we are not competent to lament with befitting sorrow each of the books which has perished in various parts of the world by the hazards of war. We may, however, record with a tearful pen the horrible havoc that happened through the auxiliary soldiers in the second Alexandrine war in Egypt, where 700,000 volumes, collected by the Ptolemies, kings of Egypt, during a long course of time, were consumed by fire, as Aulus Gellius relates (Attic Nights, B. 6, c. 17). What an Atlantic progeny is supposed to have then perished! comprehending the motions of the spheres, all the conjunctions of the planets, the nature and generation of the galaxy, the prognostications of comets, and whatsoever things are done in heaven or in the air. Who is not horrified by such an evil-omened holocaust, in which ink is offered up instead of blood, where glowing sparks spring from the blood of crackling parchment; where voracious flames consume so many thousands of innocents in whose mouths no falsehood is found; where fire that knows not when to spare, converts so many shrines of eternal truth into fetid ashes! The pious virgin daughters of Jephthah and Agamemnon, murdered for the glory of their fathers, may be thought victims of a minor crime. How many labours of the celebrated Hercules, who, for his skill in astronomy, is described as having supported the heavens upon his shoulders, may we imagine to have perished, when he was now for the second time thrown into the flames! The secrets of heaven, that Inachus neither learned from man nor by human means, but received by divine inspiration, whatsoever his half-brother Zoroaster, the servant of unclean spirits, disseminated amongst the Brahmins; whatsoever holy Enoch, the governor of Paradise, prophesied before he was transferred from the world; yea, whatsoever the first Adam taught his sons, as he had previously seen it in the book of eternity, when rapt in an ecstasy—may with probability be thought to have been destroyed by those impious flames. The religion of the Egyptians, which the book called Logistoricus so highly commends; the polity of the ancient Athenians, who preceded the Athenians of Greece 9000 years; the verses of the Chaldeans; the astronomy of the Arabs and Indians; the ceremonies of the Jews; the architecture of the Babylonians; the Georgics of Noah; the divinations of Moses; the trigonometry of Joshua; the enigmas of Samson; the problems of Solomon, most clearly argued from the cedar of Lebanon to the hyssop; the antidotes of Æsculapius; the grammatics of Cadmus; the poems of Parnassus; the Oracles of Apollo; the Argonautics of Jason: the stratagems of Palamedes; and an infinity of other secrets of science— are believed to have been lost in like manner by fires.

Would the demonstrative syllogism of the quadrature of the circle have been concealed from Aristotle, if wicked wars had permitted the books of the ancients, containing the methods of the whole of Nature, to be forthcoming? Or would he have left the problem of the eternity of the world undecided, or have at all doubted about the plurality of human intellects, and of their perpetuity, as he is with some reason believed to have done, if the perfect sciences of the ancients had not been exposed to the pressure of odious wars? For by wars we are dispersed in foreign countries, dismembered, wounded, and enormously mutilated, buried in the earth, drowned in the sea, burned in the fire, and slain by every species of violent slaughter. How much of our blood did the warlike Scipio shed, when earnestly bent upon the overthrow of Carthage, the emulous assailant of the Roman empire? How many thousands of thousands did the ten years Trojan war send out of the world! How many, upon the murder of Tully by Anthony, went into the recesses of remote provinces! How many of us, when Boëthius was banished by Theodoric, were dispersed into the various regions of the world like sheep whose shepherd is slain! How many, when Seneca fell by the malice of Nero, and willingly or unwillingly went towards the gates of death, withdrew weeping, and not knowing where we ought to take up our abode when separated from him. Fortunate was that transfer of books which Xerxes is described to have made from the Athenians to the Persians, and which Zeleucus brought back from the Persians to Athens. O, what becoming pride, what admirable exultation might you behold, when the mother, leaping for joy, met her children, and the bride-chamber of the now aged parent was once more pointed out to her offspring as the lodging assigned to its former tenants! Now cedar shelves with light beams and supporters are most neatly planed, labels are designed in gold and ivory for each partition, in which the volumes themselves are reverently deposited and most nicely arranged, so that no one can impede the entrance of another, or injure its brother by over-pressure.

In all other respects, indeed, the damages which are brought on by the tumults of war, especially upon the race of books, are infinite; and forasmuch also as it is a property of the infinite that it can neither be stepped over nor passed through, we will here finally set up the pillars of our complaints, and, drawing in our reins, return to the prayers with which we set out, suppliantly beseeching the ruler of Olympus and the most high Dispenser of all the world, that he may abolish war, establish peace, and bring about tranquil times under his own special protection.

CHAPTER VIII.

*Of the numerous Opportunities of the Author of Collecting
Books from all Quarters.*

As there is a time and opportunity for every purpose, as
Ecclesiastes witnesseth (ch. iii.), we will now proceed to
particularize the numerous opportunities we have enjoyed,
under divine propitiation, in our proposed acquisition of
books. For, although from our youth we have ever been
delighted to hold special and social communion with literary
men and lovers of books, yet prosperity attending us,
having obtained the notice of his Majesty the King, and
being received into his own family, we acquired a most
ample facility of visiting at pleasure and of hunting as it
were some of the most delightful coverts, the public and
private libraries both of the regulars and seculars. Indeed,
while we performed the duties of Chancellor and Treasurer
of the most invincible and ever magnificently triumphant
King of England, Edward III. (of that name) after the
Conquest—whose days may the Most High long and tran-
quilly deign to preserve!—after first inquiring into the
things that concerned his Court, and then the public affairs
of his kingdom, an easy opening was afforded us, under the
countenance of royal favour, for freely searching the hiding-
places of books. For the flying fame of our love had already
spread in all directions, and it was reported not only that
we had a longing desire for books and especially for old
ones, but that anybody could more easily obtain our favour
by quartos than by money. Wherefore when supported by
the bounty of the aforesaid prince of worthy memory, we
were enabled to oppose or advance, to appoint or discharge,
crazy quartos and tottering folios, precious however in our
sight as well as in our affections, flowed in most rapidly
from the great and the small, instead of new year's gifts

and remunerations, and instead of presents and jewels. Then the cabinets of the most noble monasteries were opened, cases were unlocked, caskets were unclasped, and astonished volumes which had slumbered for long ages in their sepulchres were roused up, and those that lay hid in dark places were overwhelmed with the rays of a new light. Books heretofore most delicate, now become corrupted and abominable, lay lifeless, covered indeed with the excrements of mice and pierced through with the gnawing of worms; and those that were formerly clothed with purple and fine linen, were now seen reposing in dust and ashes, given over to oblivion, the abodes of moths. Amongst these nevertheless, as time served, we sat down more voluptuously than the delicate physician could do amidst his stores of aromatics; and where we found an object of love, we found also an assuagement. Thus the sacred vessels of science came into the power of our disposal—some being given, some sold, and not a few lent for a time.

Without doubt, many who perceived us to be contented with gifts of this kind, studied to contribute those things freely to our use which they could most willingly do without themselves. We took care, however, to conduct the business of such so favourably that the profit might accrue to them; justice therefore suffered no detriment.

Moreover, if we would have amassed cups of gold and silver, excellent horses, or no mean sums of money, we could in those days have laid up abundance of wealth for ourselves; but indeed we wished for books, not bags; we delighted more in folios than florins, and preferred paltry pamphlets to pampered palfreys. In addition to this, we were charged with the frequent embassies of the said prince of everlasting memory, and, owing to the multiplicity of State affairs, were sent first to the Roman Chair, then to the Court of France, then to various other kingdoms of the world, on tedious embassies and in perilous times, carrying about with us,

however, that fondness for books which many waters could
not extinguish; for this, like a certain drug, sweetened
the wormwood of peregrination; this, after the perplexing
intricacies, scrupulous circumlocutions of debate, and almost
inextricable labyrinths of public business, left an opening for
a little while to breathe the temperature of a milder atmosphere. O blessed God of gods in Sion! what a rush of the
flood of pleasure rejoiced our heart as often as we visited
Paris, the Paradise of the world! There we longed to
remain, where, on account of the greatness of our love, the
days ever appeared to us to be few. There are delightful
libraries in cells redolent of aromatics; there flourishing
greenhouses of all sorts of volumes; there academic meads
trembling with the earthquake of Athenian Peripatetics
pacing up and down; there the promontories of Parnassus,
and the porticos of the Stoics. There is to be seen Aristotle
the surveyor of arts and sciences, to whom alone belongs all
that is most excellent in doctrine in this transitory world.
There Ptolemy extends cycles and eccentrics; and Gen-
sachar plans out the figures and numbers of the planets.
There Paul reveals his Arcana; and Dionysius arranges and
distinguishes the hierarchies. There whatsoever Cadmus
the Phœnician collected of grammatics, the virgin Carmentis
represents entire in the Latin character. There in very
deed, with an open treasury and untied purse-strings, we
scattered money with a light heart, and redeemed inesti-
mable books with dirt and dust. Every buyer is apt to boast
of his great bargains; but consider, how good, how agreeable
it is to collect the arms of the clerical militia into one pile,
that it may afford us the means of resisting the attacks of
heretics if they rise against us. Furthermore, we are
conscious of having seized the greatest opportunity in this—
namely, that from an early age, bound by no matter what
partial favour, we attached ourselves with most exquisite
solicitude to the society of masters, scholars, and professors
of various arts, whom perspicacity of wit and celebrity in

learning had rendered most conspicuous; encouraged by
whose consolatory conversation, we were most deliciously
nourished, sometimes with explanatory investigation of
arguments, at others with recitations of treatises on the
progress of physics, and of the Catholic doctors, as it were,
with multiplied and successive dishes of learning. Such
were the comrades we chose in our boyhood; such we
entertained as the inmates of our chambers; such the
companions of our journeys; such the messmates of our
board; and such entirely our associates in all our fortunes.
But as no happiness is permitted to be of long duration, we
were sometimes deprived of the personal presence of some
of these luminaries, when, Justice looking down upon
them from heaven, well-earned ecclesiastical promotions and
dignities fell in their way; whence it came to pass, as it
shculd do, that, being incumbents of their own cures,
they were compelled to absent themselves from our
courtesies.

Again. We will add a most compendious way by which
a great multitude of books, as well old as new, came into
our hands. Never indeed having disdained the poverty of
religious devotees, assumed for Christ, we never held them
in abhorrence, but admitted them from all parts of the
world into the kind embraces of our compassion; we allured
them with most familiar affability into a devotion to our
person, and, having allured, cherished them for the love of
God with munificent liberality, as if we were the common
benefactor of them all, but nevertheless with a certain propriety of patronage, that we might not appear to have given
preference to any—to these under all circumstances we
became a refuge; to these we never closed the bosom of our
favour. Wherefore we deserved to have those as the most
peculiar and zealous promoters of our wishes, as well by
their personal as their mental labours, who, going about by
sea and land, surveying the whole compass of the earth, and
also inquiring into the general studies of the universities of

the various provinces, were anxious to administer to our wants, under a most certain hope of reward.

Amongst so many of the keenest hunters, what leveret could lie hid? What fry could evade the hook, the net, or the trawl of these men? From the body of divine law, down to the latest controversial tract of the day, nothing could escape the notice of these scrutinizers. If a devout sermon resounded at the fount of Christian Faith, the most holy Roman Court, or if an extraneous question were to be sifted on account of some new pretext; if the dulness of Paris, which now attends more to studying antiquities than to subtly producing truth; if English perspicacity overspread with ancient lights always emitted new rays of truth, whatsoever it promulgated, either for the increase of knowledge or in declaration of the faith—this, while recent, was poured into our ears, not mystified by imperfect narration nor corrupted by absurdity, but from the press of the purest presser it passed, dregless, into the vat of our memory. When indeed we happened to turn aside to the towns and places where the aforesaid paupers had convents, we were not slack in visiting their chests and other repositories of books; for there, amidst the deepest poverty, we found the most exalted riches treasured up; there, in their satchels and baskets, we discovered not only the crumbs that fell from the master's table for the little dogs, but indeed the shewbread without leaven, the bread of angels, containing in itself all that is delectable—yea, the granaries of Joseph full of corn and all the furniture of Egypt, and the richest gifts that the Queen of Sheba brought to Solomon. These are the ants that lay up in harvest, the laborious bees that are continually fabricating cells of honey; the successors of Belzaleel, in devising whatsoever can be made by the workman in gold, silver and precious stones, with which the Temple of the church may be decorated; these, the ingenious embroiderers who make the ephod and breastplate of the Pontiff, as also the various garments of the priests.

These keep in repair the curtains, cloths, and red ram skins with which the tabernacle of the church militant is covered over. These are the husbandmen that sow, the oxen that tread out the corn, the blowers of the trumpets, the twinkling Pleiades, and the stars remaining in their order, which cease not to fight against Sisera. And that truth may be honoured (saving the opinion of any man), although these may have lately entered the Lord's vineyard at the eleventh hour, as our most beloved books anxiously alleged in the sixth chapter, they have nevertheless in that shortest hour trained more layers of the sacred books than all the rest of the vine-dressers, following the footsteps of Paul, who, being the last in vocation but the first in preaching, most widely spread the Gospel of Christ. Amongst these we had some of two of the orders—namely, Preachers and Minors, who were raised to the pontifical state, who had stood at our elbows, and been the guests of our family; men in every way distinguished as well by their morals as by their learning, and who had applied themselves with un-wearied industry to the correction, explanation, indexing, and compilation of various volumes.

Indeed, although we had obtained abundance both of old and new works through an extensive communication with all the religious orders, yet we must in justice extol the Preachers with a special commendation in this respect; for we found them above all other religious devotees ungrudging of their most acceptable communications, and overflowing with a certain divine liberality ; we experienced them, not to be selfish hoarders, but meet professors of enlightened knowledge. Besides all the opportunities already touched upon, we easily acquired the notice of the stationers and librarians, not only within the provinces of our native soil, but of those dispersed over the kingdoms of France, Germany, and Italy, by the prevailing power of money; no distance whatever impeded, no fury of the sea deterred them ; nor was cash wanting for their expenses when they

sent or brought us the wished-for books; for they knew to
a certainty that their hopes reposed in our bosom could not
be disappointed, but ample redemption with interest was
secure with us.   Lastly, our common captivatrix of the love
of all men (money) did not neglect the rectors of country
schools nor the pedagogues of clownish boys; but rather,
when we had leisure to enter their little gardens and pad-
docks, we culled redolent flowers upon the surface, and dug
up neglected roots (not, however, useless to the studious),
and such coarse digests of barbarism as with the gift of eloquence might be made sanative to the pectoral arteries.
Amongst productions of this kind we found many most
worthy of renovation, which when the foul rust was skilfully polished off and the mask of old age removed, deserved
to be once more remodelled into comely countenances, and
which, we having applied a sufficiency of the needful means,
resuscitated for an exemplar of future resurrection, having
in some measure restored them to renewed soundness.
Moreover, there was always about us in our halls no small
assemblage of antiquaries, scribes, bookbinders, correctors,
illuminators, and generally of all such persons as were qualified to labour advantageously in the service of books.

To conclude.   All of either sex of every degree, estate or
dignity, whose pursuits were in any way connected with
books, could with a knock most easily open the door of our
heart, and find a convenient reposing place in our bosom.
We so admitted all who brought books, that neither the
multitude of first-comers could produce a fastidiousness of
the last, nor the benefit conferred yesterday be prejudicial
to that of to-day.   Wherefore, as we were continually re-
sorted to by all the aforesaid persons as to a sort of adamant
attractive of books, the desired accession of the vessels of
science, and a multifarious flight of the best volumes were
made to us.   And this is what we undertook to relate at
large in the present chapter.

CHAPTER IX.

The Ancient Students surpassed the Modern in Fervency of Learning.

ALTHOUGH the novelties of the moderns were never the burthen of our desires, we have always with grateful affection honoured those who found leisure for the studies and opinions of the primitive Fathers, and ingeniously or usefully added anything to them. We have nevertheless coveted with a more undisturbed desire the well-digested labours of the ancients. Whether they were naturally invigorated with the capacity of a more perspicacious mind, whether they addicted themselves perhaps to more intense study, or whether they succeeded by the support of both these aids, we have clearly discovered this one thing—that their successors are scarcely competent to discuss the discoveries of those who preceded them, or to comprehend those things by the shorter way of instruction which the ancients quarried up by their own roundabout contrivances.

For as we read that they possessed a more excellent proportion of body than what modern times are known to exhibit, so there is no absurdity in believing that most of the ancients were more refulgent in the clearness of their understandings, as the works they performed, by both appear alike unattainable by their successors. Whence Phocas in the prologue of his Grammar writes:

> Omnia cum veterum sint explorata libellis
> Multa loqui breviter sit novitatis opus.

As in the books of the ancients all things have been explored,
Be it the work of novelty to say much in few words.

For certainly if the question is about ardour in learning and diligence in study, these devoted their whole life entirely to philosophy ; but the contemporaries of our age negligently apply a few years of ardent youth, burning by turns with the fire of vice; and when they have attained the acumen of discerning a doubtful truth, they immediately become involved in extraneous business, retire, and say farewell to the schools of philosophy; they sip the frothy must of juvenile wit over the difficulties of philosophy, and pour out the purified old wine with economical care.

Further, as Ovid justly laments, De Vetula:

> Omnes declinant ad ea quæ lucra ministrant,
>   Utque sciant discunt pauci; plures ut abundent.
> Sic te prostituunt, O virgo Scientia, sic te
>   Venalem faciunt, castis amplexibus aptam,
> Non te propter te quærentes, sed lucra pro te:
>   Ditarique volunt potius quam philosophari.

> All men incline to things affording gain;
>   Few study wisdom, more for riches strain;
> Thee they prostitute, O virgin Science;
>   Thee venal make, whose chaste compliance
> None for thy own sake ask. Man rather tries
>   Through thee to thrive than to philosophize.

And thus as the love of wisdom is doomed to exile, the love of money rules, which is evidently the most violent poison of discipline. In what manner indeed the ancients set no other limit to their studies than that of their life, Valerius Maximus shows to Tiberius by the examples of many (lib. 8, cap. 7). Carneades (he says) was a laborious and constant soldier of science; for having completed his ninetieth year, that same was the end of his living and philosophizing. Socrates during his ninety-fourth year wrote a most noble book. Sophocles being nearly one hundred years old wrote his Œdipodæon, that is, the Book of the Acts of Œdipus. Simonides wrote verses in his eightieth year. Aulus Gellius wished to live no longer than while he was competent to write, as he testifies in the prologue of his Attic Nights. But the philosopher Taurus, in order to excite young people to study, used to adduce the fervour of study that possessed Euclid the Socratic, as Aulus Gellius relates in his afore-

said volume (lib. 6, cap. 10). For as the Athenians hated
the Megarenses, they decreed that if any one of them should
enter Athens he should be beheaded; but Euclid, who was
a Megarensian, and had heard Socrates before that decree,
went afterwards to hear him in the night disguised as a
woman and returned, the distance from Megara to Athens
being twenty miles. Imprudent and excessive was the
fervour of Archimedes, a lover of the geometric art, who
would neither tell his name, nor raise his head from a
figure he had drawn, by doing which he might have
prolonged the fate of his mortal life; but thinking more
of his study than his life, he imbrued his favourite figure
with his vital blood. There are many more examples of
the same sort to our purpose, which the brevity we affect
does not permit us to detail. But with sorrow we say that
the celebrated clerks of these days fall into a very different
course. Labouring, indeed, under ambition at an early age,
fitting Icarian wings upon their feeble and untried arms,
they immaturely seize upon the magisterial cap, and become
worthless puerile professors of many faculties, which they
by no means pass through step by step, but ascend to
by leaps, after the manner of goats; and when they have
tasted a little of the great stream, they think they have
drunk it to the bottom, their mouths being scarcely wetted.
They raise up a ruinous edifice upon an unstable foundation, because they were not founded in the first rudiments
at the proper time: being now promoted, they are ashamed
to learn what it would have become them to have learnt
when younger, and thus in effect they are perpetually
compelled to pay the penalty of having too hastily leaped
into undue authority. For these and other similar causes
scholastic tyros do not obtain, by their scanty lucubrations,
that soundness of learning that the ancients possessed,
inasmuch as they can now be endowed with honours,
distinguished by names, authorized by the garb of office,
and solemnly placed in the chairs of their seniors, as soon

as they have crept out of their cradles, been hastily weaned, and can repeat the rules of Priscian and Donatus by rote. In their teens and beardless, they re-echo with infantine prattle the Categories and Parmenias, in the writing of which the great Aristotle is feigned to have dipped his pen in his heart's blood. Passing the routine of which faculties, with dangerous brevity and a baneful diploma, they lay violent hands upon holy Moses ; and sprinkling their faces with the dark waters of the clouds of the air, they prepare their heads, unadorned by any of the greyness of old age, for the mitre of the Pontificate. By such pernicious steps are these pests put forward, and aided in attaining to that fantastical clerkship. The Papal provision is importuned by the seductive entreaties, or rather prayers, of cardinals and powerful friends which cannot be rejected, and the cupidity of relations, who, building up Sion upon their own blood, watch for ecclesiastical dignities for their nephews and wards before they are matured by the course of nature or sufficient instruction. Hence not without shame we observe the Parisian Palladium in our woful times, suffering under the paroxysm we are deploring. There, where zeal was lately hot, it now almost freezes; where the rays of so noble a school formerly gave light to every corner of the earth, there the pen of every scribe is now at rest, the generation of books is no longer propagated, nor is there any one who can attempt to be considered as a new author. They involve their opinions in unskilful language, and are destitute of all logical propriety, excepting that with furtive vigilance they find out English subtleties which they manifestly carry off.

The admirable Minerva seems to have made the tour of the nations of mankind, and casually come in contact with them all, from one end of the world to the other, that she might communicate herself to each. We perceive her to have passed through the Indians, Babylonians, Egyptians, Greeks, Arabians, and Latins. She next deserted Athenas, and then retired from Rome; and having already given the slip to the Parisians, she has at last happily reached Britain, the most renowned of islands, or rather the Microcosm, that she may show herself indebted to Greeks and barbarians. From the accomplishment of which miracle it is conjectured by many that, as the Sophia of Gaul is now become lukewarm, so her emasculated militia is become altogether languid.

———

CHAPTER X.

Science grew to Perfection by Degrees.—The Author provided a Greek and a Hebrew Grammar.

ASSIDUOUSLY searching out the wisdom of the ancients according to the advice of the wise man (Eccl. xxxix.), who says, "A wise man searches out all the wisdom of the ancients;" we have not led ourselves into that opinion for the purpose of saying that the first founders cleared away all the rudeness of the arts, knowing that the invention of every one has been weighed, in the faithful endeavour to make a small portion of science efficient. But through the careful investigations of many, the symbols being given as it were one by one, the vigorous bodies of the sciences grew up by successive augmentations into the immense copiousness we now behold: for scholars ever melted down the opinions of their masters in renewed furnaces, running off the previously neglected dross till they became choice gold, proved, seven times purged of earth, and unalloyed by any admixture of error or doubt. Even Aristotle, although of gigantic mind, in whom it pleased Nature to try how great a portion of reason she could admit into mortality, and whom the Most High made but little inferior to the angels, who sucked those wonderful volumes out of his own fingers which the whole world scarcely comprehends, would not have flourished if he had not, with the penetrating eyes of a lynx, looked through the sacred books of the Babylonians, Egyptians, Chaldeans, Persians, and Medes, all which he transferred into his own treasuries in eloquent Greek. Receiving their correct assertions, he polished their asperities, cut off their superfluities, supplied their deficiencies, expunged their errors, and thought it right to return thanks, not only to those who taught truly, but also to those who erred, as their errors point out a way of more easily investigating truth, as he himself clearly shows (Metaph. 2). Thus many lawyers compiled the Pandect, many physicians the Tegni, and Avicenna the canon. Thus Pliny edited that mass of Natural History, and Ptolemy the Almagest; for after this manner it is not difficult to perceive in writers of annals that the last always presupposes a prior, without whom he would in no way have been competent to detail past events. The same thing holds good amongst the authors of science, as no man produced any science whatever alone; for between the more ancient and the more recent we find intermediates, old, indeed, if compared with our times, but new, if referred to the groundwork of science; and these are held to be the most learned. What would Virgil, the greatest poet of the Latins, have done if he had not at all plundered Theocritus, Lucretius, and Homer, or ploughed with their heifer? What could Horace anyhow have pored over but Parthenius and Pindar, whose eloquence he could in no way imitate? What Sallust, Tully, Boethius, Macrobius, Lactantius, Martianus, nay, the whole cohort of the Latins in general, if they had not seen the labours of the Athenians or volumes of the Greeks? Jerome, skilled in the treasures of the three languages of Scripture; Ambrose; Augustine, who, however, confessed that he hated Greek literature; and still more, Gregory, who is described as altogether ignorant of it, would certainly have contributed little to the doctrines of the Church, if they had borrowed nothing from the more learned Greeks; watered by whose rivulets,

Rome, as she first generated philosophers after the image of the Greeks, so afterwards in like form she brought forth treatisers of the orthodox faith. The creeds we chant are the sweat of the Greeks, declared in their councils and confirmed by the martyrdom of many. Native dulness, however, as it falls out, gives way to the glory of the Latins; inasmuch as, if they were less learned in their studies, so they were less wicked in their errors. For instance, the Arian malice nearly eclipsed the whole Church. The Nestorian profligacy presumed to rave against the Virgin with blasphemous madness; for it would have taken from her the name of Queen as well as the definition Theotocos, Θεοτόκος (divine genetrix), had not the invincible soldier, Cyril, been prepared to attack and extinguish it in single combat. We can neither enumerate the various kinds nor the authors of the heresies of the Greeks; for as they were the primitive cultivators of the most holy faith, so they were also the first sowers of darnel, as already said, and as they are declared to have been in histories worthy of credit. From this they afterwards proceeded to worse; for while they endeavoured to rend the seamless garment of the Lord, they entirely lost the light of philosophical doctrine; and being blind, they will fall into the abyss of new darknesses, unless He, by His hidden power, shall take care of them, whose wisdom numbers cannot measure. But enough of this, for here the power of judging is taken from us. We draw this one conclusion, however, from what has been said: namely, that ignorance of the Greek language is at this day highly injurious to the study of the Latins, without which the dogmas either of the ancient Christians or Gentiles cannot be comprehended. The same may credibly be supposed of the Arabic in many astronomical treatises, and of the Hebrew in reading the Holy Bible. Clement the Fifth providently meets these defects, if prelates would only faithfully observe what is easily ordained. Wherefore we have taken care to provide for our scholars a Hebrew as well as a Greek Grammar, with certain adjuncts, by the help of which studious readers may be instructed in writing, reading, and understanding the said languages, although the hearing alone with the ears can represent propriety of idiom to the mind.

———

CHAPTER XI.

Laws are, properly speaking, neither Sciences nor Books.

THE lucrative skill adapted to worldly dispensations in the books of positive law, is the more usefully serviceable to the sons of the world, the less it contributes to the sons of light, towards comprehending the mysteries of Holy Scripture and the arcane sacraments of the faith, inasmuch as it peculiarly disposes to the friendship of this world, by which man is made the enemy of God, as James witnesseth (iv. 4). Hence, without doubt, human cupidity produces infinite contentions, which it extends oftener than it extinguishes, by intricate laws that can be turned to either side. Positive law, however, is distinguished as having emanated from lawyers and pious princes to appease such contentions. Truly when the discipline of contraries is one and the same, and the reasoning power is available to opposites, and at the same time human feelings are most prone to mischief, it happens that the practitioners of this faculty indulge more in protracting litigation than in peace; and quote the law, not according to the intention of the legislator, but violently twist his words to the purpose of their own machinations.

Wherefore, although the master love of books possessed our mind from childhood, a longing for which we took to instead of a desire for pleasure, yet an appetite for the books of civilians took little hold of our affections, and we

bestowed but little labour and expense on acquiring volumes
of that sort. They are nevertheless useful things, like the
scorpion in treacle, as Aristotle, the sun of doctrine, said of
logic in the book, De Pomo et Morte. We have even
perceived a certain manifest difference of nature between
laws and sciences ; as every science is delightful, and desires
that, its bowels being inspected, the vitals of its principles
may be laid open, the roots of its germination appear, and
the emanation of its spring come to light ; for thus, from
the connate and consistent light of the truth of conclusion
from principles, the body itself of science will become
entirely lucid without any particle of obscurity. But laws,
indeed, as they are certain covenants and human enact-
ments for regulating civil life, or yokes of princes thrown
over the horns of their subjects, they refuse to be reduced
to the very synderesis of truth and origin of equity, and on
that account may be feared to have more of the empire of
will in them than of the judgment of reason ; for the same
reason it is the opinion of wise men that the causes of laws
are for the most part not to be discussed. For many laws
acquire strength by custom alone, not from syllogistic
necessity, like the arts, as Aristotle, the Phœbus of the
school, affirms in the second book of his Politics, where he
argues against the policy of Hippodamus, which promised
to bestow rewards upon the inventors of new laws, because
to abolish old laws and decree new, is to weaken the validity
of those that exist ; for things which receive stability from
custom alone must necessarily go to ruin by disuse.

From all which it appears sufficiently clear that as laws
are neither arts nor sciences, so neither can law books be
properly called books of science or art ; nor is this faculty
to be numbered amongst the sciences, though by an appropriate word it may be called geology ; but books of liberal
literature are so useful to Divine Scripture, that the understanding may in vain aspire to a knowledge of it, without
their help.

CHAPTER XII.

Of the Utility and Necessity of Grammar.

As we were carefully nurtured in the reading of books,
which it was our custom to read or hear daily, we duly
considered how much an imperfect knowledge even of a
single word may impede the business of the understanding,
as the meaning of a proposition, of which any part whatever is unknown, cannot be comprehended. Wherefore,
with wonderful perseverance, we ordered the interpretation
of exotic words to be noted down. We considered the
orthography, prosody, etymology, and diasynthesis of the
ancient grammarians with unyielding curiosity, and we
took care to elucidate terms becoming obscure from too
great age with suitable descriptions, so that we might
prepare a level way for our students. And this is really
the whole reason why we have laboured to renovate so
many ancient volumes of the grammarians in emended
editions; that we might so pave the king's highway with
them, that our future scholars might walk towards any of
the arts whatever without stumbling.

CHAPTER XIII.

A Vindication of Poetry, and its Utility.

THE missiles of all sorts which lovers of naked truth only
cast at poets may be warded off by a twofold shield; because
either a graceful turn of language is to be learned, where
the subject is impure, or natural or historical truth may be
traced where feigned but honest sentiments are treated of

under the eloquence of typical fiction. Although all men
certainly desire to know, yet all do not equally like to
learn. Wherefore, feeling the labour of study, and finding
it to fatigue the senses, most of them inconsiderately throw
away the nut before they have broken the shell and got at
the kernel; for there is a twofold innate love in mankind—
namely, of self-liberty in conduct, and of a certain portion
of pleasure in labour; whence no man submits himself to
the rule of another without cause, or undertakes any labour
whatever, that is tiresome, of his own freewill; for cheer-
fulness perfects labour as beauty does youth, as Aristotle
most truly affirms (Nic. Eth. 10). Wherefore the prudence
of the ancients discovered a remedy by which the wanton
part of mankind might, in a manner, be taken in by a pious
fraud, and the delicate Minerva lie hid under the dissembling mask of pleasure.

We are accustomed to allure children with gifts, to make
them willing to learn those things freely which we mean
them to apply to, even if unwilling; for does not corrupt
nature impel itself by the same instinct by which, being
prone to vice, it transmigrates to virtue? This Horace
declares to us in a short verse, where he treats of the art
of poetry, saying:

> Aut prodesse volunt aut delectare poetæ.
> Poets would improve or delight mankind.

And the same thing in another of his verses, writing,

> Omne tulit punctum qui miscuit utile dulci.
> He carries every point who mixes the useful with the
> delightful.

How many scholars has the Helleflight of Euclid repelled,
as if it were a high and steep cliff that could not be scaled
by the help of any ladder! This is crabbed language, say
they, and who can listen to it? That son of inconstancy,
who at last wished to be transformed into an ass, would

perhaps never have rejected the study of philosophy if it had familiarly fallen in his way, covered with this same veil of pleasure; but being suddenly stupefied at the chair of Crato, and thunderstruck as it were by his infinite questions, he saw no safety whatever but in flight. We have adduced this much in exculpation of poets, and will now show that those who study them with a proper intention are blameless. Ignorance indeed of a single word impedes the understanding of the most important sentences, as assumed in the preceding chapter. As the sayings therefore of the sacred poets frequently allude to fictions, it necessarily follows that the poem introduced being unknown, the whole meaning of the author is entirely obstructed; and certainly, as Cassiodorus says, in his book upon the Institution of Divine Literature, those things are not to be thought small without which great ones cannot subsist. It holds good therefore that, being ignorant of poetry, we cannot understand Jerome, Augustine, Boethius, Lactantius, Sidonius, and many others, whose joyful songs a long chapter would not contain. But Venerable Bede has in a lucid discussion settled the point of this sort of doubtfulness, as the great compiler Gratian, the repeater of many authors, recites, who, as he was niggardly in the matter, so he is found to be confused in the manner of his compilation. He writes, in Distinction 37, beginning, Turbat acumen: "Some read secular literature for pleasure, being delighted with the fictions of poets, and the ornament of their words; but others study them for erudition, that, by reading the errors of the Gentiles, they may detest them, and that they may devoutly carry off what they find in them useful for the service of sacred erudition: such as these, study secular literature laudably." Thus far Bede.

Admonished by this salutary instruction, let the detractors of poetical students be silent for the present; nor should ignorant people of this sort wish for fellow-ignoramuses, for this is like the solace of the miserable. Let every man

therefore confine himself to the feelings of a pious intention; he may thus make his study grateful to God from
any materials whatever, the circumstances of virtue being
observed. And if he should become a poet, as the great
Maro confesses himself to have done by the help of Ennius,
he has not lost his labour.

CHAPTER XIV.

Of those who ought most particularly to Love Books.

To him who recollects what has been said, it is evident and
perspicuous who ought to be the greatest lovers of books.
For who stand most in need of wisdom in fulfilling the
duties of their calling usefully? Those, without doubt, who
are most firmly bound to exhibit the most ready and
anxious affection of a grateful heart for the sacred vessels of
wisdom. But as Aristotle, the Phœbus of philosophers, who
is neither mistaken nor to be mistaken in human affairs,
says in the proem of his Metaphysics: "It is the business
of a wise man to regulate both himself and others properly."
Wherefore princes and prelates, judges and teachers, and all
other directors of public affairs whatever, as they have need
of wisdom beyond other men, so they ought to be zealous
beyond other men about the vessels of wisdom. Boethius
indeed emblematically represented Philosophy holding a
sceptre in her left hand, and a book in her right; by which
it is evidently shown to all men that no one can duly
govern a State without books. You, says Boethius, address-
ing himself to Philosophy, sanctioned this axiom by the
mouth of Plato—"That States would be happy if those
who studied wisdom ruled them, or if it could happen that
wisdom had the appointment of their rulers." Again, the

bearing of the emblem itself insinuates this to us—that inasmuch as the right hand excels the left, insomuch a contemplative life is more worthy than an active; and at the same time it is shown to be the business of a wise man, first to employ himself in the study of truth, and then in the dispensation of temporal affairs, each in its turn. We read that Philip devoutly returned thanks to the gods, because they had granted to Alexander to be born in the days of Aristotle, educated under whose tuition he might be worthy to govern his paternal kingdom. As Phaeton, become the driver of his father's chariot, was ignorant of its management, and unfortunately administered the heat of Phœbus, sometimes at too near and sometimes at too remote a distance, he justly deserved to be struck with thunder for his unsteady driving, and that all below might not be put in peril. The histories both of the Greeks and Latins relate that there were no noble princes amongst them who were unskilled in literature. The sacred Mosaic law, prescribing a rule for a king by which he must reign, commands him to have the book of Divine law written out for himself, according to the copy set forth by the priests, in which he is to read all the days of his life. Truly God himself, who made, and daily and individually fashions the hearts of men, had sufficiently known the slipperiness of human memory, and the instability of virtuous intentions in mankind. For which reason it was His will that there should be a book, an antidote as it were to all evil, of which He ordered the continued reading and use, as the most wholesome daily food of the spirit; by which the understanding, being refreshed and neither enervated nor doubtful, might be altogether fearless in action. This, John of Salisbury elegantly touches upon in his Policraticon (lib. 4). To conclude: All sorts of men who are distinguished by the tonsure or clerical name, against whom the fourth, fifth, and sixth chapters of this book complained, are bound to render service to books with perpetual veneration.

CHAPTER XV.

Of the manifold Effects of the Sciences which are contained in Books.

IT is beyond the wit of man, however deeply he may have drunk of the Pegasean fountain, perfectly to unfold the title of this present chapter. If any one can speak with the tongues of men and angels; if he can be transformed into Mercury or Tully; if he can charm with the creamy eloquence of Livy; if he can plead with the suavity of Demosthenes—even he will allege the hesitation of Moses, or confess with Jeremiah that he is a child, not yet knowing how to speak, or will imitate the echo resounding in the lofty mountains; for the love of books is evidently the love of wisdom, which has been proved to be ineffable. This love is also called by a Greek word, Philosophy, whose virtue no created intelligence comprehends, wherefore it is believed to be the mother of everything that is good (Wisd. vii.); for like a heavenly dew it extinguishes the heat of carnal vices, when the intense commotion of the animal powers abates the force of natural virtue; by entirely expelling idleness, which being removed, every particle of concupiscence will perish. Hence Plato says, in Phædo, "The philosopher is manifest in this—that he separates the soul more widely from communion with the body than other men." Love (says Jerome) the knowledge of the Scriptures, and you will not love the vices of the flesh. The godlike Zenocrates demonstrated this in the firmness of his purpose, whom the noble strumpet Phryne defined to be a statue, and not a man, as no enticement was able to shake his chastity; as Valerius relates at large (lib. 4, cap. 3). Our Origen is another example; who, that he might not chance to be effeminated by omnipotent woman, chose the medium between the two sexes by the abnegation of his extremities. A spiteful remedy truly—neither consonant to nature nor to virtue, whose business is not to make man insensible of the passions, but to check the first efforts of insubordination by the power of reason. Again : All who are affected by the love of books, hold worldly affairs and money very cheap, as Jerome writes to Vigilantius (Epist. 54), " It is not for the same man to ascertain the value of gold coins and of writings ; " which somebody thus repeated in verse :

> No tinker's hand shall dare a book to stain ;
>   No miser's heart can wish a book to gain ;
> The gold assayer cannot value books ;
>   On them the epicure disdainful looks.
> One house at once, believe me, cannot hold
>   Lovers of books and hoarders up of gold.

> Nulla libris, erit apta manus ferrugine tincta.
>   Nec nummata queunt corda vacare libris.
> Non est ejusdem nummos librosque probare.
>   Persequitur libros, grex Epicure tuus.
> Nummipetæ cum libricolis nequeunt simul esse,
>   Ambos, crede mihi, non tenet una domus.

No man therefore can serve Mammon and books. The deformities of vice are highly reprobated in books; so that they are thence said to detest vice in all its forms, who delight in perusing books. The demon who is named after Science, is most easily triumphed over by the knowledge of books; his numerous versatile frauds, and thousand pernicious meanderings, are laid open to the readers of books, that he may not fraudulently circumvent the innocent, by transforming himself into an angel of light. The divine reverence is revealed to us by books ; the virtues by which it is cultivated are most expressly divulged, and the reward is described which the truth, that neither deceives nor is deceived, promises. The contemplation of divine literature in which the Creator and the creature are alternately beheld, and which is drawn from the eternal stream of pleasure, is a perfect representation of future beatitude.

Faith is founded on the power of letters; Hope is confirmed by the solace of books, as we retain it by patience and the consolation of Scripture; Charity is not inflated, but edified by the knowledge of true literature; nay, the Church appears, in the clearest light, to be established upon the Sacred Books. Books are delightful when prosperity happily smiles; when adversity threatens, they are inseparable comforters. They give strength to human compacts, nor are grave opinions brought forward without books. Arts and sciences, the benefits of which no mind can calculate, depend upon books. How great is the wonderful power arising from books! for by them we see not only the ends of the world, but of time; and we contemplate alike things that are, and things that are not, as in a sort of mirror of eternity. In books, we ascend mountains and fathom the depths of the abyss; we behold varieties of fishes which the common atmosphere can by no means contain in soundness; we distinguish the peculiarities of rivers and springs, and different countries, in volumes. We dig up the various kinds of metals, gems, and minerals, and substances of all sorts, out of books; and we learn the virtues of herbs, trees and plants, and behold at leisure the whole offspring of Neptune, Ceres, and Pluto; for if we are pleased to visit the inhabitants of heaven, by walking up Taurus, Caucasus, and Olympus, we transcend the kingdoms of Jove, and with lines and compasses measure the territories of the seven planets, and at last survey the great firmament itself, decorated with signs, degrees, and configurations in endless variety.

There we survey the Antarctic Pole, which eye hath not seen nor ear heard, and with delectable pleasure we admire the luminous way of the Galaxy, and the Zodiac painted with celestial animals. From this we pass on, through books, to separate substances; and as the intellect greets kindred intelligences with the eye of the mind, it discerns and cleaves to the First Cause of all, the immovable Mover of infinite power, in love without end. Behold how, being led on by books, we obtain the reward of our beatitude while we are yet wayfarers : what more can we wish for? Without doubt, as Seneca teaches us in his eighty-fourth Letter, beginning Desij—"Leisure without letters is death, and the sepulture of the living man ;" so we justly conclude, from a converse meaning, that to be employed with literature and books is life.

Again, through books we intimate both to friends and enemies things that we can by no means safely entrust to messengers, inasmuch as access to the chambers of princes is generally conceded to a book, from which the voice of the author would be altogether excluded, as Tertullian says in the beginning of his Apologetics. When we are kept in prison, in chains, and entirely deprived of bodily liberty, we make use of the embassies of books to our friends, and to them we commit the expediting of our causes, and we transmit them there where access could not be made by ourselves in case of death. By books we remember the past, and in a certain manner prophesy the future, and we fix things present that are vacillating and transient in the memory of writing.

It was a felicitous studiousness and a studious felicity of the powerful eunuch, of whom it is related, in the eighth chapter of Acts, that the love of prophetic reading so vehemently excited him, that he never ceased to read on account of travelling : he had given up the form of Queen Candace to oblivion, had removed the treasures he had the charge of from the care of his heart, and was alike regardless of the road, and of the chariot in which he was carried—the love of his book alone had claimed this domicile of chastity, disposed by which he was already worthy to enter the gate of the Faith. O gratifying love of books, that by the grace of baptism made this son of Hell and nursling of Tartarus a son of the Kingdom of Heaven !

Let the impotent pen now cease to consummate the tenor

of an infinite undertaking, lest it may seem rashly to encounter what in the beginning was acknowledged to be impossible for any one to accomplish.

———

CHAPTER XVI.

Of writing New Books and repairing Old Ones.

As it is necessary for a State to provide military arms, and prepare plentiful stores of provisions for soldiers who are about to fight, so it is evidently worth the labour of the Church militant to fortify itself against the attacks of pagans and heretics with a multitude of sound books. But because everything that is serviceable to mortals suffers the waste of mortality through lapse of time, it is necessary for volumes corroded by age to be restored by renovated successors, that perpetuity, repugnant to the nature of the individual, may be conceded to the species. Hence it is that Ecclesiastes significantly says, in the 12th chapter, "There is no end of making many books." For as the bodies of books suffer continual detriment from a combined mixture of contraries in their composition, so a remedy is found out by the prudence of clerks, by which a holy book paying the debt of nature may obtain an hereditary substitute, and a seed may be raised up like to the most holy deceased, and that saying of Ecclesiasticus, chapter xxx., be verified, "The father is dead, and as it were not dead, for he hath left behind him a son like unto himself." The transcribers therefore of old books are, as it were, a sort of propagators of new sons, to whom that paternal duty has devolved, that the common stock may not be diminished. Transcribers of this sort are justly called antiquaries, whose studies Cassiodorus confessed pleased him most of all the things that are accomplished by

bodily labour, thus noticing it in his Institution of Divine
Letters, cap. 3 :—"Happy science (he says), praiseworthy
diligence, to unfold language with the fingers, to give
salvation to mortals in silence, and to fight against the
illicit temptations of the devil with pen and ink!" So far
Cassiodorus.

Moreover, our Saviour exercised the office of a writer,
when, stooping down, He wrote with His finger on the ground
(John viii.), that no man, however noble, may disdain to do
that which the wisdom of God the Father is seen to have
done. O singular serenity of writing, in the delineation of
which the artificer of the world, at whose tremendous name
every knee is bent, bowed down! O venerable invention,
singularly above all contrivances made by the hand of man,
in which the breast of the Lord was humbly inclined, in
which the finger of God was applied to perform the office of
a pen!

We do not read that the Son of God sowed or ploughed,
or wove or dug, or that any other of the mechanical arts
were becoming to the divine wisdom humanized, excepting
to trace letters by writing, that every noble man and sciolist
may learn that fingers were given to man for the business
of writing rather than for fighting. Wherefore we approve
of the opinion of many books, which deem a clergyman
unskilled in writing to be in a certain manner maimed, as
aforesaid in Chapter VI. God himself inscribes the just in
the book of the living. Moses indeed received stone tables
written upon by the finger of God. Job exclaims, " Let him
who gives judgment write a book." The trembling Bel-
shazzar saw fingers writing on the wall, "Mene, Tekel, Uphar-
sin" (Dan. v.). " I," says Jeremiah, "wrote in a volume
with ink" (Jer. xxx.). Christ thus commanded His beloved
John : "What you see, write in a book" (Apoc. i.). The
office of a writer was also enjoined by Isaiah and by Joshua,
that the practice as well as the skill might be commended
to posterity. The King of kings, and Lord of lords, Christ

himself, had writing upon His garment and upon His thigh; as without writing, the perfect regal ornament of the Omnipotent cannot be apparent.

Those who write books of holy science do not cease to teach when dead. Paul did greater service in forming the Church by writing holy Epistles, than by evangelizing verbally to the Gentiles and Jews: for the compiler continues by books from day to day what the traveller laid in the earth formerly began; and thus the prophetic words about teachers writing books are verified—"They who teach many according to righteousness shall exist like the stars to all eternity" (Dan. xii.). Moreover, Catholic doctors have determined that the deep researches of the ancients, before God deluged the original world by a general flood, are to be ascribed to miracle and not to Nature; as God granted them as much of life as was requisite for discovering and inscribing the sciences in books, amongst which, according to Josephus, the wonderful diversities of astronomy required a period of 600 years, that they might be experimentally submitted to observation. But indeed they do not insinuate that the productions of the earth did not afford a more useful aliment to mortals in those primitive times than they do now; by which not only a more exhilarating energy of body was given, but also a more durable and flourishing age; added to which, it conferred not a little to their strength, that the superfluities of voluptuousness were in every way discarded.

Therefore whosoever thou art, being endowed with the gift of God according to the counsel of the Holy Spirit (Eccles. xxxviii.), write wisdom while you have leisure, that your reward with the blessed and the length of your days may be increased. Now if we turn our discourse to the princes of the world, we find great emperors not only to have flourished by skill in the art of writing, but for the most part to have indulged in the practice of it. Julius Cæsar, the first of them all as well in time as in virtue, left

Commentaries upon the Gallic and Civil wars, written out by himself; he also made two books of Analogy, and as many against Cato (Anticatos), and a poem titled The Journey, and many other tracts. And Julius, as well as Augustus, invented secret modes of writing letters, that they might conceal what they wrote; for Julius put the fourth letter for the first, and so went through the alphabet; but Augustus put the second for the first, and the third for the second; and such was the custom afterwards. This last is said to have read and written daily, and even to have declaimed, in the greatest pressure of affairs, during the Mutinensian war. Tiberius wrote lyric verse and some Greek poems. Claudius in like manner, skilled both in the Greek and Latin languages, made various books. But in the art of writing, Titus went beyond these and others, who imitated the handwriting of whomsoever he pleased with the utmost facility, and therefore confessed that, if he had chosen, he could have become a great forger. All these things Suetonius notices in his Lives of the Twelve Caesars.

CHAPTER XVII.

Of handling Books in a cleanly Manner, and keeping them in Order.

WE not only set before ourselves a service to God, in preparing volumes of new books, but we exercise the duties of a holy piety, if we first handle so as not to injure them, then return them to their proper places, and commend them to undefiling custody, that they may rejoice in their purity while held in the hand, and repose in security when laid up in their repositories. Truly, next to the vestments and vessels dedicated to the body of the Lord, holy books deserve to be most decorously handled by the clergy, upon which injury is inflicted as often as they presume to touch them with a dirty hand. Wherefore we hold it expedient to exhort students upon various negligences, which can always be avoided, but which are wonderfully injurious to books.

In the first place, then, let there be a mature decorum in opening and closing of volumes, that they may neither be unclasped with precipitous haste, nor thrown aside after inspection without being duly closed; for it is necessary that a book should be much more carefully preserved than a shoe. But school folks are in general perversely educated, and, if not restrained by the rule of their superiors, are puffed up with infinite absurdities; they act with petulance, swell with presumption, judge of everything with certainty, and are inexperienced in anything.

You will perhaps see a stiff-necked youth lounging sluggishly in his study: while the frost pinches him in winter time, oppressed with cold, his watery nose drops, nor does he take the trouble to wipe it with his handkerchief till it has moistened the book beneath it with its vile dew. For such a one I would substitute a cobbler's apron in the place of his book. He has a nail like a giant's, perfumed with stinking ordure, with which he points out the place of any pleasant subject. He distributes innumerable straws in various places, with the ends in sight, that he may recall by the mark what his memory cannot retain. These straws, which the stomach of the book never digests, and which nobody takes out, at first distend the book from its accustomed closure, and being carelessly left to oblivion, at last become putrid. He is not ashamed to eat fruit and cheese over an open book, and to transfer his empty cup from side to side upon it; and because he has not his almsbag at hand, he leaves the rest of the fragments in his books. He never ceases to chatter with eternal garrulity to his companions; and while he adduces a multitude of reasons void of physical meaning, he waters the book, spread out upon his lap, with the sputtering of his saliva. What is worse, he next reclines with his elbows on the book, and by a short study invites a long nap; and by way of repairing the wrinkles, he twists back the margins of the leaves, to the no small detriment of the volume. He goes out in the rain, and returns, and now flowers make their appearance upon our soil. Then the scholar we are describing, the neglector rather than the inspector of books, stuffs his volume with firstling violets, roses, and quadrifoils. He will next apply his wet hands, oozing with sweat, to turning over the volumes, then beat the white parchment all over with his dusty gloves, or hunt over the page, line by line, with his forefinger covered with dirty leather. Then, as the flea bites, the holy book is thrown aside, which, however, is scarcely closed once in a month, and is so swelled with the dust that has fallen into it. that it will not yield to the efforts of the closer.

But impudent boys are to be specially restrained from meddling with books, who, when they are learning to draw the forms of letters, if copies of the most beautiful books are allowed them, begin to become incongruous annotators, and wherever they perceive the broadest margin about the text, they furnish it with a monstrous alphabet, or their unchastened pen immediately presumes to draw any other frivolous thing whatever that occurs to their imagination. There the Latinist, there the Sophist, there every sort of unlearned scribe tries the goodness of his pen, which we have frequently seen to have been most injurious to the fairest volumes, both as to utility and price. There are also certain thieves who enormously dismember books by cutting off the side margins for letter paper, leaving only the letters or text, or the fly-leaves put in for the preservation of the book, which they take away for various uses and abuses, which sort of sacrilege ought to be prohibited under a threat of anathema.

But it is altogether befitting the decency of a scholar,

that washing should without fail precede reading, as often
as he returns from his meals to study, before his fingers
besmeared with grease loosen a clasp or turn over the leaf
of a book.   Let not a crying child admire the drawings in
the capital letters, lest he pollute the parchment with his
wet fingers, for he instantly touches whatever he sees.

Furthermore, laymen, to whom it matters not whether
they look at a book turned wrong side upwards or spread
before them in its natural order, are altogether unworthy
of any communion with books.   Let the clerk also take
order that the dirty scullion, stinking from the pots, do not
touch the leaves of books unwashed; but he who enters
without spot shall give his services to the precious volumes.
The cleanliness of delicate hands, as if scabs and pustules
could not be clerical characteristics, might also be most important, as well to books as to scholars, who as often as
they perceive defects in books should attend to them instantly, for nothing enlarges more quickly than a rent, as a
fracture neglected at the time will afterwards be repaired
with increased trouble.

The most meek Moses instructs us about making cases
for books in the neatest manner, wherein they may be safely
preserved from all damage.   "Take this book," says he,
"and put it in the side of the ark of the covenant of the
Lord your God" (Deut. xxxi.).   O, befitting place, appropriate library, which was made of imperishable Shittim
wood, and covered all over inside and out with gold!   But
our Saviour also, by His own example, precludes all unseemly
negligence in the treatment of books, as may be read in
Luke iv.   For when He had read over the Scriptural
prophecy written about himself in a book delivered to Him,
He did not return it to the minister till He had first closed
it with His most holy hands; by which act students are
most clearly taught that they ought not in the smallest
degree whatever to be negligent about the custody of books.

CHAPTER XVIII.

The Author against Detractors.

NOTHING is held to be more unjust in human affairs than that those things which are most justly done should be perverted by the obloquies of the malignant, as if he who reports the news of a fault should thereby deserve the highest degree of respect. Many things are done with an honest intention; the right hand does not interfere with the left; the mass is not corrupted by any ferment, nor is the garment woven of flax and wool. A pious work, however, is mendaciously transformed into a monster by the legerdemain of perverters. This state of a sinful mind is without doubt to be reprobated, because it not only judges for the worst of acts morally doubtful, but even with iniquitous perversity very often depraves those that bear the stamp of goodness.

Now, although the love of books, in a clerical man, from the nature of the object, bears honour in the face of it, yet it made us in a wonderful manner obnoxious to the criticisms of many; traduced by whose wonderings we were sometimes remarked upon for superfluous curiosity, sometimes for earnestness in that matter alone, sometimes for a display of vanity, and sometimes for immoderate pleasure in literature; but, in truth, these vituperations no more discompose us than the barking of a lapdog, being contented with the testimony of Him to whom alone it belongs to search the reins and heart. For as the final intention of the secret will is concealed from man and exposed to God alone, the inspector of hearts, they deserve to be rebuked for pernicious rashness who, not perceiving the mainspring of human actions, so readily set the sinister mark of their baneful temerity upon them. For the end, in things practicable, sustains itself like principles in speculative, and assumptions in mathematical propositions, as Aristotle, the prince of philosophers, witnesses (Ethics, 7). Wherefore, as the truth of a conclusion is made clear from the evidence of principles, so, for the most part, moral goodness in things practicable is stamped upon the performance by the intention of an honest purpose, where on the contrary the work itself ought to be deemed indifferent as to morals. But we have for a long time held a rooted purpose in the inmost recesses of our mind, looking forward to a favourable time and divine aid, to found, in perpetual alms, and enrich with the necessary gifts, a certain Hall in the revered University of Oxford, the first nurse of all the liberal arts; and further to enrich the same, when occupied by numerous scholars, with deposits of our books, so that the books themselves and every one of them may be made common as to use and study, not only to the scholars of the said Hall, but through them to all the students of the aforesaid University for ever, according to the manner and form which the following chapter will declare. Wherefore a sincere love of study and a zeal for confirming the orthodox faith, to the edification of the Church, brought forth in us this to money-lovers stupendous solicitude in purchasing such books, collected from all parts, as were to be sold, regardless of the expense, and of causing those that ought not to be sold to be handsomely transcribed. For as the pleasures of men are diversified in many manners, according to the disposition of the heavenly bodies, to which a complexion of mixtures frequently accommodates itself, so that some choose to be conversant with architecture, some with agriculture, some with field sports, some with navigation, some with war, and some with games, so our Mercurial sort of honest pleasure about books fell under the will of right reason (in the control of which no stars are dominant), which we have so regulated in honour of the Supreme Majesty, that our mind might find the tranquillity of rest, and that the worship of God might most devoutly increase thereby.

Wherefore let detractors like the blind desist from judging of colours. Let not bats dare to argue about lights, nor those who have beams in their own eyes presume to pluck the motes out of other people's. Let those cease to defame what they know nothing of with satirical remarks, and to discuss secrets which are not open to human research, who perhaps would have commended us with a benevolent affection if we had found leisure for hunting wild beasts, playing at hazard, or for the favours of mistresses.

CHAPTER XIX.

A Provident Arrangement by which Books may be Lent to Strangers.

It was always a difficult matter so to limit men to the rules of honesty, that the knavery of the last generation might not overstep the boundaries of its predecessor, and infringe established rules by the licentiousness of liberty. Wherefore by the advice of prudent men we have devised beforehand a certain method by which we wish the communication and use of our books to descend to the service of students. In the first place, therefore, we have conceded and given with a charitable view, to a company of scholars residing in a Hall at Oxford, as a perpetual alms-deed for our own soul and for the souls of our parents, as well as for the souls of the most illustrious King of England, Edward the Third, after the Conquest, and of the most devout Lady Philippa his consort, all and singular the books of which we have made a special catalogue, that all and singular the said books may be lent out for a time to the scholars and masters, as well regulars as seculars, of the University of the said city, for the advantage and use of students, according to the manner immediately subjoined, which is to this effect.

Five of the scholars dwelling in the aforesaid Hall are to be appointed by the master of the same Hall, to whom the custody of the books is to be deputed. Of which five, three, and in no case fewer, shall be competent to lend any books for inspection and use only; but for copying and transcribing we will not allow any book to pass without the walls of the house. Therefore when any scholar, whether secular or religious, whom we have deemed qualified for the present favour, shall demand the loan of a book, the keepers must carefully consider whether they have a duplicate of that book; and if so, they may lend it to him, taking a security which in their opinion shall exceed in value the book delivered; and they shall immediately make a written memorandum both of the security and the book lent, containing the names of the persons who delivered the book, and of him who received it, with the day and year of our Lord on which the loan took place. But if the keepers shall find that there is no duplicate of the book demanded, they shall not lend such book to any one whomsoever, unless he be of the company of scholars of the said Hall, except as it may happen for inspection within the walls of the aforesaid Hall, but not to be carried beyond them. But to every scholar whatever of the aforesaid Hall, any book whatever may be available by loan; his name, and the day on which he received the book, being first noted down. He, however, is not to have the power of lending the book delivered to him to another, without the assent of three of the aforesaid keepers, and then the name of the first borrower being erased, the name of the second, with the time of delivery, is to be inscribed. For observing all these conditions each of the keepers shall pledge his faith, when a custody of this kind is deputed to him. But the receivers of a book or books shall swear in like manner that he or they shall in no way apply a book to any other use but to inspection or study, and that they will neither carry nor permit it to be carried without the city of Oxford and the suburbs. And the aforesaid keepers must render an account every year to the master of the house, and two of his scholars to be selected by him ; or if he has not leisure, he shall depute three inspectors, not being keepers, who reading over the catalogue must see that they have the whole, either in the books themselves or at least in the securities representing them. We also think the most convenient time for settling this account will be from the kalends of June to the subsequent feast of the most glorious martyr St. Thomas. But we have to add this, that every person, in every instance, to whom any book has been lent, shall exhibit the book once in the year to the keepers, and if he wishes it he shall see his security. Moreover, if any book should happen to be lost, through death, theft, fraud or carelessness, he who lost it or his administrator or executor shall in like manner pay the price of the book and receive the security; but if profit should in any way arise to the keepers themselves, it is not to be converted to any other purpose than to the aid and repairing of the books.

Here we pass over many particulars relating to the care of books, because it appears unnecessary to detail them at present.

CHAPTER XX.

The Author desires to be prayed for, and notably teaches Students to Pray.

TIME now urges us to finish the tract we are tagging together about the love of books, in which we have endeavoured to account for the amazement of our contemporaries at our taking such great delight in books. But because scarcely anything can be said to be performed by mortals that has not some sprinkling of the powder of vanity in it, we will not attempt entirely to justify the zealous love we have so constantly had for books, as it may perhaps at times have been the cause of some venial neglect on our part, although the object of our love were honourable and the intention regulated. For may we not still be bound to call ourselves unprofitable servants, when we shall have done all these things? Indeed, if the most holy Job was fearful in all his works; if, according to Isaiah, all our righteousness is as a menstruous cloth, who shall presume to boast of the perfection of any virtue whatever? or shall not deserve to be reprehended for some circumstances which perhaps he was not able to perceive of himself? For good arises out of pure causes; but evil is omnifarious (as Dionysius instructs us, on Divine Names).

Wherefore, being about to demand the aid of prayers as a remedy for the sins by which we acknowledge ourselves very often to have offended the Creator of all things, we have thought proper to exhort our future students, that they may in so far become grateful as well to ourselves as to their other future benefactors, as to recompense our providential benefactions by spiritual retributions, that we may live entombed in their memories, who being yet unborn lived in our benevolence, and now live, supported by our benefactions.

Let them, with unwearied importunity, implore the clemency of our Redeemer, to the end that He may spare our neglects; that the pious Judge may be indulgent to the guilt of our sins; that He may throw the cloak of charity over the omissions of our frailty, and through His divine benignity remit the offences which with shame and repentance we acknowledge ourselves to have committed; that He may preserve in us sufficient time for repentance, for returning thanks for His gifts, for the confirmation of

our faith, for the exaltation of our hope, and for the most
unbounded charity towards all mankind; that He may
incline our proud will to lament its errors, to deplore its
former most vain elations, retract its most bitter indigna-
tions, and detest its most insane pleasures; that His
strength may grow in us as our own decays, who alike
gratuitously consecrated our entrance into holy baptism,
and undeservedly exalted our progress to the apostolical
state. That the love of the flesh may be weakened in
our spirit, and the fear of death entirely vanish from
it; that it may desire to be set at liberty and to be
with Christ; and that when in body alone we are placed
in the earth, we may dwell in thought and earnest desire in
the eternal country!

May the Father of mercy and the God of all consolation
run to meet the prodigal son returing from the husks!
May He receive the drachm found again, and transmit it
by holy angels into the eternal treasury! May He, with
terrific countenance, castigate the spirit of darkness in the
hour of our departure, that the old serpent Leviathan,
lurking at the threshold of the gate of death, may not
prepare unlooked-for snares for our feet! But when we
shall be called up to the tremendous tribunal, that we may
relate everything that we did in the body (our conscience
bearing witness), may humanity joined to God consider the
price of His holy blood poured out for us! and may
Divinity made man advert to the composition of carnal
nature, that its fragility may pass on with impunity to
that place where clement piety is declared to be infinite,
where the spirit of mercy breathes, and where the peculiar
office of the Judge is to be exceedingly merciful! Furthermore, the refuge of our hope, next to God and the Blessed
Virgin and Queen-Mother, is that our students may always
be careful to reiterate devout salutations, that we who
deserve to meet an angry Judge may be made worthy to
find Him appeased by their ever grateful suffrages! May

a pious hand depress to an equipoise the scale in which our merits, as small as few, shall be weighed, lest (which God forbid!) the weight of crime may preponderate, and cast us to be damned in the abyss! Moreover, let them be devoutly anxious to venerate the merits of St. Cuthbert the confessor, whose flock we, though unworthy, took upon ourselves to feed, earnestly praying that he may favourably condescend to exculpate his vicar, though indeed undeserving, and that he may bring it about that the successor he admitted on earth, may be made a confessor in heaven!

Finally: Let them beseech God with holy prayers, as well bodily as mental, that He may bring back the spirit created in the image of the Trinity, after its sojourn in this life of misery, to its primordial prototype, and grant it a perpetual view of His rejoicing countenance, through our Lord Jesus Christ! Amen.

ΒΑΣΙΛΙΚΟΝ ΔΩΡΟΝ.

OR,

HIS MAIESTIES INSTRVCTIONS TO HIS DEAREST SONNE,

HENRY THE PRINCE.

Basilikon Doron.

THE ARGVMENT.

SONNET.

GOD giues not Kings the stile of Gods in vaine,
For on his throne his sceptre doe they swey :
And as their subiects ought them to obey,
So Kings should feare and serue their God againe.
If then ye would enioy a happie raigne,
Obserue the statutes of your heauenly King,
And from his Law, make all your Lawes to spring :
Since his Lieutenant here ye should remaine,
Reward the iust, be stedfast, true, and plaine,
Represse the proud, maintaining aye the right,
Walke alwaies so, as euer in his sight,
Who guards the godly, plaguing the prophane :
   And so ye shall in Princely vertues shine,
   Resembling right your mightie King Diuine.

TO HENRY,

MY DEAREST SONNE AND NATURALL SUCCESSOR.

WHOME-TO can so rightlie appertaine this booke of instructions to a Prince in all the points of his calling, as well generall, as a Christian towards God ; as particular, as a king towards his people ? Whome-to, I say, can it so justly appertaine, as vnto you my dearest Sonne ? Since I the Authour thereof as your naturall Father, must be carefull for your godly and vertuous education, as my eldest Sonne, and the first fruits of Gods blessing towards me in my posteritie : and as a King must timouslie prouide for your training vp in all the points of a Kings office; since yee are my naturall and lawfull successor therein : that being rightlie informed hereby, of the weight of your burthen, ye may in time begin to consider, that being borne to be a King, ye are rather borne to *onus*, then *honos :* not excelling all your people so farre in ranke and honour, as in daily care and hazardous paines-taking, for the dutifull administration of that great office, that God hath laid vpon your shoulders. Laying so a iust symmetrie and proportion, betwixt the height of your honourable place, and the heauie weight of your great charge : and consequentlie, in case of failing, which God forbid, of the sadnesse of your fall, according to the proportion of that height. I haue therefore for the greater ease to your memorie, and that ye may at the first, cast vp any part that ye haue to do with, deuided this treatise in three parts. The first teacheth you your dutie towards God as a Christian : the next, your dutie in your office as a King : and the third informeth you how to behaue your selfe in indifferent things, which of themselues are neither right nor wrong, but according as they are rightlie or wrong vsed, and yet will serue according to your behauiour therein, to augment or empaire your fame & authoritie at the hands of your people. Recciue and welcome this booke then, as a faithfull Preceptour and counsellor vnto you: which, because my affaires will not permit me euer to be present with you, I ordaine to be a resident faithfull admonisher of you. And because the hovvre of death is uncertaine to me, as vnto all flesh, 1 leaue it as my Testament and latter will vnto you. Charging you in the presence of GOD, and by the fatherlie authoritie I haue ouer you, that yee keepe it euer with you, as carefullie, as Alexander did the Iliads of Homer. Ye will finde it a iust and impartiall counsellor; neither flattering you in anie vice, nor importuning you at vnmeete times. It will not come vncalled, neither speake vnspeered at: and yet conferring with it when yee are at quiet, yee shall say with Scipio, that yee are *nunquam minus solus, quàm cum solus.* To conclude then, I charge you, as euer ye thinke to deserue my fatherlie blessing, to follovve and put in practice, as farre as lieth in you, the precepts hereafter following. And if yee followe the contrarie course, I take the great God to record, that this booke shall one day be a witnesse betwixt me and you; and shall procure to bee ratified in heauen, the curse that in that case here I giue vnto you. For I protest before that great God, I had rather not bee a father, and childlesse, then be a father of wicked children. But hoping, yea euen promising vnto my selfe, that God, who in his great blessing sent you vnto me; shall in the same blessing, as he hath giuen me a Sonne; so make him a good and a godlie Sonne; not repenting him of his mercie shewed vnto me: I end, with my earnest prayer to God, to worke effectualie into you, the fruites of that blessing, which here from my hart I bestow vpon you.

Your louing Father,
I. R.

TO THE READER.

CHARITABLE Reader, it is one of the golden sentences which Christ our Saviour vttred to his Apostles, that there "is nothing so couered, that shal not be reuealed, neither so hid, that shall not be knowne : and whatsoeuer they haue spoken in darknesse, should bee heard in the light : and that which they had spoken in the eare in secret place, should be publiklie preached on the tops of the houses." And since he hath said it, most true must it bee, since the authour thereof is the fountaine and very being of truth. Which should moue all godlie and honest men, to bee very warie in all their secretest actions, and what-soeuer middesses they vse for attaining to their most wished ends : least otherwaies how avowable soeuer the mark be, where-at they aime, the middesses being discouered to be shamefull, whereby they climbe ; it may turne to the disgrace both of the good work it selfe, and of the authour thereof : since the deepest of our secrets cannot be hid from that al-seeing eye, and penetrant light, pearcing through the bowels of verie darknesse it selfe.

But as this is generallie true in the actions of all men, so is it more speciallie true in the affaires of Kings. For Kings being publike persons, by reason of their office and authoritie, are as it were set (as it was sayd of old) vpon a publique stage, in the sight of all the people ; where all the beholders eyes are attentiuelie bent, to looke and pry in the least circumstance of their secretest driftes. Which should make Kings the more carefull, not to harbour the secretest thought in their minde, but such as in the owne time they shall not be ashamed openlie to avouch : assuring themselues, that time the mother of verity, will in the dewe season bring her owne daughter to perfection.

The true practice hereof, I haue as a King, oft found in

my owne person; though I thanke God, neuer to my
shame : hauing laide my count, euer to walke as in the
eyes of the Almightie, examining euer so the secretest of
my driftes, before 1 gaue them course, as how they might
some day byde the touchstone of a publike tryall.

And amongst the rest of my secret actions, which haue
(vnlooked for of me) come to publick knowledge, it hath so
fared with my Βασιλικὸν δῶρον, directed to my eldest sonne ;
which I wrote for exercise of my owne ingene, and instruction of him, who is appointed by God (I hope) to sit on my
Throne after me. For the purpose and matter thereof
being only fit for a King, as teaching him his office ; and
the person whome-for it was ordayned, a King's heire, whose
secret counsellor and faithfull admonisher it must bee ; I
thought it no waies conuenient, nor comelie, that either it
should to all be proclaymed, which to one onely appertained
(& specially being a messenger betwixt two so coniunct
persons) or yet that the moulde, whereupon he should frame
his future behauiour, when he comes both vnto the perfection of his yeeres, and possession of his inheritance, should
before the hand, bee made common to the people, the subiect
of his future happie gouernment. And therefore for the
more secret and close keeping of them, I onely permitted
seauen of them to be printed, the printer being first sworn
for secrecie : and these seauen I dispersed amongst some of
my trustiest seruants, to be keeped closelie by them : least in
case by the iniquitie, or wearing of time, any of them might
haue been lost, yet some of them might have remained after
me, as witnesses to my Sonne, both of the honest integritie
of my heart, and of my fatherlie affection' and naturall care
towards him. But since contrarie to my intention and
expectation, as I haue alreadie said, this booke is now
vented, and set foorth to the publike view of the world, and
consequently subiect to euery mans censure, as the current
of his affection leades him ; I am now forced, as well for
resisting to the malice of the children of enuie, who like

waspes, suckes venome out of euery wholsome hearbe; as for
the satisfaction of the godly honest sort, in anything that
they may mistake therein; both to publish and spred the
true copies thereof, for defacing of the false copies that are
alreadie spred, as I am enformed: as likewaies, by this
preface, to cleere such parts thereof, as in respect of the
concised shortnes of my stile, may be misinterpreted
therein.

To come then particularlie to the matter of my booke,
there are two speciall great points, which (as I am informed)
the malitious sort of men haue detracted therein; and
some of the honest sort haue seemed a little to mistake:
whereof the first and greatest is, that some sentences therein
should seeme to furnish groundes to men, to doubt of my
sinceritie in that Religion, which I haue euer constantly
professed: the other is, that in some partes thereof I should
seeme to nourish in my minde, a vindictiue resolution
against England, or at the least, some principalles there, for
the Queene my mothers quarrell.

The first calumnie (most grieuous indeede) is grounded
vpon the sharpe and bitter words, that therein are vsed in
the description of the humours of Puritanes, and rashe-
headie preachers, that thinke it their honour to contend
with Kings, & perturbe whole kingdomes. The other point
is onely grounded vpon the straite charge I giue my Sonne,
not to heare, nor suffer any vnreuerent speeches or bookes
against any of his parents or progenitors: wherein I doe
alleage my owne experience anent the Queene my mother:
affirming that I neuer founde any, that were of perfite age
the time of her raigne here, so stedfastly true to me in al
my troubles, as these that constantly kept their alleageance
to her in her time. But if the charitable reader will
aduisedlie consider, both the methode and matter of my
treatise, hee will easilie iudge, what wrong I haue sustained
by the carping at both. For my booke, suppose very small,
being deuyded in three seuerall parts, the first part thereof

onely treates of a Kings duetie towards God in Religion: wherein I haue so clearlie made profession of my Religion, calling it the Religion wherein I was brought vp, and euer made profession of, and wishing him euer to continue in the same, as the onely true forme of Gods worship; that I would haue thought my sincere plainnesse in that first part vpon that subiect, should haue ditted the mouth of the most enuious Momus, that euer hell did hatche, from barking at any other part of my booke vpon that grounde; except they would alledge me to be contrarie to my selfe, which in so small a volume would smell of too great weaknesse, and sliprinesse of memorie. And the second part of my booke, teaches my sonne howe to vse his office, in the administration of iustice, and politike gouernement: the third onely contayning a Kings outward behauiour in indifferent things; what aggreeance and conformitie he ought to keepe betwixt his outward behauiour in these things, and the vertuous qualities of his minde: & how they should serue for trunshe-men, to interprete the inwarde disposition of the minde, to the eyes of them that cannot see farther within him, and therefore must onely iudge of him by the outward appearance. So as if there were no more to be looked into, but the very methode and order of the booke, it will sufficientlie cleare me of that first and grieuousest imputation, in the point of Religion; since in the first part, where Religion is onely treated of, I speake so plainly. And what in other parts I speake of Puritanes, it is onely of their morall faults, in that part where I speake of policie: declaring when they contemne the law and soueraigne authoritie, what examplare punishment they deserue for the same. And now as to the matter it selfe where-vpon this skandale is taken, that I may sufficiently satisfie all honest men, and by a iust apologie raise vp a brasen wall or bulwark against all the darts of the enuious, I will the more narrowly rippe vp the wordes, whereat they seeme to bee somewhat stomacked.

First then, as to the name of Puritanes, 1 am not ignorant that the stile thereof doth properly belong onely to that vile sect amongst the Anabaptists, called the Familie of loue; because they thinke themselues onely pure, and in a manner, without sinne, the onely true Church, and only worthie to bee participant of the Sacraments; and all the rest of the world to be but abomination in the sight of God. Of this speciall sect I principally meane, when I speake of Puritanes; diuers of them, as Browne, Penrie, and others, hauing at sundrie times come in Scotland, to sowe their popple amongst vs (and from my heart I wish that they had left no schollers behinde them, who by their fruites will in the owne time be manifested), and partly, indeede, I giue this stile to such brainsick and headie preachers their disciples and followers, as refusing to be called of that sect, yet participates too much with their humours, in maintaining the aboue mentioned errours; not onely agreeing with the generall rule of all Anabaptists, in the contempt of the ciuill Magistrate, and in leaning to their owne dreames and reuelations; but particularly with this sect, in accounting all men prophane that sweares not to all their fantasies; in making for euerie particular question of the policie of the Church, as great commotion, as if the article of the Trinitie were called in controuersie; in making the Scriptures to be ruled by their conscience, and not their conscience by the Scripture; and he that denies the least iot of their grounds *sit tibi tanquam ethnicus & publicanus;* not worthy to enioy the benefite of breathing, much lesse to participate with them of the Sacraments : and before that any of their grounds be impugned, let King, people, law and all be tred vnder foote. Such holie warres are to be preferred to an vngodlie peace : no, in such cases, Christian princes are not only to be resisted vnto, but not to be prayed for. For prayer must come of Faith, and it is reuealed to their consciences, that God will heare no prayer for such a Prince. Iudge then, Christian reader, if 1 wrong this sort of people, in giuing

them the style of that sect, whose errours they imitate : and
since they are contented to weare their liuerie, let them not
bee ashamed to borrowe also their name.   It is onely of this
kind of men, that in this book I write so sharplie, and
whome I wishe my Sonne to punishe, in case they refuse to
obey the lawe, and will not cease to stur-vp a rebellion.
Whome against I haue written the more bitterlie, in respect
of diuers famous libels, & iniurious speaches spred by some
of them, not onely dishonourably inuectiue against all
Christian princes, but euen reprochefull to our profession
and religion, in respect they are come out vnder coullour
thereof : and yet were neuer answered but by Papists, who
generally meddle aswell against them, as the religion it
selfe ; whereby the skandale was rather doubled, then taken
away.   But on the other part, I protest vpon mine honour, I
meane it not generally of all Preachers, or others, that likes
better of the single forme of policie in our Church, then of
the many ceremonies in the Church of England, that are
perswaded, that their Bishops smels of a Papall supremacie,
that the surplise, the cornered cap, and such like, are the
outward badges of Popish errors.   No, I am so farre from
being contentious in these things (which for my owne part
I euer esteemed as indifferent), as I doe æqually loue and
honour the learned and graue men of either of these
opinions.   It can no waies become me to pronounce so
lightly a sentence, in so olde a controuersie.   We all (God
bee praised) doe agree in the grounds, and the bitternesse
of men vpon such questions doth but trouble the peace of
the Church ; and giues aduantage and entry to the Papists
by our diuision.   But towards them, I onely vse this prouision, that where the Law is otherwayes, they may content
themselues soberly and quietly with their owne opinions,
not resisting to the authoritie, nor breaking the law of the
countrie ; neither aboue all, sturring any rebellion or
schisme : but possessing their soules in peace, let them
preasse by patience, and well grounded reasons, either to

perswade all the rest to like of their iudgements ; or where they see better grounds on the other part, not to be ashamed peaceablie to incline thereunto, laying aside all preoccupied opinions.

And that this is the onely meaning of my booke, and not any coldnesse or crack in Religion, that place doth plainlie witnesse, where, after 1 haue spoken of the faults in our Ecclesiasticall estate, I exhort my sonne to bee beneficiall vnto the good men of the Ministrie ; praising God there, that there is presently a sufficient number of good men of them in this kingdome : and yet are they all knowne to be against the forme of the English Church. Yea, so farre I am in that place from admitting corruption in Religion, as I wish him in promoouing them, to vse such caution as may preserue their estate from creeping to corruption ; euer vsing that forme thorough the whole booke, where euer I speake of bad preachers, tearming them some of the ministers, and not Ministers or Ministrie in generall. And to conclude this point of Religion, what indifferencie of Religion can Momus call that in me, where, speaking of my sonnes mariage (in case it pleased God before that time to cut the threede of my life) I plainlie forewarne him of the inconueniences that were like to insue, in case he should marrie any that be of a different profession in Religion from him : notwithstanding that the number of Princes professing our Religion bee so small, as it is hard to foresee, how he can be that way meetly matched according to his ranke.

And as for the other point, that by some parts in this booke, it should appeare, that I doe nourish in my minde a vindictiue resolution against England, or some principals there ; it is surelie more then wonderfull vnto me, vpon what grounds they can haue gathered such conclusions. For as vpon the one part, I neither by name nor discription point out England in that part of my discourse ; so vpon the other, I plainly bewray my meaning to be of Scotish-

men, where I conclude that purpose in these termes : "that
the loue I beare to my Son, hath mooued me to be so
plaine in this argumět: for so that I discharge my
conscience to him in vttering the veritie, I care not what
any traitour or treason-allower doe thinke of it." And
English-men could not thereby be meant, since they could
be no traitors, where they ought no alleageance. I am not
ignorant of a wise and Princely apothegme, which the
same Queene of England vttered about the time of hir
owne coronation. But the drift of that discourse doth
fully cleare my intention, being onely grounded vpon that
precept to my Sonne, that he should not permit any vnreuerent detracting of his predecessors ; bringing in that
purpose of my mother onely for an example of my
experience anent Scottish-men, without vsing any perswad-
ing to him of reuenge. For a Kings giuing of any fault
the dew stile, inferres no reduction of the faulters pardon.
No, I am by a degree nearer of kinne vnto my mother then
he is, neither thinke I my selfe, either that vnworthie, or
that neere my ende, that I neede to make such a Dauidicall
testament; since I haue euer thought it the dutie of a
worthie Prince, rather with a pike, then a pen, to write his
iust reuenge. But in this matter I haue no delight to be
large, wishing all men to iudge of my future proiects, according to my by-past actions.

Thus hauing as much insisted in the clearing of these two
points, as will (I hope) giue sufficient satisfaction to all
honest men, and leauing the enuious to the foode of their
owne venome ; I will heartilie pray thee, louing reader,
charitablie to conceiue of my honest intention in this booke.
I knowe the greatest part of the people of this whole Ile,
haue been very curious for a sight thereof : some for the
loue they beare mee, either being particularlie acquainted
with me, or by a good report that perhappes they haue
heard of mee : and therefore longed to see any thing that
proceeded from that authour whome they so loued and

honoured; since bookes are viue Idees of the authors minde. Some onely for meere curiositie, that thinkes it their honour to know all new things, were curious to glut their eyes therewith, only that they might vaunt them to haue seene it: and some fraughted with causelesse enuie at the authour, did greedilie search out the booke, thinking their stomacke fit enough for turning neuer so wholesome foode into noysome and infectiue humours. So as this their great concurrence in curiositie (though proceeding from farre different complexions) hath inforced the vn-timous diuulgating of this booke, farre contrarie to my intention, as I haue alreadie said. To which hydra of diuerslie enclined spectators, I haue no targe to oppone but plain-nesse, patience, and sinceritie : plainnesse, for resoluing and satisfying of the first sort; patience, for to beare with the shallownesse of the next; and sinceritie to defie the malice of the third withall. Though I cannot please all men therein, I am contented so that I onely please the vertuous sort : and though they also finde not euerie thing therein, so fullie to answere their expectation, as the argument would seeme to require; although I would wish them modestly to remember that God hath not bestowed all his gifts vpon one, but parted them by a Iustice distributiue; and that many eyes sees more then one; and that the varietie of mens minds in such, that *tot capita tot sensus;* yea and that euen the very faces that God hath by nature brought foorth in the world, doe euery one in some of their particular lineaments differ from any other : yet in truth it was not my intention in handling of this purpose (as it is easie to perceiue fully to set downe here all such grounds, as might out of the best writers haue been alledged, and out of my owne invention and experience added, for the perfite institution of a King: but onely to giue some such precepts to my owne Sonne for the gouernment of this Kingdome, as was meetest for him to be instructed in, and best became me to be the informer of.

If I in this booke haue been too particularly plaine,
impute it to the necessitie of the subiect, not so much being
ordained for the institution of a Prince in generall, as I
haue said, as containing particular precepts to my Sonne in
speciall; whereof he could haue made but a generall vse, if
they had not contained the particular diseases of this
kingdome, with the best remedies for the same; which it
became me best as a King, hauing learned both the
theoricke and practicke thereof, more plainely to expresse
then any simple schoole-man, that onely knowes matters of
Kingdomes by contemplation.

But if in some places it seeme too obscure, impute it to
the shortnesse thereof, being both for the respect of my selfe,
and of my Sonne, constrained thereunto : my owne respect,
for fault of leasure, being so continually occupied in the
affaires of my office, as my great burthen, and rest-lesse
fashery is more then knowne, to all that knowes or heares
of me : for my Sonnes respect, because I knowe by my selfe,
that a Prince so long as he is young, will be so carried away
with some sorte of delight or other, that he cannot patiently
abide the reading of any large volume : and when he comes
to a full maturitie of age, he must be so busied in the
actiue part of his charge, as he will not be permitted to
bestow many houres vpon the contemplatiue part thereof.
So as it was neither fit for him, nor possible for mee, to
haue made this treatise any more ample then it is. Indeede
I am little beholden to the curiositie of some, who thinking
it too large already (as appeares) for lacke of leasure to
copie it, drew some notes out of it, for speeds sake ; putting
in the one halfe of the purpose, and leauing out the other :
not vnlike the man that alleadged that part of the Psalme,
non est Deus; but left out the preceding words, *Dixit
insipiens in corde suo.* And of these notes, making a little
pamphlet (lacking both my methode and halfe of my matter)
entituled it, forsooth, the Kings Testament : as if I had
eiked a third Testament of my owne, to the two that are in

D

the holy Scriptures. It is true that in a place thereof, for affirmation of the purpose I am speaking of to my Sonne, I bring my selfe in there, as speaking vpon my Testament: for in that sense, euery record in write of a mans opinion in anything (in respect that papers out-liues their authors) is as it were a Testament of that mans will in that case : and in that sense it is, that in that place I call this treatise a Testament. But from any particular sentence in a booke, to giue the booke itself a title, is as ridiculous as to stile the booke of the Psalmes the booke of *Dixit insipiens,* because with these words one of them doth begin.

Well, leauing these new baptisers and blockers of other mens books to their owne follies, I returne to my purpose, anent the shortnesse of this booke : suspecting that all my excuses for the shortnesse thereof, shall not satisfy some, especially in our neighbour countrie : who though, that as I haue so narrowly in this treatise touched all the principall sicknesses in our kingdome, with overtures for the remedies thereof, as I said before : so looked they to haue found something therein, that should haue touched the sicknesses of their state, in the like sort. But they will easily excuse me thereof, if they will consider the forme I haue vsed in this treatise : wherein I onely teach my Sonne, out of my owne experience, what forme of gouernment is fittest for this Kingdome : and in one part thereof speaking of the bordours, I plainely there doe excuse my selfe, that I will speake no thing of the state of England, as a matter wherein I neuer had experience. I know, indeede, no Kingdome lackes her owne diseases, and likewayes what interest I haue in the prosperitie of that state : for although I would be silent, my blood and discent doth sufficiently proclaime it. But notwithstanding, since there is a lawfull Queene there presently raigning, who hath so long with so great wisedome and felicitie gouerned her Kingdomes, as (I must in true sinceritie confesse) the like hath not been read nor heard of, either in our time, or since

the dayes of the Romane Emperour Augustus; it could no
wayes become me, farre inferiour to her in knowledge and
experience, to bee a busie-bodie in other Princes matters,
and to fish in other folkes waters, as the prouerbe is. No,
I hope by the contrairie (with Gods grace) euer to keepe
that Christian rule, To doe as I would be done to: and I
doubt nothing, yea euen in her name I dare promise, by the
bypast experience of her happie gouernment, as I haue
alreadie saide, that no good subiect shall be more carefull to
enforme her of any corruptions stolen in in her state: then
she shall be zealous for the discharge of her conscience and
honour, to see the same purged and restored to the auncient
integritie: and further, during her time, becomes me least
of any to meddle in.

And thus hauing resolued all the doubts, so farre as I can
imagine may bee mooued against this treatise; it onely
rests to praye thee (charitable reader) to interpret fauour-
ably this birth of mine, according to the integritie of the
author, and not looking for perfection in the worke it selfe.
As for my part, I onely glorie thereof in this point, that I
trust no sort of vertue is condemned, nor any degree of vice
allowed in it: and that (though it be not perhaps so
gorgeously decked and richly attired as it ought to be) it is
at the least rightly proportioned in all the members, without any monstrous deformitie in any of them: and specially
that since it was first written in secret, and is now published,
not of ambition, but of a kinde of necessitie; it must be
taken of all men, for the true image of my very mind, and
forme of the rule, which I haue prescribed to my selfe and
mine. Which as in all my actions I haue hitherto preassed
to expresse, so farre as the nature of my charge and the
condition of time would permit me: so beareth it a dis-
couerie of that, which may be looked for at my hand, and
where-to, euen in my secret thoughts, I haue engaged my
selfe for the time to come. And thus in a firme trust, that
it shall please God, who with my being and Crowne, gaue

D 2

me this minde, to maintaine and augment the same in me and my posteritie, to the discharge of our conscience, the maintenance of our honor, and weale of our people, I bid thee hartely fare-well.

The First Booke.

OF A KINGS CHRISTIAN DVTIE TOWARDS GOD.

As he cannot be thought worthy to rule and commaund others that cannot rule and dantone his owne proper affections and vnreasonable appetites, so can he not be thought worthie to gouerne a Christian people knowing and fearing God, that in his own person and heart, feareth not and loueth not the Diuine Majestie. Neither can anie thing in his gouernment succeed wel with him (deuise and labour as he list) as comming from a filthie spring, if his person be vnsanctified: for (as that royall Prophet saith) "Except the Lord build the house, they labour in vaine that build it : except the Lord keepe the Citie, the keepers watch it in vaine :" in respect the blessing of God hath only power to giue the successe thereunto : and as Paul saith, "he planteth, Apollos watereth ; but it is God onely that giueth the increase." Therefore (my sonne) first of all things, carne to know and loue that GOD, whome-to yee haue a double obligation ; first, for that hee made you a man, and next, for that he made you a little God to sitte on his Throne, and rule ouer other men. Remember, that as in dignitie hee hath erected you aboue others, so ought yee in thankfulnesse towards him, goe as farre beyond all others. A moate in anothers eye, is a beame into yours : a blemish in another, is a leprouse byle into you : and a veniall sinne (as the Papists call it) in another, is a great crime into you.

Thinke not therefore, that the highnes of your dignitie
diminisheth your faults (much lesse giueth you a licence to
sin), but by the contrarie, your fault shal be aggrauated,
according to the height of your dignitie; any sinne that ye
commit, not being a single sin, procuring but the fall of one;
but being an exemplare sinne, and therefore drawing with it
the whole multitude to bee guiltie of the same. Remember
then, that this glistring worldlie glorie of Kings is giuen them
by God, to teach them to preasse so to glister and shine
before their people, in al works of sanctification & righteousnes, that their persons as bright lampes of godlines and
vertue may, going in and out before their people, giue light
to al their steps. Remēber also, that by the right knowledge and feare of God (which is "the beginning of wisedome," as Salomon saith) ye shall knowe all the things
necessarie for the discharge of your dutie, both as a
Christian and as a King; seeing in him, as in a mirrour,
the course of all earthlie things, whereof he is the spring
and only moouer.

Now, the onely way to bring you to this knowledge, is
diligentlie to reade his word, and earnestly to pray for the
right vnderstanding thereof. "Search the Scriptures," saith
Christ, "for they beare testimonie of me :" and "the whole
Scripture," saith Paul, "is giuen by inspiration of God, and
is profitable to teach, to conuince, to correct, & to instruct
in righteousnes; that the man of God may be absolute,
being made perfit vnto al good workes." And most
properlie of any other, belongeth the reading thereof
vnto kings, since in that part of Scripture, where the
godlie Kings are first made mention off, that were ordained
to rule ouer the people of God, there is an expresse and
most notable exhortation and commaundement giuen them,
to reade and meditate in the law of God. I ioyne to this,
the carefull hearing of the doctrine with attendance and
reuerence : For "faith commeth by hearing," saith the same
Apostle. But aboue all, beware yee wrest not the word to

your owne appetite, as ouer manie doe, making it like a bell to sound as ye please to interprete : but by the contrarie, frame all your affections, to follow precisely the rule there set downe.

The whole Scripture chieflie containeth two things : a command, and a prohibition ; to do such things, and to abstaine from the contrarie. Obey in both ; neither thinke it enough to abstaine from euill, and do no good : nor thinke not that if ye doe manie good things, it may serue you for a cloake to mixe euill turns therewith. And as in these two points, the whole Scripture principallie consisteth : so in two degrees standeth the whole seruice of God by man : interiour, or vpward ; exteriour, or downward : the first, by prayer in faith towards God ; the next, by workes flowing therefra before the world : which is nothing else but the exercise of Religion towards God, and of equitie towards your neighbour.

As for the particular poynts of Religion, I neede not to dilate them ; I am no hypocrite, follow my footesteppes, and your owne present education therein. I thanke God, I was neuer ashamed to giue account of my profession, how-soeuer the malitious lying tongues of some haue traduced me : and if my conscience had not resolued me, that all my Religion presently professed by me and my kingdome, was grounded vpon the plaine wordes of the Scripture, without the which all points of Religion are superfluous, as anie thing contrarie to the same is abomination, I had neuer outwardlie avowed it, for pleasure or awe of any flesh.

And as for the points of equitie towards your neighbour (because that will fall in properlie, vpon the second part concerning a kings office) I leaue it to the owne roome.

For the first part then of mans seruice to his God, which is Religion, that is, the worshippe of God according to his reuealed will, it is wholic grounded vpon the Scripture, as I haue alreadie sayd, quickened by faith, and conserued by conscience. For the Scripture, I haue now spoken of it in generall : but that ye may the more readilie make choise of any part thereof, for your instruction or comfort, remember shortlie this methode.

The whole Scripture is dited by Gods spirit, thereby, as by his liuely word, to instruct and rule the whole Church militant to the ende of the world. It is composed of two parts, the Olde and new Testament. The grounde of the former is the Law, which sheweth our sinne, and containeth justice: the ground of the other is Christ, who pardoning sinne containeth grace. The summe of the Law is the tenne Commandements, more largelie dilated in the bookes of Moses, interpreted and applied by the Prophets, and by the histories, are the examples shewed of obedience or disobedience thereto, and what *præmium* or *pœna* was accordinglie giuen by God. But because no man was able to keepe the Law, nor any part thereof, it pleased God of his infinite wisedome and goodnesse to incarnate his onely Sonne in our nature, for satisfaction of his iustice in his suffering for vs: that since we could not be saued by doing, wee might at least, be saued by beleeuing.

The ground therefore of the word of grace, is contained in the foure histories of the birth, life, death, resurrection, and ascension of Christ. The larger interpretation and vse thereof, is contained in the Epistles of the Apostles: and the practise in the faithfull or vnfaithfull, with the historie of the infancie and first progresse of the Church is contained in their acts.

Would ye then know your sinne by the Law? Reade the bookes of Moses containing it. Would yee haue a commentarie thereupon? Reade the Prophets, and likewise the bookes of the Prouerbs and Ecclesiastes, written by that great paterne of wisedome Salomon; which will not only serue you for instruction, how to walke in the obedience of the Law of God, but is also so full of golden sentences, and morall precepts, in all things that can concerne your conuersation in the world, as among all the prophane Philosophers and Poets, ye shall not finde so rich a storehouse of precepts of naturall wisedome, agreeing with the will and diuine wisdome of God. Would ye see how good men are rewarded, and wicked punished? looke the historicall partes of these same bookes of Moses, together with the histories of Iosua, the Iudges, Ezra, Nehemiah, Esther, and Iob : but especially the bookes of the Kings, and Chronicles, wherewith ye ought to be familiarlie acquainted : for there shall ye see your selfe, as in a mirrour, in the catalogue either of the good or the euill Kings.

Would yee knowe the doctrine, life and death of our Sauiour Christ? reade the Euangelists. Would ye be more particularlie trained vp in his schoole? meditate vpon the Epistles of the Apostles. And would yee be acquainted with the practizes of that doctrine in the persons of the Primitiue Church? Cast vp the Apostles Acts. And as to the Apocryphe bookes, I omit them, because I am no Papist, as I said before, and indeede some of them are no waies like the ditement of the Spirit of God.

But when yee reade the Scripture, reade it with a sanctified & chast hart : admire reuerentlie such obscure places as ye vnderstand not, blaming only your own capacitie : reade with delight the plaine places, and study carefully to vnderstand those that are somewhat difficile : preasse to be a good textuare; for the Scripture is euer the best interpreter of it selfe. But preasse not curiously to seek out farther then is contained therein ; for that were ouer vnmannerly a presumption, to striue to be further vpon Gods secrets, then he hath will ye be : for what he thought needfull for vs to know, that hath he reuealed there. And delight most in reading such partes of the Scripture, as may best serue for your instruction in your calling ; rejecting foolish curiosities vpon genealogies and contentions, " which are but vaine and profit not," as Paul saith.

Now, as to faith, which is the nourisher and quickner of Religion, as I haue alreadie said, it is a sure perswasion and

apprehension of the promises of God, applying them to
your soule: and therefore may it iustly bee called the
golden chaine that linketh the faithfull soule to Christ·
And because it groweth not in our garden, but "is the free
gift of God," as the same Apostle saith, it must bee nourished
by prayer, which is nothing else but a friendly talking with
God.

As for teaching you the forme of your prayers, the
Psalmes of Dauid are the meetest schoole-master that ye
can be acquainted with (next the prayer of our Sauiour,
which is the onely rule of prayer) whereout of as of most
rich and pure fountaines, ye may learne all forme of prayer,
necessarie for your comfort at all occasions. And so much
the fitter are they for you then for the common sort, in
respect the composer thereof was a king : and therefore
best behooued to know a kings wants, and what things
were meetest to be required by a king at Gods hand for
remedie thereof.

Vse often to pray when yee are quietest, especiallie forget
it not in your bed, how oft soeuer yee doe it at other times:
for publique prayer serueth as much for example as for any
particular comfort to the supplicant.

In your prayer, bee neither ouer straunge with God,
like the ignorant common sort, that prayeth nothing but
out of books ; nor yet ouer homelie with him, like some of
the vaine Pharisaicall Puritanes, that think they rule him
vpon their fingers. The former way will breed an vncouth
coldnes in you towards him, the other will breede in you a
contempt of him. But in your prayer to God speak with
all reuerence : for if a subject will not speake but reuerentlie to a King, much lesse should any flesh presume to
talke with God as with his companion.

Craue in your prayer, not onelie things spirituall, but
also things temporall, sometimes of greater, & sometimes of
lesse consequence ; that yee may lay vp in store his grant
of these thinges, for confirmation of your faith, and to bee

an arles-penny vnto you of his loue. Pray, as ye find your heart moueth you, *pro re nata* : but see that ye sute no vnlawfull things, as reuenge, lust, or such like : for that prayer cannot come of faith : "and whatsoeuer is done without faith is sinne," as the Apostle saith.

When yee obtaine your prayer, thanke him joyfully therefore : if otherwaies, beare patientlie, preassing to win him with importunitie, as the widow did the vnrighteous Iudge : and if notwithstanding thereof ye be not heard, assure your selfe God foreseeth that which yee aske is not for your weale : and learne in time, so to interprete all the aduersities that God shall send vnto you; so shall ye in the middest of them, not onelie bee armed with patience, but joyfullie lift vp your eyes from the present trouble to the happie ende that God will turne it to. And when ye finde it once so fall out by proofe, arme your selfe with the experience thereof against the next trouble, assuring your selfe, though yee cannot in time of the showre see thorough the clowd, yet in the end, shall ye find, God sent it for your weale, as yee found in the former.

And as for conscience, which I called the conseruer of Religion, it is nothing else but the light of knowledge that God hath planted in man, which euer watching ouer all his actions, as it beareth him a joyfull testimonie when he does right, so choppeth it him with a feeling that hee hath done wrong when euer he committeth any sinne. And surely, although this conscience bee a great torture to the wicked, yet is it as great a comfort to the godlie, if wee will consider it rightly. For haue we not a great aduantage, that haue within our selues while wee liue heere, a count booke and inuentarie of al the crimes that wee shall be accused of, either at the houre of our death, or at the great day of judgement; which when wee please (yea though wee forget) will chop, and remember vs to look vpon it; that while we haue leasure and are here, wee may remember to amend; and so at the day of our triall, compeare with "new and white garments

washed in the bloud of the Lambe," as S. Iohn saith.
Aboue all then, my Sonne, labour to keepe sound this
conscience, which many prattle of, but ouer few feele:
especiallie be carefull to keepe it free from two diseases,
wherewith it vseth oft to be infected: to wit, Leaprosie, and
Superstition: the former is the mother of Atheisme, the
other of Heresies. By a leaprouse conscience, I meane "a
cauterized conscience," as Paul calleth it, being become
senselesse of sinne, through sleeping in a carelesse securitie,
as King Dauids was, after his murther and adulterie, euer till
he was wakened by the Prophet Nathans similitude. And by
superstition, I meane, when one restraines himselfe to any
other rule in the seruice of God then is warranted by the
word, the onelie true square of Gods seruice.

As for a preseruatiue against this leaprosie, remember
euer once in the foure and twentie houres, either in the
night, or when yee are at greatest quiet, to call your selfe
to account of all your last daies actions, either wherein yee
haue committed things ye should not, or omitted the things
ye should doe, either in your Christian or Kingly calling:
and in that account, let not your selfe be smoothed ouer
with that flattering φιλαυτία, which is ouer kindlie a sicknes
to all mankinde: but censure your selfe as sharply, as if ye
were your owne enemie: "For if ye iudge your selfe, ye
shall not be iudged," as the Apostle saith: and then
according to your censure, reforme your actions as far as
yee may; eschewing euer wilfully and wittinglie to contrarie
your conscience. For a small sinne wilfullie committed,
with a deliberate resolution to breake the bridle of conscience
therein, is farre more grieuous before God then a greater
sinne committed in a suddaine passion, when conscience is a
sleepe. Remember therefore in all your actions, of the
great account that yee are one daie to make: in all the
daies of your life euer learning to die, and liuing euery day
as it were your last;

Omnem crede diem tibi diluxisse supremum.

And therefore, I would not haue you to pray with the Papists, to bee preserued from suddaine death, but that God would giue you grace so to liue, as ye may euerie houre of your life be readie for death : so shall ye attaine to the vertue of true Fortitude, neuer being affraid for the horror of death, come when he list. And especiallie beware to offend your conscience, with vse of swearing or lying, suppose but in jest ; for oathes are but an vse, and a sinne cloathed with no delight nor gaine, and therefore the more inexcusable euen in the sight of men : and lying commeth also much of a vile vse, which bannisheth shame. Therefore beware euen to denie the truth, which is a sorte of lie, that may best bee eschewed by a person of your ranke. For if any thing bee asked at you that yee thinke not meete to reueale, if yee say that question is not pertinent for them to aske, who dare examine you further? and vsing sometimes this answere both in true and false things that shal be asked at you, such vnmannerly people will neuer be the wiser thereof.

And for keeping your conscience sound from that sicknes of superstition, ye must neither lay the safetie of your conscience vpon the credit of your owne conceites, nor yet of other mens humours, how great doctors of Diuinitie that euer they bee : but ye must onely ground it vpon the expresse Scripture : for conscience not grounded vpon sure knowledge, is either an ignorant fantasie or an arrogant vanitie. Beware therefore in this case with two extremities : the one, to beleeue with the Papists, the Churches authoritie, better then your owne knowledge : the other to leane, with the Anabaptistes, to your owne conceites and dreamed reuelations.

But learne wisely to discerne betwixt points of saluation and indifferent thing, betwixt substance and ceremonies ; and betwixt the expres commaundement and will of God in his word, and the invention or ordinance of man : since all that is necessarie for saluation is contained in the Scripture.

For in any thing that is expresly commanded or prohibited in the booke of God, ye cannot be ouer precise, euen in the least thing; counting euery sinne, not according to the light estimation and common vse of it in the world, but as the booke of God counteth of it. But as for all other things not contained in the Scripture, spare not to vse or alter them, as the necessitie of the time shall require. And when any of the spirituall office-bearers in the Church speaketh vnto you any thing that is well warranted by the word, reuerence and obey them as the Heraulds of the most high God : but, if passing that bounds, they vrge you to embrace any of their fantasies in the place of Gods word, or would colour their particulars with a pretended zeale, acknowledge them for no other then vaine men, exceeding the bounds of their calling; and according to your office, grauely and with authoritie redact them in order againe.

To conclude then, both this purpose of conscience and the first part of this booke; Keepe God more sparingly in your mouth, but aboundantly in your heart : be precise in effect, but sociall in shew : kythe more by your deedes then by your words the loue of vertue and hatred of vice : and delight more to bee godlie and vertuous in deede then to be thought and called so ; expecting more for your praise and reward in heauen then heere : and apply to all your outward actions Christes commaunde, to pray and giue your almes secretly : so shall ye on the one part be inwardly garnished with true Christian humility, not outwardly (with the proud Pharisie) glorying in your godlines : but saying, as Christ commandeth vs all, when we haue done all that we can, *Inutiles serui sumus.* And on the other part, ye shall eschew outwardly before the world, the suspition of filthie proud hypocrisie and deceitfull dissimulation.

The Second Booke.

OF A KINGS DVTIE IN HIS OFFICE.

Bvt as ye are clothed with two callings, so must ye be alike carefull for the discharge of them both: that as yee are a good Christian, so ye may bee a good King, discharging your office (as I shewed before) in the points of justice and equitie: which in two sundrie waies ye must doe: the one, in establishing and executing (which is the life of the law) good lawes among your people: the other, by your behauiour in your owne person, and with your seruants, to teach your people by your example: for people are naturally inclined to counterfaite (like apes) their Princes maners, according to the notable saying of Plato, expressed by the Poet:

> Componitur orbis
> Regis ad exemplum, necsic inflectere sensus
> Humanos edicta valent, quàm vita regentis.

For the part of making and executing of lawes, consider first the true difference betwixt a lawfull good King and an vsurping Tyrant, and ye shall the more easily vnderstand your dutie herein: for *contraria iuxta se posita magis elucescunt*. The one acknowledgeth himselfe ordained for his people, hauing receiued from God a burthen of gouernment whereof he must bee countable: the other thinketh his people ordained for him, a pray to his passions and inordinate appetites, as the fruites of his magnanimitie. And therefore, as their ends are directlie contrarie, so are their whole actions, as meanes, whereby they preasse to attaine to their endes: A good King, thinking his highest honor to consist in the due discharge of his calling, employeth all his studie and paines to procure and maintaine, by the making and execution of good lawes, the well-fare and peace of his people; and as their naturall father and kindly maister, thinketh his greatest contentment standeth in their prosperitie, and his greatest suretie in hauing their hearts, subiecting his owne priuate affections and appetites to the weale and standing of his subiects, euer thinking the common interesse his chiefest particular : where by the contrarie, an vsurping Tyrant, thinking his greatest honour and felicitie to consist in attaining *per fas, vel nefas,* to his ambitious pretenses, thinketh neuer himselfe sure, but by the dissention and factions among his people ; and counterfeiting the Sainte while hee once creepe in credit, will then (by inuerting all good lawes to serue onely for his vnrulie priuate affections) frame the Commonweale euer to aduance his particular : building his suretie vpon his peoples miserie : and in the end (as a step-father and an vncouth hireling) make vp his owne hand vpon the ruines of the Republicke. And according to their actions, so receiue they their reward. For a good King (after a happie and famous reigne) dieth in peace, lamented by his subiects, and admired by his neighbours ; and leauing a reuerent renowne behinde him in earth, obtaineth the crowne of eternall felicitie in heauen. And although some of them (which falleth out verie rarely) may bee cut off by the reason of some vnnaturall subiects, yet liueth their fame after them, and some notable plague faileth neuer to ouer-take the committers in this life, besides their infamie to all posterities hereafter. Whereby the contrarie, a Tyrannes miserable and infamous life, armeth in end his owne subjects to become his burreaux : and although that rebellion be euer vnlawfull on their part, yet is the world so wearied of him, that his fall is little meaned by the rest of his subjects, and but smyled at by his neighbours. And besides the infamous memorie he leaueth behinde him here, and the endles paine hee sustaineth hereafter, it oft falleth out that the committers not onely escape vnpunished, but farther, the fact will remaine as allowed by the law in diuers ages thereafter. It is easie then for you

(my Sonne) to make a choyse of one of these two sortes of
rules, by following the way of vertue to establish your
standing ; yea, in case ye fell in the highway, yet should it
be with the honourable report, and just regrate of all honest
men.

And therefore to returne to my purpose anent the
gouernment of your subjects, by making and putting good
lawes to execution ; I remitte the making of them to your
owne discretion, as yee shall finde the necessitie of new-
rising corruptions to require them : for, *ex malis moribus
bonæ leges natæ sunt :* besides, that in this countrie, we haue
alreadie moe good lawes then are well execute, and am
onely to insist in your forme of gouernment anent their
execution.   Onlie remember, that as Parliaments haue been
ordained for making of lawes, so yee abuse not their institution, in holding them for any mens particulars.   For as
a Parliament is the honorablest and highest judgement in
the land (as being the Kings head Courte) if it bee well
vsed, which is by making of good lawes in it ; so is it the
in-justest judgement-seate that may bee, being abused to
mens particulars : irreuocable decreits against particular
parties being giuen therein vnder colour of generall lawes,
and ofttimes the Estates not knowing themselues whom
thereby they hurt.   And therefore hold no Parliaments
but for necessitie of new lawes, which would be but
seldome : for few lawes and well put in execution, are
best in a well ruled Common-weale.   As for the matter of
fore-faltures, which also are done in Parliament, it is not
good tigging with these things ; but my aduice is, ye fore-
fault none but for such odious crimes as may make them
vnworthie euer to bee restored againe.   And for smaller
offences, ye haue other penalties sharpe enough to be vsed
against them.

And as for the execution of good lawes, whereat I left,
remember that among the differences that I put betwixt the
formes of the gouernment of a good **King** and an vsurping

Tyrant; I shew how a Tyrant would enter like a Saint while hee found himselfe fast vnder-foote, and then would suffer his vnrulie affections to burst foorth. Therefore be ye contrarie at your first entrie to your Kingdome, to that *Quinquennium Neronis*, with his tender hearted wish, *Vellem nescirem literas*, in giuing the lawfull execution against all breakers thereof but exception. For since yee come not to your Reigne *precario* nor by conquest, but by right and due discent; feare no vproares for doing of justice, since yee may assure your selfe the most part of your people will euer naturally fauour justice: prouiding alwaies, that ye doe it onely for loue to justice, and not for satisfying any particular passions of yours, vnder colour thereof: otherwise, how justlie that euer the offender deserue it, ye are guiltie of murther before God. For ye must consider that God euer looketh to your inward intention in all your actions.

And when ye haue by the seueritie of justice once setled your countries, and made them knowe that ye can strike, then may ye thereafter all the dayes of your life mixe justice with mercie, punishing or sparing, as ye shall finde the crime to haue been wilfullie or rashlie committed, and according to the by-past behauiour of the committer. For if otherwise ye kyth your clemencie at the first, the offences would soone come to such heapes, and the contempt of you growe so great, that when ye would fall to punish, the nomber of them to be punished would exceede the innocent; and ye would be troubled to resolue whome-at to begin: and against your nature would be compelled then to warcke manie, whom the chastisement of fewe in the beginning might haue preserued. But in this, my ouer-deare bought experience may serue you for a sufficient lesson. For I confesse, where I thought (by being gracious at the beginning) to win all mens heartes to a louing and willing obedience, I by the contrarie found the disorder of tho countrie and the losse of my thankes to be all my rewarde.

But as this seuere justice of yours vpon all offences would be but for a time (as I haue alreadie sayd), so is there some horrible crimes that ye are bound in conscience neuer to forgiue : such as Witch-craft, wilfull murther, Incest (especially within the degrees of consanguinitie), Sodomy, Poysoning, and false coine. As for offences against your owne person and authority, since the fault concerneth your selfe, I remit to your owne choyse to punish or pardon therein as your heart serueth you, and according to the circumstances of the turne and the qualitie of the committer.

Here would I also eike another crime to be vnpardonable, if I should not bee thought partiall : but the fatherly loue I beare you will make me breake the bounds of shame in opening it vnto you. It is then, the false and vnreuerent writing or speaking of malicious men against your Parents and Predecessors : ye know the commaund in Gods law, " Honour your Father and Mother : " and consequently, sen yee are the lawfull magistrate, suffer not both your Princes and your Parents to be dishonoured by any; especially, sith the example also toucheth your selfe, in leauing thereby to your successors the measure of that which they shall mette out againe to you in your like behalfe. I graunt we haue all our faults, which, priuately betwixt you and God, should serue you for examples to meditate vpon, and mend in your person ; but shoulde not bee a matter of discourse to others what-soeuer. And sith yee are come of as honourable Predecessoures as anie Prince liuing, represse the insolence of such, as vnder pretence to taxe a vice in the person, seekes craftily to staine the race, and to steale the affection of the people from their posteritie. For howe can they loue you, that hated them whome of yee are come. Wherefore destroy men innocent yong sucking Wolues and Foxes, but for the hatred they beare to their race ; and why will a coult of a Courser of Naples giue a greater price in a market then an Asse-

colt, but for loue of the race? It is therefore a thing
monstrous, to see a man loue the childe and hate the
Parentes : as on the other parte, the infaming and making
odious of the parent, is the readiest way to bring the sonne
in contempt. And for conclusion of this point, I may also
alledge my owne experience. For besides the judgements
of God, that with my eyes I haue seene fall vpon all them
that were chief traitours to my parents, I may justly affirme,
I neuer found yet a constant byding by me in all my straits,
by any that were of perfite age in my parentes dayes, but
only by such as constantly bode by them. I meane specially
by them that serued the Queene my mother : for so that I
discharge my conscience to you, my Son, in reuealing to
you the trueth, I care not what any traitour or treason-
allower thinke of it.

And although the crime of oppression be not in this
ranke of vnpardonable crimes, yet the ouer-common vse of
it in this nation, as if it were a vertue, especially by the
greatest rank of subiects in the land, requireth the King to
be a sharpe censurer thereof. Be diligent therefore to try,
and awfull to beate downe the hornes of proude oppressours :
embrace the quarrell of the poore and distressed, as your
owne particular, thinking it your greatest honour to
represse the oppressours : care for the pleasure of none,
neither spare yee any paines in your own person, to see
their wrongs redressed : & remember of the honourable
stile giuen to my grand-father of worthy memorie, in being
called "the poore mans King." And as the most part of a
Kings office standeth in deciding that question of *Meum*
and *Tuum* among his subiects ; so remember when yee sit
in iudgement, that the Throne ye sit on is Gods, as Moses
sayeth, and sway neither to the right hand nor to the left,
either louing the rich, or pittying the poore. Iustice should
bee blinde and friendlesse : it is not there ye should
rewarde your friends, or seek to crosse your enemies.

Heere nowe speaking of oppressours and of justice, the

people leadeth mee to speake of Hie-lande and Bordour oppressions. As for the Hie-lands, I shortly comprehend them all in two sortes of people: the one, that dwelleth in our maine land, that are barbarous for the most parte, and yet mixed with some shewe of ciuilitie: the other, that dwelleth in the Iles, & are all vtterly barbarous, without any sort or shewe of ciuilitie. For the first sorte, put straitely to execution the lawes made already by mee against the Ouer-lords, and the chiefes of their Clannes, and it will bee no difficultie to danton them. As for the other sort, follow forth the course that I haue intended, in planting Colonies among them of answerable In-lands subiects, that within short time may reforme and ciuilize the best inclined among them: rooting out or transporting the barbarous and stubborne sort, and planting ciuility in their rooms.

But as for the Bordours, because I knowe, if yee enjoy not this whole Ile, according to Gods right and your lineal discent, ye will neuer get leaue to brooke this north and barrenest parte thereof, no, not your owne head whereon the Crowne shoulde stand: I neede not in that case trouble you with them: for then they will bee the middest of the Ile, and so as easily ruled as any part thereof.

And that ye may the readier with wisedome and justice gouerne your subjects, by knowing what vices they are naturally most inclined to, as a good physitian, who must first knowe what peccant humours his patient naturally is most subject vnto, before hee can beginne his cure: I shall therefore shortly note vnto you, the principall faults that euery ranke of the people of this country is most affected vnto. And as for England, I will not speake by-gesse of them, neuer hauing beene among them; although I hope in that God, who euer fauoureth the right, before I die, to be as well acquainted with their fashions.

As the whole Subjectes of our Country (by the auncient and fundamentall policie of our Kingdome) are diuided into three estates; so is euery estate heereof generally subject to some speciall vices; which in a manner by long habitude are thought rather vertue then vice among them: not that euery particular man, in any of these rankes of man, is subject vnto them; for there is good and euill of all sortes: but that I meane, I haue found by experience these vices to haue taken greatest holde with these rankes of men.

And first, that I prejudge not the Church of her ancient priviledges, reason would shee should haue the first place, for orders sake, in this catalogue.

The naturall sickenesse that haue euer troubled, and beene the decay of all the Churches, since the beginning of the world, changing the candle-sticke from one to another, as Iohn saith, haue beene Pride, Ambition, and Auarice: and now last, these same infirmities wrought the ouerthrowe of the Popish Church, in this country and diuerse others. But the reformation of Religion in Scotland, being extraordinarily wrought by God, wherein many things were inordinately done by a populare tumult and Rebellion, of such as blindely were doing the worke of God, but clogged with their owne passions and particular respects, as well appeared by the destruction of our policie; and not proceeding from the Princes order, as it did in our neighbour country of England, as likewise in Denmarke, and sundrie partes of Germanie; some fierie spirited men in the ministerie, gotte such a guyding of the people at that time of confusion, as finding the gust of gouernement sweete, they begouth to fantasie to themselues a Democraticke forme of gouernement: and hauing (by the iniquitie of time) bin ouer-well baited vpon the wracke, first of my Grandmother, and next of my owne Mother, and after vsurping the liberty of the time in my long minoritie, settled themselues to fast vppon that imagined Democracie, as they fed themselues with the hope to become *Tribuni plebis:* and so in a populare gouernment by leading the people by the nose, to beare the sway of all the rule. And for this cause, there neuer rose faction in the time of my minoritie, nor trouble sen-syne, but they that were vppon that factious parte, were euer carefull to perswade and allure these vnruly spirites among the ministerie, to spouse that quarrell as their owne : where-through I was ofttimes calumniated in their populare sermons, nor for any euill or vice in me, but because I was a King, which they thought the highest euill. And because they were ashamed to professe this quarrell, they were busie to looke narrowly in al my actions, and I warrant you a moate in my eye, yea a false reporte was matter ynough for them to worke vppon : and yet for all their cunning, whereby they pretended to distinguish the lawfulnesse of the office, from the vice of the person, some of them would some-times snapper out well grosely with the truth of their intentions : informing the people, that all Kings and Princes were naturally enemies to the libertie of the Church, and could neuer patiently beare the yoke of Christ, with such sound doctrine fed they their flockes. And because the learned, graue, and honest men of the ministery were euer ashamed and offended with their temeritie and presumption, preassing by all good meanes by their authority and example, to reduce them to a greater moderation, there could be no way found out so meete in their conceit, that were turbulent spirites among them, for maintaining their plottes, as paritie in the Church : whereby the ignorants were emboldened (as bayards) to cry the learned, godly and modest out of it : paritie the mother of confusion, and ennemy to Vnitie which is the mother of order. For if by the example thereof, once established in the Ecclesiasticall gouernment, the Politicke and ciuill estate should be drawne to the like, the great confusion that there-vppon would arise, may easily be discerned. Take heede therefore (my Sonne) to suche Pvritans, very pestes in the Church, and common-weale : whom no deserts can oblige ; neither oathes or promises binde ; breathing nothing but sedition and calumnies, aspyring without measure, rayling without reason, and making their owne imagina-

tions (without any warrant of the worde) the square of
their conscience. I protest before the great God, and since
I am heere as vpon my Testament, it is no place for me to
lie in, that ye shall neuer finde with any Hie-land or Bordor
theeues greater ingratitude, and moe lies and vile perjuries,
then with these phanatick spirites. And suffer not the
principalles of them to brooke your land, if ye like to sit at
rest : except ye would keepe them for trying your patience,
as Socrates did an euill wife.

And for preseruatiue against their poison, entertaine
and aduance the godlie, learned, and modest men of the
ministry, whom-of (God be praised) there lacketh not a
sufficient number : and by their prouision to Bishopricks
and Benefices (annulling that vile act of Annexation, if ye
find it not done to your hand) ye shal not onely bannish
their conceited Paritie, whereof I haue spoken, and their
other imaginarie groundes ; which can neither stand with
the order of the Church, nor the peace of a common-weale,
and well ruled Monarchie : but also shall yee re-establish
the olde institution of three Estates in Parliament, which
can no otherwise be done. But in this I hope (if God spare
me daies) to make you a faire entry ; alwaies where I leaue,
followe yee my steps.

And to end my aduice anent the Church estate, cherishe
no man more than a good Pastor, hate no man more than a
proude Puritane : thinking it one of your fairest stiles to
bee called a louing nourish-Father to the Church ; seeing
all the Churches within your dominions planted with good
Pastors, the Schooles (the seminary of the church) maintained, the doctrine and discipline preserued in puritie,
according to Gods word, a sufficient prouision for their
sustentation, a comely order in their policie, pride punished,
humilitie aduaunced, and they so to reuerence their
superiors, and their flockes them, as the flourishing of your
Church in pietie, peace, and learning, may be one of the
chiefe points of your earthly glorie : being euer alike ware

with both the extremities, as well as yee represse the vaine Puritane, so not to suffer prowde Papall Bishops: but as some for their qualities will deserue to be preferred before others, so chaine them with such bonds as may preserue that estate from creeping to corruption.

The next estate now that by order commeth in purpose, according to their rankes in Parliament, is the Nobilitie, although second in ranke, yet ouer-farre first in greatnesse and power, either to doe good or euill, as they are inclined.

The naturall sickenesse that I haue perceiued this estate subject to in my time, hath beene a fectlesse arrogant conceit of their greatnesse & power: drinking in with their very noursmilke, that their honor stood in committing three points of iniquitie : to thrall, by oppression, the meaner sorte that dwelleth neere them, to their seruice and following, although they hold nothing of them : to maintaine their seruants and dependers in anie wrong, although they be not answerable to the lawes (for any body will maintaine his man in a right cause) and for any displeasure, that they apprehend to be doone vnto them by their neighbour, to take vp a plaine seide against him, and (without respect to God, King, or common-weale) to bang it out brauely, he and all his kinne, against him and all his : yea they will thinke the King farre in their common, in-case they agree to graunt an assurance to a short daie, for keeping of the peace : where, by their naturall duetie, they are obliged to obey the lawe, and keepe the peace all the dayes of their life, vpon the peril of their very cragges.

For remeid to these euils in their estate, teach your Nobilitie to keepe your lawes as precizely as the meanest : feare not their orping or beeing discontented, as long as yee rule well, for their pretended reformation of Princes taketh neuer effect, but where euill gouernement proceedeth. Acquaint your selfe so with all the honest men of your Barrones and Gentlemen, and be in your giuing accesse so open and affable to euery ranke of honest persons,

as may make them pearte without scarring at you, to make
their owne sutes to you themselues, and not to employ the
great Lordes their intercessours, for intercession to Saints
is Papistry : so shall yee bring to a measure their monstrous
backes.   And for their barbarous feids, put the lawes to due
execution made by me there-anent, beginning euer rathest
at him that yee loue best, and is most obliged vnto you,
to make him an example to the rest.   For ye shall
make all your reformations to begin at your elbowe,
and so by degrees to flowe to the extremities of the land.
And rest not, vntill yee roote out these barbarous feides,
that their effectes may bee as well smoared downe, as their
barbarous name is vnknowne to any other nation.   For if
this treatise were written eyther in Frenche or Latine, I
could not get them named vnto you but by circumlocution.
And for your easier abolishing of them, put sharpely to
execution my Lawes made against Gunnes and traiterous
Pistolots, thinking in your heart, terming in your speach,
and vsing by your punishments all such as weare and vse
them, as brigands and cut-throates.

On the other part, eschewe the other extreamitie, in
lightlying & contemning your Nobilitie.   Remember howe
that errour brake the King my grand-fathers hart.   But
consider that vertue followeth oftest noble blood: the
worthinesse of their antecessours craueth a reuerent regarde
to bee had vnto them : honour them therefore that are
obedient to the lawe among them, as Peeres and Fathers of
your land : the more frequently that your Court can be
garnished with them, thinke it the more your honour,
acquainting and employing them in all your greatest
affaires, sen it is they must be your armes and executers
of your lawes: and so vse your selfe louingly to the
obedient, and rigourously to the stubborne, as may make
the greatest of them to thinke, that the chiefest point of
their honour standeth in striuing with the meanest of the
land in humilitie towards you, and obedience to your lawes:

beating euer in their eares, that one of the principall points
of seruice that yee owne of them, is, in their persons to
practise, and by their power to procure due obedience to
the law, without the which no seruice they can make can
be agreeable vnto you.

But the greatest hinderance to the execution of our
Lawes in this countrie, are these heritable Shirefdomes and
Regalities, which being in the handes of the great men,
do wracke the whole Countrie. For which I knowe no
present remedy, but by taking the sharper account of them
in their offices; vsing all punishment against the slouthfull,
that the lawe wil permit: and euer as they vaike, for any
offences committed by them, dispone them neuer heritablie
againe: pressing, with time, to draw it to the laudable
custome of England : which yee may the easilier doe, being
King of both, as I hope in God ye shall.

And as to the third and last estate, which is our Burghes
(for the small Barrones are but an interiour parte of the
Nobilitie and of their estate), they are composed of twoo
sortes of men, Merchants and Craftes-men : either of
these sorts bceing subiect to their owne infirmities.

The Merchants thinke the whole common-weale ordained
for making them vp, and accounting it their lawfull gaine
and trade to enrich themselues vppon the losse of all the
rest of the people, they transporte from vs thinges necessarie ;
bringing backe some-times vnnecessary things, and at other
times nothing at all. They buy for vs the worst wares,
and sell them at the dearest prices : and albeit the victualles
fall or rise of their prices, according to the aboundance or
skantnesse thereof ; yet the prices of their wares euer rise,
but neuer fall : being as constant in that their euill custome,
as if it were a sealed lawe for them. They are also the
speciall cause of the corruption of the coyne ; transporting
all our owne, and bringing in forraine, vpon what price
they please to set on it. For order putting to them, put
the good Lawes in execution already made anent these

abuses : but especially do three things. Establish honest, diligent, but few searchers, for many handes make slight worke ; and haue an honest and diligent Thesaurer to take count of them. Permit and allure forraine merchants to trade heere : so shall yee haue best and best cheape wares, not buying them at the third hand. And set euerie yeare downe a certaine price of all things, considering first, howe it is in other Countries : and the price being set reasonablie downe, if the Merchants will not bring them home on the price, cry forrainers free to bring them.

And because I haue made mention heere of the coyne, make your money of fine Golde and Siluer, causing the people bee payed with substance, and not abused with number : so shall yee enrich the common-weale, and haue a great treasure laide vp in store, if yee fall in warres or in any straits. For the making it baser will breede your commodity, but it is not to be vsed, but at a great necessity.

And the Craftes-men thinke, we should be content with their worke, howe bad and deare so euer it be : and if they in any thing be controlled, vp goeth the blew-blanket. But for their part take example by England, howe it hath flourished both in wealth and policie, since the strangers Craftes-men came in among them. Therefore not only permit, but allure strangers to come heere also : taking as straite order for repressing the mutining of ours at them, as was done in England at their first in-bringing there.

But vnto one fault is all the common people of this Kingdome subject, as well burgh as land, which is, to judge and speake rashly of their Prince : setting the common-weale vpon foure proppes, as wee call it, euer wearying of the present estate, and desirous of nouelties. For remedie whereof (besides the execution of lawes that are to be vsed against vnreuerent speakers) I knowe no better meane, then so to rule as may justly stoppe their mouthes, from all such

idle and vnreuerent speeches : and so to proppe the weale of
your people, with prouident care for their good gouernement, that justly Momus himselfe may haue no grounde to
grudge at: and yet so to temper and mixe your seueritie
with myldenesse, that as the vnjust railers may be restrayned
with a reuerent awe ; so the good and louing subjects may
not onely liue in suretie and wealth, but be stirred vp and
inuited by your benigne courtesies, to open their mouthes in
the just praise of your so well moderated regiment.   In
respect whereof, and therewith also the more to allure them
to a common amitie among themselues, certaine dayes in
the yeare would be appointed, for delighting the people
with publike spectacles of all honest games, and exercise of
armes: as also for conueening of neighbours, for entertaining
friendship and hartlinesse, by honest feasting and merri-
nesse.   For I cannot see what greater superstition can be
in making playes and lawfull games in Maie, and good
cheere at Christmasse, then in eating fish in Lent, and
vpon fridayes ; the Papists as well vsing the one as the
other : so that alwayes the Sabbothes be kept holie, and no
vnlawfull pastime be vsed.   And as this forme of contenting
the peoples mindes hath beene vsed in all well gouerned
Republickes, so will it make you performe in your gouernement that olde good sentence,

Omne tulit punctum, qui miscuit vtile dulci.

Ye see nowe (my Sonne) howe for the zeale I beare to
acquaint you with the plaine and single verity of all
things, I haue not spared to be something satyrick, in
touching wel quickly the faultes in all the estate of my
kingdome.   But I protest before God I do it with the
fatherly loue that I owe to them all : onely hating their
vices, whereof there is a good number of honest men free
in euery estate.

And because, for the better reformation of all these
abuses among your estates, it will be a great helpe vnto

you, to be well acquainted with the nature and humours of all your subjects, and to knowe particularlie the estate of euery part of your dominions; I would therefore counsel you, once in the yeare to visite the principall parts of the country ye shall be in for the time : and because, I hope ye shall bee King of moe countries than this, once in the three yeares to visite all your Kingdomes : not lipening to Vice-roies, but hearing your selfe their complaints, and hauing ordinary councels and justice-seates in euery kingdome, of their own countrimen : and the principall matters euer to be decided by your selfe when ye come in those parts.

Ye haue also to consider, that yee must not onely be carefull to keepe your subjects from receiuing anie wrong of others within; but also yee must be carefull to keepe them from the wrong of any forraigne Prince without : sen the sword is giuen you by God, not onely to revenge vpon your owne subjectes the wrongs committed amongst themselues; but further, to reuenge and free them of forrain injuries done vnto them. And therefore warres vppon just quarrells are lawfull : but aboue all, let not the wrong cause be on your side.

Vse all other Princes, as your brethren, honestly and kindely : Keepe precisely your promise vnto them, although to your hurte : Striue with euery one of them in courtesie and thankfulnes : and as with all men, so especially with them, be plaine and trueth-full, keeping euer that Christian rule, " to doe as ye would be done to : " especially in count-ing rebellion against any other Prince, a cryme against your owne selfe, because of the preparatiue. Supplie not there-fore, nor trust not other Princes rebelles, but pittie and succour all lawfull Princes in their troubles. But if any of them will not abstaine, notwithstanding whatsoeuer your good deserts, to wrong you or your subjects, craue redresse at leasure, heare and do all reason : and if no offer that is lawfull or honourable can make him to abstaine, nor repaire his wrong doing, then-for last refuge, commit the justnesse of your cause to God : giuing first honestly vp with him, and in as publicke and honourable forme.

But omitting nowe to teach you the forme of making warres, because that arte is largely treated of by many, and is better learned by practise then speculation, I will onely set downe to you heere a fewe precepts therein. Let first the justnesse of your cause be your greatest strength, and then omitte not to vse all lawfull meanes for backing of the same. Consult therefore with no Necromancer nor false Prophet vpon the successe of your warres, remembering on King Saules miserable end : but keepe your land cleane of all Sooth-sayers, according to the command in the Lawe of God, dilated by Ieremie. Neither commit your quarrell to be tried by a Duell : for beside that generally all Duell appeareth to be vnlawfull, committing the quarrell, as it were, to a lot, whereof there is no warrant in the Scripture, since the abrogating of the old Lawe : it is specially most vnlawfull in the person of a King : who being a publike person hath no power therefore to dispose of himselfe, in respect, that to his preseruation or fall, the safety or wracke of the whole common-weale is necessarily coupled, as the body is to the head.

Before ye take on warre, play the wise Kings part described by Christ, fore-seeing how yee may beare it out with all necessarie provision : especially remember, that money is *Nervus belli.* Choose olde experimented Captaines, and yoong able souldiers. Be extreamely straite and seuere in Martiall Discipline, as well for keeping of order, which is as requisit as hardinesse in the wars, and punishing of slouth, which at a time may put the whole army in hazard ; as likewise for repressing of mutinies which in warres are wonderfull dangerous. And looke to the Spaniard, whose great successe in all his warres, hath onely come through straitenesse of Discipline and order : for such errours may bee committed in the warres as cannot bee gotten mended againe.

Bee in your owne person walkrife, diligent, & paineful, vsing the aduice of such as are skilfullest in the craft, as ye must also doe in all other. Be homelie with your souldiers as your companions, for winning their harts, and extreamly liberall, for then is no time of sparing. Be colde & foreseeing the deuising, constant in your resolutions, and forward and quicke in your executions. Fortifie well your Campe, and assaile not rashly without an aduantage : neyther feare lightly your enemie. Bee curious in deuising Stratagems, but alwaies honestly : for of any thing they worke greatest effects in the warres, if secrecie be joyned to invention. And once or twice in your owne person hazard your selfe fairely, but, hauing acquired so the fame of courage and magnanimitie, make not a daylie Souldier of your selfe, exposing rashly your person to euerie perill : but conserue your selfe thereafter for the weale of your people ; for whose sake ye must more care for your selfe then for your owne.

And as I haue counselled you to be slowe in taking on a warre, so aduise I you to be slowe in peace-making. Before yee agree, looke that the grounde of your warres be satisfied in your peace, and that yee see a good suretie for you and your people : otherwaies, a honourable and just war is more tollerable then a dishonourable and disaduantageous peace.

But it is not enough to a good King, by the scepter of good lawes well execute to gouerne, and by force of armes to protect his people, if he joyne not therewith his vertuous life in his own person, and in the person of his Court and companie : by good example alluring his Subjects to the loue of vertue, and hatred of vice. And therefore (my Sonne) sith all people are naturally inclined to followe their Princes example (as I shewed you before), let it not be said that ye command others to keepe the contrarie course to that, which in your owne person yee practise : making so your wordes and deedes to fight together : but by the contrarie, let your owne life be a law-booke and a mirrour to your people, that therein they may reade the practise of their owne lawes; and therein they may see, by your image, what life they should leade.

And this example in your owne life and person, I likewise diuide in two partes: The first, in the gouernement of your Court and followers, in all godlinesse and vertue: the next, in hauing your owne minde decked and enriched so with al vertuous qualities, that therewith yee may worthilie rule your people. For it is not enough that yee haue and retaine (as prisoners) within your selfe neuer so many good qualities and vertues, except yee employ them, and set them on worke, for the weale of them that are committed to your charge: *Virtutis enim laus omnis in actione consistit.*

First then, as to the gouernement of your Court and followers, King Dauid sets downe the best precepts, that any wise and christian King can practise in that point. For as ye ought to haue a great care for the ruling well of all your subjects, so ought yee to haue a double care for the ruling well of your owne seruants, since vnto them ye are both a Politick and Oeconomick gouernour. And as euery one of the people will delight to followe the example of any of the Courtiers, as well in euill as in good: so what crime so horrible can there be committed & ouer-seene in a courteour, that will not bee an exemplare excuse for any other boldely to commit the like? And therefore in twoo poynts haue yee to take good heed anent your Court and householde. First, in choosing them wisely: next, in carefully ruling them whom ye haue chosen.

It is an olde and true saying, that a kindelie Auer will neuer become a good horse: for albeit good education and companie bee great helpes to Nature, and education bee therefore most justly called *Altera natura:* yet is it euill to get out of the flesh that is bred in the bone, as the olde prouerb sayeth. Be very ware then in making choyse of your seruantes and companie:

Nam
Turpius eiicitur, quam non admittitur hospes :

and many respects may lawfully let an admission, that will not be sufficient causes of depriuation.

All your seruantes and Courte must be composed partly of minors, such as young Lordes, to be broght vp in your company, or Pages and such like ; and partly of men of perfite age, for seruing you in such roomes, as ought to be filled with men of wisdome and discretion. For the first sorte, yee can doe no more but choose them within age, that are come of a good and vertuous kinde, *In fide parentum*, as baptisme is vsed. For though *anima non venit ex traduce*, but is immediately created by God, and infused from aboue : yet it is most certaine that vertue or vice will oftentimes, with the heritage, be transferred from the parents to the posteritie, and runne on a blood (as the Prouerbe is), the sickenesse of the minde becomming as kindely to some races, as these sickenesses of the body, that infects in the seede. Especially choose such minors as are come of a true and honest race, and haue not had the house whereof they are descended infected with falshoode.

And as for the other sorte of your companie and seruaunts that ought to be of perfect age, first, see that they be of a good fame, and without blemish : otherwise, what can the people thinke, but that ye haue chosen a company vnto you, according to your owne humour, and so haue preferred these men, for the loue of their vices and crimes, that ye knew them to be guiltie of ? For the people that see you not within, cannot iudge of you but according to the outwarde appearance of your actions and companie, which onely is subiect to their sight. And next, see that they be indued with such honest qualities as are meete for such offices, as yee ordaine them to serue in ; that your judgement may bee knowne in imploying euery man according to his gifts. And shortly, follow good king Dauids counsell in the

E

choise of your seruants, by setting your eies vpon the faithfull and vpright of the land to dwell with you.

But heere I must not forget to remember, and according to my fatherlie authoritie, to charge you to preferre speciallie to your seruice, so many as haue truelie serued me, and are able for it : the rest, honorably to reward them, preferring their posteritie before others, as kindliest : so shall yee not onely be best serued (for if the haters of your parents cannot loue you, as I shewed before, it followeth of necessitie their louers must loue you), but further, yee shall kyth your thankfull memorie of your father, and procure the blessing of these old seruants, in not missing their old master in you; which otherwaies would be turned in a praier for mee, and a curse for you. Vse them therefore when God shall call me, as the testimonies of your affection towards me : trusting and advancing those farthest, whom I found faithfullest : which yee must not discerne by their rewards at my hande (for rewards, as they are called *Bona fortunœ*, so are they subject vnto fortune), but according to the trust I gaue them; hauing oft-times had better hart then hap to the rewarding of sundry. And on the other part, as I wish you to kyth your constant loue towardes them that I loued, so desire I you to kyth in the same measure, your constant hatred to them that I hated : I meane, bring not home, nor restore not such, as yee finde standing bannished or forefaulted by me. The contrarie would kyth in you ouer great a contempt of me, and lightnesse in your owne nature : for how can they bee true to the Sonne, that were false to the Father.

But to returne to the purpose anent the choise of your seruants, yee shall by this wise forme of doing, eschew the inconuenients that in my minoritie I fell in, anent the choise of my seruants. For by them that had the command where I was brought vp, were my seruants put vnto me; not choosing them that were meetest to serue me, but whom they thought meetest to serue their turne about me; as

kythed well in many of them at the first rebellion raised
against me : which compelled mee to make a great alteration
among my seruants.   And yet the example of that corruption, made me to be long troubled there-after with solliciters,
recommending seruants vnto me, more for seruing in effect,
their friendes that put them in, then their maister that
admitted them.   Let my example then teach you to follow
the rules heere set downe : choosing your seruantes for your
owne vse, and not for the vse of others.   And since yee
must be *communis parens* to all your people, so choose
your seruantes indifferentlie out of all quarters; not re-
specting other mens appetites, but their owne qualities.   For
as yee must command all, so reason would yee should be
serued out of all, as yee please to make choise.

But speciallie take good heede to the choise of your
seruants, that yee præferre to the offices of the crowne and
estate : for in other offices ye haue onely to take heede to
your owne weale ; but these concerne likewise the weale of
your people ; for the which yee must bee answerable to
God.   Choose then for all these offices, men of knowne
wisedome, honestie, and good conscience ; well practised in
the points of the craft, that yee ordaine them for ; and
free of all factions and partialities : but speciallie free of
that filthy vice of Flattery, the pest of all Princes, and
wracke of Republickes.   For since in the first part of this
treatise, I for-warned you to be warre with your owne
inward flatterer φιλαυτία ; howe much more should yee be
warre with outwarde flatterers, who are nothing so sib to
you as your selfe is ; by the selling of such counterfeit
wares, onely preassing to ground their greatnesse vpon your
ruines ?   And therefore be carefull to præferre none, as ye
will be answerable to God, but onely for their woorthinesse.
But speciallie choose honest, diligent, meane, but responsall
men, to be your receauers in money matters : meane I say
that yee may when ye please, take a sharpe account of their
intromission, without perill of their breeding any trouble to

I. 2

your estate : for this ouer-sight hath beene the greatest cause of my mis-thriuing in money matters. Especially, but neuer a forrainer, in any principall office of estate : for that will neuer faille to stirre vp sedition and enuy in the countrie-mens harts, both against you and him. But (as I said before) if God prouide you with moe countries then this, choose the borne men of euery countrey, to be your chiefe counsellers therein.

And for conclusion of my aduice, anent the choise of your seruaunts, delight to be serued with men of the noblest blood that may be had : for besides that their seruice shall breede you great good-will and least enuie, contrary to that of start-ups ; ye shall oft finde vertue follow noble races, as I haue said before speaking of the Nobilitie.

Now, as to the other point, anent your gouerning of your seruants when yee haue chosen them ; make your Court and companie to be a paterne of godlinesse and all honest vertues, to all the rest of the people. Be a daily watch-man ouer your seruants, that they obey your lawes præciselie : for howe can your lawes be kept in the countrey, if they be broken at your eare ? Punishing the breache therof in a Courteour, more seuearly, then in the person of any other of your subjects : and aboue all, suffer none of them (by abusing their credite with you) to oppresse or wrong any of your subjects. Bee homelie or strange with them, as yee thinke their behauiour deserueth, and their nature may beare with. Thinke a quarrellous man a pest in your companie. Bee carefull euer to præferre the gentilest natured and trustiest, to the inwardest offices about you ; especially in your chalmer. Suffer none about you to meddle in anie mens particulars ; but like the Turkes Ianisares, let them know no Father but you, nor particular but yours. And if any will meddle in their kin or friends quarrelles giue them their leaue : for since yee must be of no surname nor kinne, but æquall to all honest men ; it becommeth you not to be followed with partiall or factious seruantes. Teach obedience to your seruantes, and not to thinke themselues ouer-wise: and, as when any of them deserueth it, yee must not spare to put them away; so, without a seene cause change none of them. Paie them, as as all others your subjects, with *præmium* or *pœna* as they deserue; which is the very ground-stone of good gouernement. Employ euery man as yee thinke him qualified, but vse not one in all things, lest he waxe proud, and be enuied by his fellowes. Loue them best that are plainnest with you, and disguise not the trueth for all their kinne: suffer none to be euill tongued, nor back-biters of them they hate: commaund a hartly and brotherly loue among all them that serue you. And shortly, maintaine peace in your Court, bannish enuie, cherish modestie, bannish deboshed insolence, foster humilitie, and represse pride: setting downe such a comelie and honourable order in all the points of your seruice; that when strangers shall visit your Court, they may with the Queene of Sheba, admire your wisdome in the glorie of your house, and comelie order among your seruants.

But the principall blessing that ye can get of good companie, will stand in your marying of a godly and vertuous wife: for she must be nearer vnto you then any other company, being " Flesh of your flesh, and bone of your bone," as Adam said of Heuah. And because I know not but God may call me, before ye be ready for Mariage; I will shortly set downe to you heere my aduice therein.

First of all consider, that Mariage is the greatest earthly felicitie or miserie, that can come to a man, according as it pleaseth God to blesse or cursse the same. Since then without the blessing of GOD, ye can not looke for a happie successe in Mariage; ye must be carefull both in your præparation for it, and in the choise and vsage of your wife, to procure the same. By your præparation, I meane, that ye must keepe your bodie cleane and vnpolluted, till ye giue it to your wife; whome-to onelie it belongeth. For how can yee justlie craue to be joined with a pure Virgine, if your body be polluted? Why should the one halfe be cleane, and the other defiled? And althogh I knowe, Fornication is thought but a light and a veniall sinne, by the most part of the world; yet remember well what I saide to you in my first booke anent conscience: and count euerie sinne and breache of Gods law, not according as the vaine world esteemeth of it; but as God the judge and maker of the lawe accounteth of the same. Ieare God commanding by the mouth of Paule, to "abstaine from Fornication," declaring that the "Fornicator shall not inherite the king- dome of heauen:" and by the mouth of Iohn, reckoning out Fornication amongst other greeuous sinnes, that debarres the committers amongst "Dogges and Swine, from entrie in that spirituall and heauenly Ierusalem." And consider, if a man shall once take vpon him, to count that light, which God calleth heauie; and veniall that, which God calleth greeuous; beginning first to measure any one sinne by the rule of his lust and appetites, and not of his conscience; what shall let him to doe so with the next, that his affec- tions shall stirre him to, the like reason seruing for all: and so to go for-ward till he place his whole corrupted affections in Gods roome? And then what shall come of him; but, as a man giuen ouer to his owne filthie affections, shall perish into them? And because we are all of that nature, that sibbest examples touche vs neerest, consider the difference of successe that God granted in the Mariages of the King my grandfather, and me your owne father: the reward of his incontinencie (proceeding from his euill education) being the suddaine death, at one time, of two pleasant young Princes; and a daughter onely born to succeed to him, whome he had neuer the hap so much as once to see or blesse before his death: leauing a double cursse behinde him to the land, both a Woman of sex, and a newe borne babe of age to raigne ouer them. And as for the blessing God hath bestowed on me, in granting me both a greater continencie, and the frutes following there-upon ; your selfe, and sib folkes to you, are (praise be to God) sufficient witnesses : which, I hope the same God of his infinite mercy, shall continue and increase, without repentance to me and my posteritie. Be not ashamed then, to keepe cleane your bodie, which is the Temple of the holy Spirit, notwithstanding all vaine allurements to the contrarie ; discerning truely and wisely of euery vertue and vice, according to the true qualities thereof ; and not according to the vaine conceits of men.

As for your choise in Mariage, respect chiefly the three causes, wherefore Mariage was first ordained by God : and then ioyne three accessories, so far as they may be obtained, not derogating to the principalles.

The three causes it was ordeined for, are, for staying of lust, for procreation of children, and that man should by his wife get a helper like himselfe. Deferre not then to Marie till your age ; for it is ordained for quenching the lust of your youth. Especiallie a King must tymouslie Marie for the weale of his people. Neither Marie ye, for any accessory cause or worldly respects, a woman vn-able, either through age, nature, or accident, for procreation of children : for in a king, that were a double fault, aswell against his owne weale, as against the weale of his people. Neither also Marie one of knowne euill conditions, or vicious education : for the woman is ordeined to be a helper, and not a hinderer to man.

The three accessories (which as I haue saide, ought also to be respected, without derogating to the principall causes) are beautie, riches, and friendship by alliance, which are all blessings of God. For beautie increaseth your loue to your Wife, contenting you the better with her, without caring for others : and riches and great alliance, doe both make her the abler to be a helper vnto you. But if, ouer great respect being had to these accessories ; the principall causes be ouer-seene (which is ouer oft practised in the worlde) as of themselues they are a blessing being well vsed; so the abuse of them will turne them in a curse. For what can all these worldlie respects auaile, when a man shall finde himselfe coupled with a Diuell, to be one flesh with him, and the halfe marrow in his bed? Then (though too late) shall he finde that beautie without bountie, wealth without wisedome, and great friendship without grace and honestie; are but faire shewes, and the deceatfull masques of infinite miseries.

But haue yee respect, my Sonne, to these three speciall causes in your Mariage, which flowe from the first institution thereof, *& cætera omnia adjicientur vobis*. And therefore I would rathest haue you to Marie one that were fully of your owne Religion; her ranke and other qualities beeing agree-able to your estate. For although that to my great regrate, the number of any Princes of power and account, professing our Religion, be but very small; and that therefore this aduice seemes to be the more straite and difficile: yet yee haue deepelie to weigh & consider vpon these doubts: how yee and your wife can be of one flesh, and keepe vnitie betwix you, beeing members of two opposite Churches: disagreement in Religion bringeth euer with it, disagreement in manners; and the dissention betwixt your Preachers and hers, will breede and foster a dissention among your subjects, taking their example from your familie; besides the perrill of the euill education of your children. Neither pride you that yee will be able to frame and make her as yee please: that deceaued Salomon the wisest King that euer was: the grace of Perseuerance not being a flowre that groweth in our garden.

Remember also that Mariage is one of the greatest actions that a man doth in all his time, especially in taking of his first Wife: and if he Marie first basely beneath his ranke, he will euer be the lesse accounted of there-after. And lastlie, remember to choose your Wife as I aduised you to choose your seruants: that she be of a whole and cleane

race, not subject to the hereditary sicknesses, either of the
soule or the body. For if a man will be carefull to breed
horses and dogs of good kindes; howe much more carefull
should hee be, for the breed of his owne loines? So shall
yee in your Mariage haue respect to your conscience, honour,
and naturall weale in your successours.

When yee are Maried, keep inviolablie your promise
made to God in your Mariage; which standeth all in
dooing of one thing, and abstaining from another: to treat
her in all thinges as your Wife and the halfe of your selfe;
and to make your bodie (which then is no more yours, but
properly hers) common with none other. I trust I neede
not to insist heere to disswade you from the filthy vice
of adulterie: remember onely what solemne promise yee
make to God at your Mariage: and since it is onely by
the force of that promise that your children succeede to you,
which otherwaies they could not doe; æquitie and reason
would, yee should keepe your part thereof. God is euer
a seueare avenger of all perjuries; and it is no oath made
in ieste, that giueth power to children to succeed to great
kingdomes. Haue the King my grand-fathers example
before your eies, who by his adulterie, bred the wracke of
his lawfull daughter and heire; in begetting that bastard,
who vnnaturally rebelled, and procured the ruine of his
owne Souerane and sister. And what good her posteritie
hath gotten sen-syne, of some of that vn-lawfull generation,
Bothuell his treacherous attemptes can beare witnesse.
Keepe precisely then your promise made at Mariage, as ye
would wish to bee partaker of the blessing therein.

And for your behauiour to your Wife, the Scripture can
best giue you counsell therein. Treate her as your owne
flesh, commaund her as her Lord, cherish her as your
helper, rule her as your pupill, and please her in all things
reasonable; but teach her not to bee curious in things that
belonges her not. Yee are the head, she is your bodie: it is
your office to command, and hers to obey; but yet with such

a sweete harmonie, as shee should be as readie to obey as yee to commaund; as willing to follow as yee to goe before: your loue being wholly knit vnto her, and all her affections louingly bent to followe your will.

And to conclude, keepe specially three rules with your Wife: first, suffer her neuer to meddle with the politicke gouernement of the Common-weale, but holde her at the Oeconomicke rule of the house; and yet all to be subject to your direction: keepe carefully good and chaste companie a' out her; for wemen are the frailest sexe: and bee neuer both angrie at once; but when yee see her in passion, yee should with reason danton yours. For both when yee are setled, yee are meetest to judge of her errours; and when she is come to her selfe, she may bee best made to apprehend her offence, and reuerence your rebuke.

If God send you succession, bee carefull for their vertuous education: loue them as yee ought, but let them know as much of it, as the gentlenesse of their nature will deserue; contayning them euer in a reuerent loue and feare of you. And in case it please God to prouide you to all these three kingdomes, make your eldest sonne Isaac, leauing him all your kingdomes; and prouide the rest with priuate possessions. Otherwaies by diuiding your kingdomes, ye shal leaue the seede of diuision and discord among your posteritie: as befell to this Ile: by the diuision and assignment thereof, to the three sonnes of Brutus, Locrine, Albanact, and Camber. But if God giue you not succession, defraud neuer the nearest by right, whatsoeuer conceit yee haue of the person. For Kingdomes are euer at Gods disposition, and in that case wee are but liue-rentars, lying no more in the Kings nor peoples hands to dispossesse the righteous heire.

And as your company should bee a paterne to the rest of the people, so should your person bee a lampe and mirrour to your companie: giuing light to your seruants to walke in the path of vertue, and representing vnto them such woorthie qualities, as they should preasse to imitate.

I neede not to trouble you with the particular discourse of the foure Cardinall vertues, it is so troden a path : but I will shortly say vnto you, make one of them, which is Temperance, Queene of all the rest within you. I mean not by the vulgar interpretation of Temperance, which onely consists in *gustu & tactu,* by the moderating of these two senses : but I meane of that wise moderation, that first commaunding your selfe, shall as a Queene commaund all the affections and passions of your mind ; and, as a Physician, wisely mixe all your actions according therto. Therfore, not onely in all your affections and passions, but euen in your most vertuous actions, make euer moderation to bee the chiefe ruler. For although holinesse be the first and most requisite qualitie of a Christian, as proceeding from a feeling feare and true knowledge of God : yet yee remember how in the conclusion of my first booke, I aduised you to moderate all your outwarde actions flowing there-fra. The like say I now of Iustice, which is the greatest vertue, that properly belongeth to a Kinges office.

Vse Iustice, but with such moderation, as it turne not in tyrannie : otherwaies *summum ius* is *summa iniuria.* As for example : if a man of a knowne honest life, be in-uaded by brigandes or theeues for his purse, and in his owne defence slaie one of them, they being both moe in number, and also knowne to be deboshed and insolent liuers ; where by the contrarie, he was single alone, being a man of sounde reputation : yet because they were not at the horne, or there was no eie-witnesse present that could verifie their first inuading of him ; shall hee therefore lose his head? And likewise, by the lawe-burrowes in our lawes, men are prohibited vnder great pecuniall paines, from any waies inuading or molesting their neighbours person or boundes : if then his horse breake the halter, and pasture in his neigbours medow, shall hee pay two or three thousand poundes, for the wantonesse of his horse, or the weakenesse of his halter? Surelie no. For lawes are ordained as rules of vertuous and sociall liuing, and not to be snares to trap your good subjectes: and therefore the lawe must be interpreted according to the meaning, and not to the literall sense thereof: *Nam ratio est anima legis.*

And as I saide of Iustice, so say I of Clemencie, Magnanimitie, Liberalitie, Constancie, Humilitie, and all other Princelie vertues: *Nam in medio stat virtus.* And it is but the craft of the Diuell that falselie coloureth the two vices that are on either side thereof, with the borrowed titles of it, albeit in very deede they haue no affinitie therewith: and the two extremities themselues, although they seeme contrarie, yet growing to the height, runnes euer both in one. For *in infinitis omnia concurrunt;* and what difference is betwixt extreame tyrannie, delighting to destroy all mankinde; and extreame slacknesse of punishment, permitting euery man to tyrannize ouer his companion? Or what differeth extreame prodigalitie, by wasting of all to possesse nothing; from extreame niggardnesse, by hoarding vp all to enjoy nothing; like the Asse that carrying victuall on her backe, is like to sterue for hunger, and will bee glad of thrissels for her part? And what is betwixt the pride of a glorious Nebuchadnezzar, and the præposterous humilitie of one of the Proud Puritanes, claiming to their Paritie, and crying, Wee are all but vile wormes; and yet will judge and giue lawe to their King, but will bee judged nor controlled by none? Surelie, there is more pride vnder such a ones blacke bonnet then vnder Alexander the great his Diademe, as was said of Diogenes in the like case.

But aboue all vertues, studie to knowe well your owne craft, which is to rule your people. And when I say this, I bid you know all craftes. For except yee knowe euerie one, howe can yee controlle euerie one, which is your proper office? Therefore besides your education, it is necessarie

yee delight in reading, and seeking the knowledge of all
lawfull things; but with these two restrictions: first, that
ye choose idle houres for it, not interrupting therewith the
discharge of your office: and next, that ye studie not for
knowledge nakedly; but that your principall end be, to
make you able thereby to vse your office; practising according to your knowledge in all the points of your calling: not
like these vaine Astrologians, that studie night and day on
the course of the starres, only that they may, for satisfying
their curiositie, knowe their course. But since all artes
and sciences are linked euerie one with other, their greatest
principles agreeing in one (whiche mooued the Poets to
faine the nine Muses to be all sisters), studie them, that out
of their harmonie, ye may sucke the knowledge of all
faculties; and consequently, be on the counsell of all
craftes, that yee may be able to containe them all in
order, as I haue alreadie saide. For knowledge and learning is a light burthen, the waight whereof will neuer presse
your shoulders.

First of all then, studie to be well seene in the Scriptures,
as I remembred you in the first booke; aswell for the
knowledge of your owne saluation, as that ye may be able
to containe your Churche in their calling, as *Custos
vtriusque Tabulæ.* For the ruling them well, is no small
point of your office; taking specially heede, that they
vague not from their text in the Pulpit: and if euer yee
would haue peace in your land, suffer them not to meddle
in that place with the estate or policie: but punish seuearlie
the first that præsumeth to it. Doe nothing towards them
without a good ground and warrant; but reason not much
with them: for I haue ouer-much surfaited them with that,
and it is not their fashion to yeeld. And suffer no conuen-
tions nor meetings among Church-men, but by your knowledge and permission.

Next the Scriptures, studie well your owne lawes: for
how can yee discerne by the thing yee know not? But

preasse to drawe all your lawes and processes, to be as short & plaine as ye can : assure your selfe the long-somnesse both of rights and processes, breedeth their vn-sure loose-nesse and obscuritie : the shortest being euer both the surest and plainnest forme : and the long-somnesse seruing onely for the enriching of the Aduocates and Clerks, with the spoile of the whole countrey. And therefore delight to haunt your Session, and spie carefullie their proceedings; taking good heed, if any briberie may bee tried among them, which can not ouer-seuearly be punished. Spare not to go there, for gracing that farre any that ye fauour, by your præsence to procure them expedition of justice: although that should be speciallie done, for the poore that can not wait on, or are debarred by mightier parties. But when ye are there, remember the throne is Gods, and not yours, that ye sit in, and let no fauour, nor whatsoeuer respects mooue you from the right. Ye sit not there, as I shew before, for reward-ing of friends or seruants; nor for crossing of contemners, but only for doing of justice. Learne also wiselie to discerne, betwixt justice and æquitie ; and for pittie of the poore, rob not the riche, because he may better spare it ; but giue the little-man the larger coat if it be his : eschewing the errour of young Cyrus therein. For justice, by the law, giueth euery man his owne ; and æquitie in things arbitrall, giueth euerie one that which is meetest for him.

Be an ordinarie sitter in your secret Counsell: that judicature is onelie ordained for matters of estate, and repressing of insolent oppressions. Make that judgement as compendious and plaine as ye can ; and suffer no Aduo-cates to bee heard there with their dilatours, but let euerie partie tell his owne tale himselfe : and wearie not to heare the complaints of the oppressed, *aut ne Rex sis*. Remit euerie thing to the ordinarie judicature, for eschewing of confusion : but let it be your owne craft, to take a sharpe account of euerie man in his office.

And next the lawes, I would haue you to be well versed

in authenticke histories, and in the Chronicles of all nations; but speciallie in our owne histories (*Ne sis peregrinus domi*), the example whereof most neerely concernes you. I meane not of such infamous inuectiues, as Buchanans or Knoxes Chronicles: and if any of these infamous libels remaine vntill your daies, vse the law vpon the keepers thereof. For in that point I would haue you a Pythagorist, to thinke that the verie spirites of these archibellouses of rebellion, haue made transition in them that hoardes their bookes, or maintaines their opinions; punishing them, euen as it were their authours risen againe. But by reading of authenticke histories and chronicles, yee shall learne experience by Theoricke, applying the by-past things to the present estate, *quia nihil norum sub Sole:* such is the continuall volubilitie of things earthlie, according to the roundnesse of the worlde, and revolution of the heauenly circles: which is expressed by the wheeles in Ezechiels visions, and counterfaited by the Poets *in rota Fortunæ.* And likewise by the knowledge of histories, yee shall knowe howe to behaue your selfe to all Embassadours and strangers; being able to discourse with them vpon the estate of their owne countrie. And among all profane histories, I must not omitte most speciallie to recommend vnto you, the Commentaries of Cæsar; both for the sweete flowing of the stile, as also for the worthinesse of the matter it selfe. For I haue euer beene of that opinion, that of all the Ethnicke Emperours, or great Captaines that euer was, he hath farthest excelled, both in his practise and in his præcepts in martiall affaires.

As for the studie of other liberall artes and sciences, I would haue you reasonablie versed in them, but not preassing to bee a passe-maister in any of them: for that can not but distract you from the points of your calling, as I shewed you before: and when, by the enemie winning the towne, yee shall bee interrupted in your demonstration, as Archimedes was; your people (I thinke) will looke very bluntly vpon it. I graunt it is meete yee haue some entrance, specially in the Mathematickes; for the knowledge of the arte militarie, in situation of Campes, ordering of battels, making fortifications, placing of batteries, or suchlike. And let not this your knowledge bee deade without fruites, as S. Iames speaketh of Faith : but let it appeare in your daily conuersation, and in all the actions of your life.

Embrace true Magnanimitie, not in being vindictiue, which the corrupted judgementes of the worlde thinkes to bee true Magnanimitie; but by the contrary, in thinking your offender not woorthy of your wrath, empyring ouer your owne passion, and triumphing in the commanding your selfe to forgiue : husbanding the effects of your courage and wrath, to be rightly emploied vpon repelling of injuries within, by reuenge taking vpon the oppressours; and in reuenging injuries without, by just warres vpon forraine enemies. And so, where yee finde a notable injury, spare not to giue course to the torrents of your wrath. "The wrath of a King, is like to the roring of a Lyon."

Foster true Humility, in bannishing pride not onely towardes God (considering yee differ not in stuffe, but in vse, and that onely by his ordinance, from the basest of your people), but also towards your Parents. And if it fall out that my Wife shall out-liue me, as euer yee thinke to purchase my blessing, honour your Mother : set Beersheba in a throne on your right hand : offend her for nothing, much lesse wrong her : remember her

> Quae longa decem tulerit fastidia menses;

and that your flesh and bloode is made of hers : and beginne not, like the young lordes and lairdes, your first warres vpon your Mother; but preasse earnestlie to deserue her blessing. Neither deceaue your selfe with many that say, they care not for their Parents curse, so they deserue it not. O inuert not the order of nature, by judging your

superiours, chieflie in your owne particular! But assure
your selfe, the blessing or cursse of the Parents, hath
almost euer a Propheticke power joined with it: and if
there were no more, honour your Parents, for the lengthen-
ing of your owne daies, as God in his lawe promiseth.
Honour also them that are *in loco Parentum* vnto you,
such as your gouernours, vp-bringers, and Præceptours: be
thankfull vnto them and reward them, which is your dewty
and honour.

But on the other part, let not this true humilitie staie
your high indignation to appeare, when any great oppressours shall præsume to come in your presence; then frowne
as yee ought. And in-case they vse a colour of law in
oppressing their poore ones, as ouer-manie do; that which
yee cannot mend by law, mend by the withdrawing of your
countenance from them: and once in the yeere crosse them,
when their erands come in your way, recompencing the op-
pressour, according to Christs parable of the two debtors.

Keepe true Constancie, not onely in your kindenesse
towardes honest men; but being also *invicti animi* against
all aduersities: not with that Stoicke insensible stupiditie,
wherewith manie in our daies, preassing to winne honor, in
imitating that auncient sect, by their inconstant behauiour
in their owne liues, belyes their profession. But although
yee are not a stocke, not to feele calamities; yet let not the
feeling of them so ouerrule and doazen your reason, as may
stay you from taking and vsing the best resolution for
remedie that can be found out.

Vse true Libertie in rewarding the good, and bestowing
frankly for your honour and weale: but with that propor-
tionall discretion, that euerie man may be serued according
to his measure: wherein respect must bee had to his ranke,
desertes, and necessitie. And prouide how to haue, but cast
not awaie without cause. In speciall empaire not by your
Liberalitie the ordinarie rents of your crowne; whereby
the estate royall of you, and your successours, must be

maintained, *ne exhaurias fontem liberalitatis:* for that would euer be kept *sacrosanctum & extra commercium:* otherwaies, your Liberalitie woulde decline to Prodigalitie, in helping others with your and your successors hurt. And aboue all, enrich not your selfe with exactions vpon your subjectes; but thinke the riches of your people your best treasure, by the sinnes of offenders, where no præuention can auaile, making justlie your commoditie. And in case necessitie of warres or other extraordinaries compell you to lift Subsidies, doe it as rarely as yee can: employing it onely to the vse it was ordained for; and vsing your selfe in that case, as *fidus depositarius* to your people.

And principallie, exercise true Wisedome; in discerning wiselie betwixt true and false reportes: firste considering the nature of the person reporter; next, what entresse he can haue in the weale or euill of him, of whome hee maketh the report; thirdlie, the likeli-hoode of the purpose it selfe; and last, the nature and by-past life of the dilated person: and where yee finde a tratler, awaie with him. And although it be true that a Prince can neuer without secrecie doe great things, yet it is better ofttimes to trie reportes, then by credulitie to foster suspicion vpon a honest man. For since suspicion is the Tyrants sicknesse, as the fruites of an euill Conscience, *potiùs in alteram partem peccato:* I meane, in not mistrusting one, whom to no such vn-honestie was knowne before. But as for such as haue slipped before, former experience may justly breed prevention by foresight.

And to conclude my aduice anent your behauiour in your person; consider that God is the authour of all vertue, hauing imprinted in mens mindes by the very light of nature, the loue of all morall vertues; as was seene by the vertuous liues of the olde Romaines: and preasse then to shine as farre before your people, in all vertue and honestie, as in greatnesse of ranke: that the vse thereof in all your actions, may turne, with time, to a naturall habitude in you;

and as by their hearing of your lawes, so by their sight of your person, both their eies and their eares, may leade & allure them to the loue of vertue, and hatred of vice.

The Third Booke.

OF A KINGS BEHAVIOR IN INDIFFERENT THINGS.

It is a true olde saying, That a King is as one set on a stage, whose smallest actions and gestures all the people gazinglie doe beholde: and therefore although a King be neuer so præcise in the discharging of his office, the people, who seeth but the outward part, will euer judge of the substance by the circumstances; and according to the outward appearance, if his behauiour be light or dissolute, will conceiue præ-occupied conceits of the Kings inward intention: which although with time, the trier of all trueth, it will euanish, by the euidence of the contrarie effects, yet *interim patitur iustus ;* and præ-judged conceits will, in the meane time, breed contempt, the mother of rebellion and disorder. And besides that, it is certaine that all the indifferent actions and behauiour of a man, haue a certaine holding and dependance, either vpon vertue or vice, according as they are vsed or ruled: for there is not a middes betwixt them, no more then betwixt their rewards, heauen and hell.

Be carefull then, my Sonne, so to frame all your indifferent actions and outward behauiour, as they may serue for the furtherance and forth-setting of your inward vertuous disposition.

The whole indifferent actions of a man, I diuide in two sorts: in his behauiour in things necessarie, as food, sleep-

ing, raiment, speaking, writing, and gesture; and in things
not necessarie, though conuenient and lawfull, as pastimes
or exercises, and vsing of companie for recreation.

As to the indifferent things necessary, although that of
themselues they can not be wanted, and so in that case are
not indifferent; as like-waies in-case they be not vsed with
moderation. declining so to the extremitie which is vice;
yet the qualitie and forme of vsing them, may smell of
vertue or vice, and be great furtherers to any of them.

To beginne then at the things necessary; one of the
publickest indifferent actions of a King, and that maniest,
especially strangers, will narrowlie take heed to, is his
manner of refection at his Table, and his behauiour thereat.
Therefore, as Kings vse oft to eat publicklie, it is meet and
honourable that ye also doe so, as well to eschew the opinion
that yee loue not to haunt companie, which is one of the
markes of a Tyrant; as likewise, that your delight to eate
priuatlie, be not thought to be for priuate satisfying of
your gluttonie; which yee would be ashamed should be
publicklie scene. Let your Table be honourablie serued;
but serue your appetite with few dishes, as young Cyrus
did: whiche both is holesommest, and freest from the vice
of delicacie, which is a degree of gluttonie. And vse most
to eat of reasonablie-grosse and common-meats; aswell for
making your bodie strong and durable for trauell at all
occasions, either in peace or in warre: as that ye may be
the hartlier receaued by your meane subjects in their
houses, when their cheere may suffice you: which otherwaies would be imputed to you for pride and daintinesse,
and breed coldnesse and disdaine in them. Let all your
food bee simple, without composition or sauces; which
are more like medecines then meat. The vsing of them
was counted amongst the auncient Romanes a filthie vice
of delicacie; because they serue onely for pleasing of the
taste, and not for satisfying of the necessity of nature;
abhorring Apicius their owne citizen, for his vice of delicacie

and monstrous gluttony. Like as both the Græcians and Romanes had in detestation the very name of Philoxenus, for his filthie wish of a Crane-craig. And therefore was that sentence vsed amongst them against these artificiall false appetites, *optimum condimentum fames.* But be warre with vsing excesse of meat and drinke; and chiefly, be warre of drunkennesse, which is a beastlie vice, namelie in a King: but speciallie be warre with it, because it is one of those vices that increaseth with age. In the forme of your meat-eating, be neither vnciuill, like a grosse Cynicke; nor affectatlie mignarde, like a daintie dame; but eat in a manlie, round, and honest fashion. It is no waies comelie to dispatch affaires, or to be pensiue at meat: but keepe then an open and cheerefull countenance: causing to reade pleasant histories vnto you, that profit may be mixed with pleasure: and when ye are not disposed, entertaine pleasant, quicke, but honest discourses.

And because meat prouoketh sleeping, be also moderate in your sleepe; for it goeth much by vse: and remember that if your whole life were diuided in foure parts, three of them would be found to be consumed on meat, drinke, sleepe, and vnnecessarie occupations.

But albeit ordinarie times woulde commonlie be kept in meat and sleepe, yet vse your selfe some-times so, that any time in the foure and twentie houres may be alike to you for any of them, that thereby your diet may be accommodate to your affaires, and not your affaires to your diet: not therefore vsing your selfe to ouer great softnesse and delicacie in your sleepe, more then in your meat; and specially in-case ye haue ado with the warres.

Let not your Chalmer be throng and common in the time of your rest, aswell for comelinesse as for eschewing of carrying reports out of the same. Let them that haue the credite to serue in your Chalmer, be trustie and secret: for a King will haue need to vse secrecie in manie thinges: but yet behaue your selfe so in your greatest secrets, as yee neede not be ashamed, suppose they were all proclaimmed at the mercate crosse. But specially see that those of your Chalmer be of a sounde fame, and without blemish.

Take no heede to anie of your dreames: for all Prophecies, visions, and propheticke dreames are accomplished and ceased in Christ. And therefore take no heede to freets either in dreames, or anie other things: for that errour proceedeth of ignorance, and is vnwoorthie of a Christian; who shoulde bee assured, *Omnia esse pura puris*, as Paule saieth; all daies and meates being alike to Christians.

Next followeth to speake of rayment, the on-putting whereof is the ordinarie action that followeth next to sleepe. Bee also moderate in your raiment; neither ouer superfluous, like a deboshed waister; nor yet ouer base, like a miserable wretch; not artificiallie trimmed and decked, like a Courtizane; nor yet ouer-sluggishly clothed, like a country-clowne; not ouer lightly, like a Candie-souldier, or a vaine young Courtier; nor yet ouer grauelie, like a Minister. But in your garments be proper, cleanlie, comely and honest: wearing your cloathes in a carelesse, yet comelie forme: keeping in them a midde forme, *inter Togatos & Paludatos;* betwixt the grauitie of the one, and lightnesse of the other. Thereby to signifie, that by your calling yee are mixed of both the professions; *Togatus*, as a judge making and pronouncing the lawe; *Paludatus*, by the power of the sword: as your office is likewise mixed, betwixt the Ecclesiasticall and ciuill estate. For a King is not *merè laicus*, as both the Papistes and Anabaptistes would haue him; to the which error also the Puritanes incline ouer-farre. But to returne to the purpose of garments, they ought to be vsed according to their first institution by God; which was for three causes: first to hide our nakednesse and shame; next and consequentlie, to make vs more comelie; and thirdlie, to preserue vs from the injuries of heate and colde. If to hide our nakednesse and shamefull parts, then

these naturall parts ordained to be hid, should not be
represented by any vn-decent formes in the cloathes: and
if they shoulde helpe our comlinesse, they should not then
by their painted preened fashion, serue for baites to filthie
lechery; as false haire and fairding does amongst vnchaste
women: and if they shoulde preserue vs from the injuries of
heate and colde, men should not, like senselesse stones
contemne God, in light-lying the seasons; glorying to
conquer honour on heat and colde. And although it bee
praise-woorthy, and necessarie in a prince, to be *patiens
algoris & astus,* when he shall haue adoe with warres vpon
the fieldes; yet I thinke it meeter that yee go both clothed
and armed, than naked to the battell; except you woulde
make you light for away-running: and yet for cowards,
metus addit alas. And shortlie, in your cloathes keepe a
proportion, as well with the seasons of the yeare as of your
age: in the fashions of them being carelesse, vsing them
according to the common forme of the time, some-times
richelier, some-times meanlier clothed as occasion serueth,
without keeping any præcise rule therein. For if your
minde be founde occupied vpon them, it will be thought
idle otherwaies, and yee shall bee accompted in the number
• of one of these *compti iuuenes;* which will make your spirit
and judgement to bee lesse thought of. But speciallie
eschewe to be effœminate in your cloathes, in perfuming,
preening, or such like: and faile neuer in time of warres to
be galliardest and brauest, both in cloathes and countenance.
And make not a foole of your selfe in disguysing or wearing
long haire or nailes, which are but excrements of nature,
and bewray such misusers of them, to be either of vindictiue,
or a vaine light naturall. Especiallie, make no vowes in
such vaine and outward things, as concerne either meate or
clothes.

Let your selfe and all your Court weare no ordinarie
armour with your cloathes, but such as is knightlie and
honourable: I meane rapier-swordes & daggers. For toyle-

some weapons in the Court betokens confusion in the
countrie. And therfore bannishe not onelie from your
Courte, all traiterous offensiue weapons, forbidden by the
lawes, as gunnes and such like (whereof I spake alreadie),
but also all traiterous defensiue armes, as secretes, plate-
sleeues, and such like vnseene armour. For, besides that
the wearers thereof may be præsupposed to haue a secrete
euill intention, they want both the vses that defensiue
armour is ordained for: which is, to be able to holde out
violence, and by their outwarde glaunsing in their enemies
eyes, to strike a terrour in their harts. Where by the contrarie, they can serue for neither; being not onely vnable
to resit, but dangerous for shots, and giuing no outwarde
showe against the enemie: being onlie ordained for be-
traying vnder trust; whereof honest men should be ashamed
to beare the outwarde badge, not resembling the thing they
are not. And for answer against these arguments, I know
none but the olde Scottes fashion: which if it be wrong, is
no more to be allowed for auncientnesse, then the olde
Masse is, which also our forefathers vsed.

The next thing that yee haue to take heede to, is your
speaking and language; wherevnto I joyne your gesture,
since action is one of the cheefest qualities, that is required
in an oratour: for as the tongue speaketh to the eares, so
doth the gesture speake to the eyes of the auditour. In
both your speaking and your gesture, vse a naturall and
plaine forme, not fairded with artifice: for (as the French-
men say) *Rien contre-faict fin:* but eschewe all affectate
formes in both.

In your language be plaine, honest, naturall, comelie, cleane,
short, and sentencious: eschewing both the extremities,
aswell in not vsing any rusticall corrupt leide, as booke-
language, and Pen and Inkehorne tearmes: and least of all
mignard & effeminate termes. But let the greatest parte
of your eloquence consist in a naturall, cleare, and sensible
forme of the deliuerie of your minde, builded euer vpon

certaine and good groundes; tempering it with grauitie, quicknesse, or merinesse, according to the subject and occasion of the time; not taunting in Theology, nor alleadging and prophaning the Scripture in drinking purposes, as ouer many doe.

Vse also the like forme in your gesture; neither looking sillely, like a stupide pedant, nor vnsetledlie, with an vncouth morgue, like a new-com-ouer Cavalier: but let your behauior be naturall, graue, and according to the fashion of the countrie. Be not ouer-sparing in your courtesies; for that will be imputed to in-civility & arrogancie: nor yet ouer-prodigal in jowking or nodding at euery step; for that forme of being populare, becommeth better aspiring Absolons then lawfull Kings: framing euer your gesture according to your present actions: looking grauelie & with a majestie when ye sit in judgement, or giues audience to Embassadours; homely, when ye are in priuate with your owne seruants; merelie, when yee are at any pastime or merrie discourse; and let your countenance smell of courage and magnanimitie when yee are at the warres. And remember (I say ouer againe) to be plaine & sensible in your language: for besides that it is the tongues office to be the messenger of the mind, it may bee thought a point of imbecillitie of spirite in a King to speake obscurely; muche more vntruly: as if he stoode in awe of any in vttering his thoughts.

Remember also, to put a difference betwixt your forme of language in reasoning, and your pronouncing of sentences, or declaratour of your will in judgement, or any other waies in the pointes in your office. For in the former case, ye must reason pleasantly and paciently, not like a king, but like a priuate man and a scholler: other waies, your impacience of contradiction will be interpreted to be for lacke of reason on your parte. Where in the points of your office, ye should ripely aduise indeede, before ye giue forth your sentence, but fra it be giuen forth, the suffering of any contradiction diminisheth the Majesty of your authority, and maketh the processes endlesse. The like forme would also be obserued by all your inferiour judges and Magistrates.

Now as to your writing, which is nothing else but a forme of en-registrate speeche; vse a plaine, shorte but stately stile, both in your Proclamations and missiues, especially to forraine Princes. And if your engine spurre you to write any workes, eyther in verse or in prose, I cannot but alowe you to practise it: but take no longsome workes in hande, for distracting you from your calling.

Flatter not your selfe in your laboures, but before they be set forth, let them first be priuilie censured by some of the best skilled men in that craft, that in these workes yee meddle with. And because your writes will remaine as true pictures of your minde, to all posterities; let them be free of all vncomelinesse and vn-honestie: and according to Horace his counsell:

Nonumque premantur in annum.

I meane both your verse and your prose; letting first that fury & heate, wherewith they were written, coole at leasure; and then as an vncouth judge and censor, reuising them ouer againe, before they be published, *quia nescit vox missareuerti.*

If yee would write worthely, choose subjectes worthie of you, that be not full of vanity, but of vertue; eschewing obscurity, and delighting euer to be plaine and sensible. And if ye write in verse, remember that it is not the principall parte of a poëme to rime right, and flowe well with many pretty wordes: but the chiefe commendation of a poëme is, that when the verse shall bee shaken sundry in prose, it shall bee found so ritch in quicke inuentions, & poëticke floures, and in faire and pertinent comparisons; as it shall retaine the lustre of a poëme, although in prose. And I would also aduise you to write in your owne language;

for there is nothing left to bee saide in Greeke and Latine already; and ynewe of poore schollers would match you in these languages; and besides that, it best becommeth a King to purifie and make famous his owne tongue; wherein he may goe before all his subjectes; as it setteth him well to doe in all honest & lawfull things.

And amongst all vnnecessarie things that are lawfull and expedient, I thinke exercises of the bodie most commendable to be vsed by a young Prince, in such honest games or pastimes, as may further abilitie & maintaine health. For albeit I grant it to be most requisite for a King to exercise his engine, which surely with idlenesse will rouste and become blunt; yet certainly bodily exercises and games are very commendable; aswell for banishing of idlenesse (the mother of all vice) as for making his body able and durable for trauell, which is very necessarie for a King. But from this count I debarre all rough & violent exercise, as the foot-ball; meeter for laming, then making able the vsers thereof: as likewise such tumbling trickes as onely serue for Comedians & Balladines, to win their breade with. But the exercises that I would haue you to vse (although but moderately, not making a craft of them) are running, leaping, wrastling, fencing, dauncing, & playing at the caitche or tennise, archery, palle maillè, & such like other faire & pleasant field games. And the honourablest and most commendable games that yee can vse, are on horse-backe: for it becommeth a Prince best of any man to be a faire and good horse-man. Vse therefore to ride and danton great and courageous horses; that I may say of you, as Phillip saide of great Alexander his sonne, Μαχεδυνìα οὐσε χωρεῖ. And specially vse such games on horse-backe, as may teach you to handle your armes thereon; such as the tilt, the ring, and lowe-ryding for handling of your sworde.

I cannot omit heere the hunting, namelye with running houndes; which is the most honourable and noblest sorte thereof: for it is a theeuish forme of hunting to shoote with gunnes and bowes : and greyhound hunting is not so martiall a game. But because I would not bee thoght a partiall praiser of this sport, I remit you to Xenophon, an olde and famous writer, who had no minde of flattering you or me in this purpose : & who also setteth downe a faire patern for the education of a young king, vnder the supposed name of Cyrus.

As for hawking I condemne it not, but I must praise it more sparingly ; because it neither resembleth the warres so neere as hunting doth, in making a man hardy, and skilfully ridden in all groundes ; and is more vncertaine and subject to mischances : and (which is worst of all) is there-through an extreame stirrer vp of passions. But in vsing either of these games obserue that moderation, that yee slip not there-with the houres appointed for your affaires, which yee ought euer præciselie to keepe : remembring that these games are but ordayned for you, in enabling you for your office, for the which ye are ordayned.

And as for fitting house pastimes, where-with men by driuing time, spurre a free and fast ynough running horse (as the prouerbe is), although they are not profitable for the exercise eyther of minde or body, yet can I not vtterly condemne them ; since they may at times supply the roome, which beeing empty, would be parent to pernitious idlenes, *quia nihil potest esse vacuum.* I will not therefore agree with the curiosity of some learned men in our age, in . forbidding cardes, dice, and other such like games of hazard ; although other waies surely I reuerence them, as notable & godly men. For they are deceiued therein, in founding their argument vppon a mistaken grounde ; which is, that the playing at such games is a kinde of casting of lot, and therefore vnlawfull, wherein they deceiue themselues. For the casting of lot was vsed for triall of the trueth in any obscure thing, that other wayes could not be gotten cleared ; and therfore was a sorte of prophesie : where by the contrary, no man goeth to anie of these plaies, to cleare any obscure trueth, but onely to gage so much of his owne money, as hee pleaseth, vpon the hazarde of the running of the cardes or dice; aswell as he would doe vpon the speede of a Horse or a Dog, or any such like gaigeour. And so, if they be vnlawfull, all gaigeours vpon vncertainties must likewayes be condemned. Not that thereby I take the defence of vaine carders and dicers, that waste their money and their time (whereof fewe consider the preciousnesse) vpon prodigall and continuall playing: no, I would rather alowe it to bee discharged, where such corruption cannot bee eschewed. But onlye I cannot condemne you at some-times, when yee haue no other thing a doe (as a good King will be seldome) & are wearie of reading, or euill disposed in your person, and when it is foule and stormy weather; then, I say, may ye lawfully play at the cards or tables. For as to dyeing, I thinke it becommeth best deboshed souldiers to play at, on the head of their drums, being onely ruled by hazarde, and subject to knauish cogging. And as for the chesse, I thinke it ouer fonde, because it is ouer wise and Philosophicke a follie. For where all such light plaies are ordained to free mens heades for a time, from the fashious thoughts on their affaires; it by the contrarie filleth and troubleth mens heades, with as many fashious toyes of the playe, as before it was filled with thoughts on his affaires.

But in your playing I would haue you to keepe three rules: first or yee play, consider yee doe it onely for your recreation, and resolue to hazard the losse of all that ye play; and next, for that cause play no more then yee care to cast among Pages; & last, play alwaies faire play pre-cisely, that yee come not in vse of tricking and lying in jeste: otherwise, if ye cannot keepe these rules, my counsell is that ye all-uterly abstain from these plaies. For neither a mad passion for losse, nor falshood vsed for desire of gaine, can be called a play.

Nowe, it is not onely lawfull, but necessarie, that yee

haue companie meete for euery thing yee take on hand, aswell in your games and exercises, as in your graue and earnest affaires. But learne to distinguishe time according to th'occasion; chosing your companye accordinglie. Conferre not with hunters at your counsell, nor in your counsell affaires; nor dispatche not affaires at hunting or other games. And haue the like respect to the seasons of your age; vsing your sortes of recreation and companie therefore, aggreeing there-unto. For it becometh best, as kindliest, euery age to smell of their owne qualitie, insolence and vnlawfull things beeing alwaies eschewed: & not that a colte should drawe the plough, and an old horse run away with the harrowes. But take heede specially, that your company for recreation be chosen of honest persons; not defamed or vicious, mixing filthy talk with merrines; *Corrumpunt bonos mores colloquia praua.* And chieflie abstaine from haunting before your mariage the idle company of dames, which are nothing else but *irritamenta libidinis.* Beware likewise to abuse your selfe, in making your sporters your counsellers: and delight not to keepe ordinarilie in your companie, Comœdians or Balladines: for the Tyrants delighted most in them, glorying to be both authors & actors of Comœdies & Tragœdies themselues. Where-vpon the answer that the poët Philoxenus disdainfully gaue to the Tyrant of Syracuse, there-anent, is nowe come in a prouerbe, *reduc me in latomias.* And al the ruse that Nero made of himselfe when he dyed, was *Qualis artifex pereo?* meaning of his skill in menstrallie, and playing of Tragœdies: as indeede his whole life and death was all but one Tragœdie.

Delight not also to bee in your owne person a player vpon instruments, especiallye on suche as commonly men winne their liuing with: nor yet to be fine of any mechanick craft: *Leur esprit s'en fuit au bout des doigts,* saith Du Bartas: whose works, as they are all most worthie to be red by any Prince, or other good Christian, so would I

especially wish you to be well versed in them. But spare
not some-times by merie companie, to bee free from importunitie: for yee should be euer mooued with reason, which
is the onely qualitie whereby men differ from beasts; and
not with importunitie. For the which cause (as also for
augmenting your Majestie) ye shall not be so facile of
accesse-giuing at all times, as I haue bene: and yet not
altogether retired or locked vp, like the Kings of Persia:
appointing also certaine houres for publick audience.

And since my trust is, that GOD hath ordayned you for
moe Kingdomes then this (as I haue alreadie saide), preasse
by the outward behauiour aswell of your owne person, as of
your courte, in all indifferent things, to allure peece & peece,
the rest of your kingdomes, to followe the fashions of that
Kingdome of yours, that ye finde moste ciuill, easiest to be
ruled, and most obedient to the lawes. For these outward and indifferent things will serue greatly for allurements to the people, to embrace and follow vertue. But
beware of thrawing or constraining them thereto; letting
it be brought on with time, and at leasure: specially by so
mixing through alliance and daily conuersation, the inhabitants of euery Kingdome with other, as may with time make
them to growe and weld all in one. Which may easily be
done betwixt these two nations, being both but one Ile of
Britaine, and alreadie joyned in vnitie of Religion, and
language. So that euen as in the times of our Ancestors,
the long warres and many bloody battles betwixt these two
countries, bred a naturall and hereditarie hatred in euery
of them against the other: the vniting and welding of
them hereafter in one, by all sort of friendship, commerce,
and alliance; will by the contrarie, produce and maintaine
a naturall and inseparable vnitie of loue amongst them. As
we haue alreadie (praise be to God) a great experience of
the good beginning hereof, and of the quenching of the olde
hate in the hearts of both the people; procured by the
meanes of this long and happie amitie, betweene the Queene

my dearest sister and me; which during the whole time of both our raignes hath euer been inuiolablie obserued.

And for conclusion of this my whole treatise, remember, my Sonne, by your true and constant depending vpon God, to looke for a blessing to all your actions in your office : by the outward vsing thereof, to testifie the inward vprightnes of your heart; and by your behauiour in all indifferent things, to set forth the viue image of your vertuous disposition : and in respect of the greatnes and waight of your burthen, to be patient in hearing, keeping your heart free from preoccupation; ripe in concluding, and constant in your resolution. For better it is to bide at your resolution, although there were som defect in it, then by daily changing to effectuate nothing. Taking the paterne thereof from the microcosme of your owne body : wherein ye haue two eyes, signifying great foresight and prouidence with a narrow looking in all things; and also two eares, signifying patient hearing, and that of both the parties : but ye haue but one tongue, for pronouncing a plaine, sensible, and vniforme sentence; and but one head, and one heart, for keeping a constant and vniforme resolution, according to your apprehension : hauing two hands and two feete, with many fingers and toes for quicke execution, in employing all instruments meete for effectuating your deliberations.

But forget not to digest euer your passion, before ye determine vpon any thing, since *Ira furor breuis est:* vttering onely your anger according to the Apostles rule, *Irascimini, sed ne peccetis:* taking pleasure, not onely to reward, but to advance the good; which is a chiefe poynt of a Kings glorie (but make none ouergreat, but according as the power of the countrie may beare), and punishing the euill; but euery man according to his owne offence; not punishing nor blaming the Father for the Sonne, nor the brother for the brother; much lesse generally to hate a whole race for the fault of one : for *noxa caput sequitur.*

And aboue all, let the measure of your loue to euery one, be according to the measure of his vertue; letting your fauour be no longer tyed to any, then the continuance of his vertuous disposition shall deserue: not admitting the excuse vpon a just revenge, to procure ouer-sight to an injurie. For the first injurie is committed against the partie: but the parties reuenging thereof at his owne hand, is a wrong committed against you, in vsurping your office, whom-to onely the sword belongeth, for revenging of all the injuries committed against any of your people.

Thus hoping in the goodnesse of God, that your naturall inclination shall haue a happie Sympathie with these precepts, making the wise-mans schoolemaister, which is the example of others, to be your teacher, according to that old verse,

Felix quem faciunt aliena pericula cautum;

eschewing so the ouerlate repentance by your owne experience, which is the schoole-maister of fooles; I will for end of all, require you, my Sonne, as euer yee thinke to deserue my fatherly blessing, to keepe continually before the eyes of your minde, the greatnes of your charge: making the faithfull and due discharge thereof, the principall butte ye shoote at in all your other actions: counting it euer the principall, and all your other actions but as accessories, to be employed as middesses for the furthering of that principall. And being content to let others excell in other things, let it be your chiefest earthly glorie to excell in your owne craft: according to the worthie counsell and charge of Anchises to his posteritie, in that sublime and heroicall Poet, wherein also my diction is included;

Excudent alij spirantia mollius æra,
Credo equidem, & viuos ducent de marmore vultus,
Orabunt causas melius, cœlique meatus
Describent radio, & surgentia syder a dicent.
Tu. regere imperio populos, Romane, memento
(Hæ tibi erunt artes) pacique imponere morem,
"Parcere subjectis, & debellare superbos."

F

PROSPECTUS AND SPECIMEN OF AN

INTENDED NATIONAL WORK.

BY

WILLIAM AND ROBERT WHISTLECRAFT,

Of Stow Market, in Suffolk, Harness and Collar Makers.

**INTENDED TO COMPRISE THE MOST INTERESTING PARTICULARS
RELATING TO**

KING ARTHUR AND HIS ROUND TABLE.

AN
INTENDED NATIONAL WORK.

THE following stanzas being for the most part the production of my late brother, William Whistlecraft, as composed by him in the year 1813, I have judged (by the advice of my friends) that it would be more suitable to publish them without alteration in any respect, and to which I have adhered strictly, as may be seen by a reference to the thirteenth stanza. This I thought it due to have stated, in consideration of our having proposed the Two Boards for Verse and Prose, which in the present crisis might be stigmatized; but it is well known that the public opinion was more consonant to magnificence and useful encouragement at that time than it has been for the last twelve months, or is likely to be the case again, unless the funds should experience a further advance, together with an improvement in the branches of Customs and Excise. The occasion of their remaining unpublished was in compliance with the advice of friends, though at present, in conformity with the pressure of the times, they have thought it advisable that the following publication should take place, which, if an indulgent public should espouse it, it is intended that it should be followed in due course with a suitable continuation.

I.

I'VE often wished that I could write a book,
    Such as all English people might peruse ;
I never should regret the pains it took,
    That's just the sort of fame that I should choose :
To sail about the world like Captain Cook,
    I'd sling a cot up for my favourite Muse,
And we'd take verses out to Demarara,
To New South Wales, and up to Niagara.

II.

Poets consume exciseable commodities,
    They raise the nation's spirit when victorious,
They drive an export trade in whims and oddities,
    Making our commerce and revenue glorious ;
As an industrious and painstaking body 'tis
    That poets should be reckoned meritorious :
And therefore I submissively propose
To erect one Board for Verse and one for Prose.

III.

Princes protecting sciences and art
    I've often seen, in copper-plate and print ;
I never saw them elsewhere, for my part,
    And therefore I conclude there's nothing in't ;
But everybody knows the Regent's heart ;
    I trust he won't reject a well-meant hint ;
Each Board to have twelve members, with a seat
To bring them in per ann. five hundred neat.

IV.

From princes I descend to the nobility :
    In former times all persons of high stations,
Lords, baronets, and persons of gentility.
    Paid twenty guineas for the dedications :

This practice was attended with utility;
  The patrons lived to future generations,
The poets lived by their industrious earning,—
So men alive and dead could live by learning.

V.

Then, twenty guineas was a little fortune;
  Now, we must starve unless the times should mend:
Our poets now-a-days are deemed importune
  If their addresses are diffusely penned;
Most fashionable authors make a short one
  To their own wife, or child, or private friend,
To show their independence, I suppose;
And that may do for gentlemen like those

VI.

Lastly, the common people I beseech—
  Dear people! if you think my verses clever,
Preserve with care your noble parts of speech,
  And take it as a maxim to endeavour
To talk as your good mothers used to teach,
  And then these lines of mine may last for ever;
And don't confound the language of the nation
With long-tailed words in *osity* and *ation*.

VII.

I think that poets (whether Whig or Tory,
  Whether they go to meeting or to church)
Should study to promote their country's glory
  With patriotic, diligent research;
That children yet unborn may learn the story,
  With grammars, dictionaries, canes, and birch:
It stands to reason—this was Homer's plan,
And we must do—like him—the best we can.

VIII.

Madoc and Marmion, and many more,
  Are out in print, and most of them have sold;
Perhaps together they may make a score;
  Richard the First has had his story told,
But there were lords and princes long before,
  That had behaved themselves like warriors bold;
Among the rest there was the great KING ARTHUR,
What hero's fame was ever carried farther?

IX.

King Arthur, and the Knights of his Round Table,
  Were reckoned the best king, and bravest lords,
Of all that flourished since the Tower of Babel,
  At least of all that history records;
Therefore 1 shall endeavour, if I'm able,
  To paint their famous actions by my words:
Heroes exert themselves in hopes of fame,
And having such a strong decisive claim,

X.

It grieves me much, that names that were respected
  In former ages, persons of such mark,
And countrymen of ours, should lie neglected,
  Just like old portraits lumbering in the dark:
An error such as this should be corrected,
  And if my Muse can strike a single spark,
Why then (as poets say) I'll string my lyre;
And then I'll light a great poetic fire;

XI.

I'll air them all, and rub down the Round Table,
  And wash the canvas clean, and scour the frames,
And put a coat of varnish on the fable,
  And try to puzzle out the dates and names;

Then (as I said before) I'll heave my cable,
    And take a pilot, and drop down the Thames—
These first eleven stanzas make a proem,
And now I must sit down and write my poem.

———

Canto I.

I.

BEGINNING (as my bookseller desires,
    Like an old minstrel with his gown and beard,
" Fair ladies, gallant knights, and gentle squires,
    Now the last service from the board is cleared,
And if this noble company requires,
    And if amidst your mirth I may be heard,
Of sundry strange adventures I could tell,
    That oft were told before, but never told so well."

II.

The great King Arthur made a sumptuous feast,
    And held his royal Christmas at Carlisle,
And thither came the vassals, most and least,
    From every corner of this British Isle;
And all were entertained, both man and beast,
    According to their rank, in proper style;
The steeds were fed and littered in the stable,
The ladies and the knights sat down to table.

III.

The bill of fare (as you may well suppose)
    Was suited to those plentiful old times,
Before our modern luxuries arose,
    With truffles and ragouts, and various crimes;

And, therefore, from the original in prose
  I shall arrange the catalogue in rhymes :
They served up salmon, venison, and wild boars
By hundreds, and by dozens, and by scores.

IV.

Hogsheads of honey, kilderkins of mustard,
  Muttons, and fatted beeves, and bacon swine ;
Herons and bitterns, peacock, swan and bustard,
  Teal, mallard, pigeons, widgeons, and in fine
Plum-puddings, pancakes, apple-pies and custard :
  And therewithal they drank good Gascon wine,
With mead, and ale, and cider of our own ;
For porter, punch, and negus were not known.

V.

The noise and uproar of the scullery tribe,
  All pilfering and scrambling in their calling,
Was past all powers of language to describe—
  The din of manful oaths and female squalling :
The sturdy porter, huddling up his bribe,
  And then at random breaking heads and bawling.
Outcries, and cries of order, and contusions,
Made a confusion beyond all confusions ;

VI.

Beggars and vagabonds, blind, lame, and sturdy,
  Minstrels and singers with their various airs,
The pipe, the tabor, and the hurdy-gurdy,
  Jugglers and mountebanks with apes and bears,
Continued from the first day to the third day,
  An uproar like ten thousand Smithfield fairs ;
There were wild beasts and foreign birds and creatures,
And Jews and foreigners with foreign features.

VII.

All sorts of people there were seen together,
  All sorts of characters, all sorts of dresses;
The fool with fox's tail and peacock's feather,
  Pilgrims, and penitents, and grave burgesses;
The country people with their coats of leather,
  Vintners and victuallers with cans and messes;
Grooms, archers, varlets, falconers and yeomen,
Damsels and waiting-maids, and waiting-women.

VIII.

But the profane, indelicate amours,
  The vulgar, unenlightened conversation
Of minstrels, menials, courtezans, and boors
  (Although appropriate to their meaner station)
Would certainly revolt a taste like yours;
  Therefore I shall omit the calculation
Of all the curses, oaths, and cuts and stabs,
Occasioned by their dice, and drink, and drabs.

IX.

We must take care in our poetic cruise,
  And never hold a single tack too long;
Therefore my versatile ingenious Muse
  Takes leave of this illiterate, low-bred throng,
Intending to present superior views,
  Which to genteeler company belong,
And show the higher orders of society
Behaving with politeness and propriety.

X.

And certainly they say, for fine behaving
  King Arthur's Court has never had its match;
True point of honour, without pride or braving,
  Strict etiquette for ever on the watch:

Their manners were refined and perfect—saving
  Some modern graces which they could not catch,
As spitting though the teeth, and driving stages,
  Accomplishments reserved for distant ages.

XI.

They looked a manly generous generation;   [thick,
  Beards, shoulders, eyebrows, broad, and square, and
Their accents firm and loud in conversation,
  Their eyes and gestures eager, sharp, and quick,
Showed them prepared, on proper provocation,
  To give the lie, pull noses, stab and kick;
And for that very reason, it is said,
They were so very courteous and well-bred.

XII.

The ladies looked of an heroic race—
  At first a general likeness struck your eye,
Tall figures, open features, oval face,
  Large eyes, with ample eyebrows arched and high;
Their manners had an odd, peculiar grace,
  Neither repulsive, affable, nor shy,
Majestical, reserved, and somewhat sullen;
Their dresses partly silk, and partly woollen.

XIII.

In form and figure far above the rest,
  Sir Launcelot was chief of all the train,
In Arthur's Court an ever welcome guest;
  Britain will never see his like again.
Of all the knights she ever had the best,
  Except, perhaps, Lord Wellington in Spain:
I never saw his picture nor his print,
From Morgan's Chronicle I take my hint.

XIV.

For Morgan says (at least as I have heard,
 And as a learned friend of mine assures),
Beside him all that lordly train appeared
 Like courtly minions, or like common boors,
As if unfit for knightly deeds, and reared
 To rustic labours or to loose amours ;
He moved amidst his peers without compare,
So lofty was his stature, look, and air.

XV.

Yet oftentimes his courteous cheer forsook
 His countenance, and then returned again,
As if some secret recollection shook
 His inward heart with unacknowledged pain ;
And something haggard in his eyes and look
 (More than his years or hardships could explain)
Made him appear, in person and in mind,
Less perfect than what Nature had designed.

XVI.

Of noble presence, but of different mien,
 Alert and lively, voluble and gay,
Sir Tristram at Carlisle was rarely seen,
 But ever was regretted while away ;
With easy mirth, an enemy to spleen,
 His ready converse charmed the wintry day ;
No tales he told of sieges or of fights,
Or foreign marvels, like the foolish knights,

XVII.

But with a playful imitative tone
 (That merely seemed a voucher for the truth)
Recounted strange adventures of his own,
 The chances of his childhood and his youth,

Of churlish giants he had seen and known,
   Their rustic phrase and courtesies uncouth,
The dwellings, and the diet, and the lives
Of savage monarchs and their monstrous wives:

XVIII.

Songs, music, languages, and many a lay
   Asturian or Armoric, Irish, Basque,
His ready memory seized and bore away;
   And ever when the ladies chose to ask,
Sir Tristram was prepared to sing and play,
   Not like a minstrel earnest at his task,
But with a sportive, careless, easy style,
As if he seemed to mock himself the while.

XIX.

His ready wit and rambling education,
   With the congenial influence of his stars,
Had taught him all the arts of conversation,
   All games of skill and statagems of wars;
His birth, it seems, by Merlin's calculation,
   Was under Venus, Mercury, and Mars;
His mind with all their attributes was mixt,
And, like those planets, wandering and unfixt;

XX.

From realm to realm he ran—and never stayed:
   Kingdoms and crowns he wan—and gave away;
It seemed as if his labours were repaid
   By the mere noise and movement of the fray:
No conquests nor acquirements had he made;
   His chief delight was on some festive day
To ride triumphant, prodigal, and proud,
And shower his wealth amidst the shouting crowd:

XXI.

His schemes of war were sudden, unforeseen,
   Inexplicable both to friend and foe ;
It seemed as if some momentary spleen
   Inspired the project and impelled the blow ;
And most his fortune and success were seen
   With means the most inadequate and low ;
Most master of himself, and least encumbered
When overmatched, entangled, and outnumbered.

XXII.

Strange instruments and engines he contrived
   For sieges, and constructions for defence,
Inventions some of them that have survived,
   Others were deemed too cumbrous and immense :
Minstrels he loved, and cherished while he lived,
   And patronized them both with praise and pence ;
Somewhat more learned than became a knight,
It was reported he could read and write.

XXIII.

Sir Gawain may be painted in a word —
   He was a perfect loyal cavalier ;
His courteous manners stand upon record,
   A stranger to the very thought of fear.
The proverb says, " As brave as his own sword ; "
   And like his weapon was that worthy peer,
Of admirable temper, clear and bright,
Polished yet keen, though pliant yet upright.

XXIV.

On every point, in earnest or in jest,
   His judgment, and his prudence, and his wit,
Were deemed the very touchstone and the test
   Of what was proper, graceful, just, and fit ;

A word from him set everything at rest,
   His short decisions never failed to hit;
His silence, his reserve, his inattention,
Were felt as the severest reprehension :

XXV.

His memory was the magazine and hoard,
   Where claims and grievances, from year to year,
And confidences and complaints were stored,
   From dame and knight, from damsel, boor, and peer:
Loved by his friends, and trusted by his lord,
   A generous courtier, secret and sincere,
Adviser-general to the whole community,
He served his friend, but watched his opportunity.

XXVI.

One riddle I could never understand--
   But his success in war was strangely various;
In executing schemes that others planned,
   He seemed a very Cæsar or a Marius;
Take his own plans, and place him in command,
   Your prospect of success became precarious :
His plans were good, but Launcelot succeeded
And realized them better far than he did.

XXVII.

His discipline was steadfast and austere,
   Unalterably fixed, but calm and kind;
Founded on admiration, more than fear,
   It seemed an emanation from his mind :
The coarsest natures that approached him near
   Grew courteous for the moment and refined :
Beneath his eye the poorest, weakest wight
Felt full of point of honour like a knight.

XXVIII.

In battle he was fearless to a fault.
    The foremost in the thickest of the field ;
His eager valour knew no pause nor halt,
    And the red rampant lion in his shield
Scaled towns and towers, the foremost in assault,
    With ready succour where the battle reeled :
At random like a thunderbolt he ran,
And bore down shields, and pikes, and horse, and man.

Canto II.

I.

I've finished now three hundred lines and more,
    And therefore I begin Canto the Second,
Just like those wand'ring ancient bards of yore ;
    They never laid a plan, nor ever reckoned
What turning they should take the day before ;
    They followed where the lovely Muses beckoned :
The Muses led them up to Mount Parnassus,
And that's the reason that they all surpass us.

II.

The Muses served those heathens well enough—
    Bold Britons take a tankard, or a bottle,
And when the bottle's out, a pinch of snuff,
    And so proceed in spite of Aristotle—
Those rules of his are dry, dogmatic stuff,
    All life and fire they suffocate and throttle—
And therefore I adopt the mode I mention,
Trusting to native judgment and invention.

III.

This method will, I hope, appear defensible—
    I shall begin by mentioning the giants,
A race of mortals, brutal and insensible
    (Postponing the details of the defiance,
Which came in terms so very reprehensible
    From that barbarian sovereign King Ryence),
Displaying simpler manners, forms, and passions,
Unmixed by transitory modes and fashions.

IV.

Before the feast was ended, a report
    Filled every soul with horror and dismay;
Some ladies, on their journey to the Court,
    Had been surprised, and were conveyed away
By the aboriginal giants, to their fort—
    An unknown fort—for Government, they say,
Had ascertained its actual existence,
But knew not its direction, nor its distance.

V.

A waiting damsel, crooked and misshaped,
    Herself the witness of a woful scene,
From which, by miracle, she had escaped,
    Appeared before the ladies and the Queen;
Her figure was funereal, veiled and craped,
    Her voice convulsed with sobs and sighs between,
That with the sad recital, and the sight,
Revenge and rage inflamed each worthy knight.

VI.

Sir Gawain rose without delay or dallying—
    "Excuse us, madam, we've no time to waste;"
And at the palace-gate you saw him sallying,
    With other knights, equipped and armed in haste;

And there was Tristram making jests, and rallying
   The poor misshapen damsel, whom he placed
Behind him on a pillion, pad, or pannel;
He took, besides, his falcon and his spaniel.

VII.

But what with horror, and fatigue, and fright,
   Poor soul, she could not recollect the way.
They reached the mountains on the second night,
   And wandered up and down till break of day,
When they discovered, by the dawning light,
   A lonely glen, where heaps of embers lay;
They found unleavened fragments, scorched and toasted,
And the remains of mules and horses roasted.

VIII.

Sir Tristram understood the giants' courses:
   He felt the embers, but the heat was out;
He stood contemplating the roasted horses,
   And all at once, without suspense or doubt,
His own decided judgment thus enforces:
   "The giants must be somewhere here about!"
Demonstrating the carcasses, he shows
That they remained untouched by kites or crows;

IX.

" You see no traces of their sleeping here,
   No heap of leaves or heath, no giant's nest;
Their usual habitation must be near:
   They feed at sunset, and retire to rest,
A moment's search will set the matter clear."
   The fact turned out precisely as he guessed;
And shortly after, scrambling through a gully,
He verified his own conjecture fully.

X.

He found a valley, closed on every side,
   Resembling that which Rasselas describes;
Six miles in length, and half as many wide,
   Where the descendants of the giant tribes
Lived in their ancient fortress undescried
   (Invaders tread upon each other's kibes).
First came the Britons, afterwards the Roman,
Our patrimonial lands belong to no man :

XI.

So Horace said; and so the giants found,
   Expelled by fresh invaders in succession ;
But they maintained tenaciously the ground
   Of ancient, indefeasible possession,
And robbed and ransacked all the country round ;
   And ventured on this horrible transgression,
Claiming a right reserved to waste and spoil,
As lords and lawful owners of the soil.

XII.

Huge mountains of immeasurable height
   Encompassed all the level valley round,
With mighty slabs of rock, that sloped upright,
   An insurmountable, enormous mound ;
The very river vanished out of sight,
   Absorbed in secret channels under ground :
That vale was so sequestered and secluded,
All search for ages past it had eluded.

XIII.

High over head was many a cave and den,
   That with its strange construction seemed to mock
All thought of how they were contrived, or when :
   Hewn inward in the huge suspended rock,

The tombs and monuments of mighty men :
  Such were the patriarchs of this ancient stock.
Alas ! what pity that the present race
Should be so barbarous and depraved and base !

XIV.

For they subsisted (as I said) by pillage,
  And the wild beasts which they pursued and chased
Nor house, nor herdsman's hut, nor farm, nor village,
  Within the lonely valley could be traced,
Nor roads, nor bounded fields, nor rural tillage,
  But all was lonely, desolate, and waste.
The castle which commanded the domain
Was suited to so rude and wild a reign :

XV.

A rock was in the centre, like a cone,
  Abruptly rising from a miry pool,
Where they beheld a pile of massy stone,
  Which masons of the rude primæval school
Had reared by help of giant hands alone,
  With rocky fragments unreduced by rule,
Irregular, like Nature more than art,
Huge, rugged, aad compact in every part.

XVI.

But on the other side a river went,
  And there the craggy rock and ancient wall
Had crumbled down with shelving deep descent ;
  Time and the wearing stream had worked its fall :
The modern giants had repaired the rent,
  But poor, reduced, and ignorant withal,
They patched it up, contriving as they could,
With stones, and earth, and palisades of wood.

XVII.

Sir Gawain tried a parley, but in vain—
    A true bred giant never trusts a knight—
He sent a herald, who returned again
    All torn to rags and perishing with fright;
A trumpeter was sent, but he was slain,
    To trumpeters they bear a mortal spite:
When all conciliatory measures failed,
The castle and the fortress were assailed.

XVIII.

But when the giants saw them fairly under,
    They shovelled down a cataract of stones,
A hideous volley like a peal of thunder,
    Bouncing and bounding down, and breaking bones
Rending the earth, and riving rocks asunder;
    Sir Gawain inwardly laments and groans,
Retiring last, and standing most exposed;
Success seemed hopeless, and the combat closed.

XIX.

A council then was called, and all agreed
    To call in succour from the country round;
By regular approaches to proceed,
    Intrenching, fortifying, breaking ground.
That morning Tristram happened to secede:
    It seems his falcon was not to be found;
He went in search of her, but some suspected
He went lest his advice should be neglected.

XX.

At Gawain's summons all the country came;
    At Gawain's summons all the people aided;
They called upon each other in his name,
    And bid their neighbours work as hard as they did.

So well beloved was he, for very shame
   They dug, they delved, intrenched, and palisaded,
Till all the fort was thoroughly blockaded,
And every ford where giants might have waded.

XXI.

Sir Tristram found his falcon, bruised and lame,
   After a tedious search, as he averred,
And was returning back the way he came
   When in the neighbouring thicket something stirred,
And flashed across the path, as bright as flame ;
   Sir Tristram followed it, and found a bird
Much like a pheasant, only crimson red,
With a fine tuft of feathers on his head.

XXII.

Sir Tristram's mind—invention—powers of thought,
   Were occupied, abstracted, and engaged,
Devising ways and means to have it caught
   Alive—entire—to see it safely caged :
The giants and their siege he set at nought
   Compared with this new warfare that he waged.
He gained his object after three days wandering,
And three nights watching, meditating, pondering,

XXIII.

And to the camp in triumph he returned :
   He makes them all admire the creature's crest,
And praise and magnify the prize he earned.
   Sir Gawain rarely ventured on a jest,
But here his heart with indignation burned :
   " Good cousin, yonder stands an eagle's nest !
A prize for fowlers such as you and me."
Sir Tristram answered mildly, " We shall see."

XXIV.

Good-humour was Sir Tristram's leading quality,
  And in the present case he proved it such ;
If he forbore, it was that in reality
  His conscience smote him with a secret touch,
For having shocked his worthy friend's formality—
  He thought Sir Gawain had not said too much ;
He walks apart with him, and he discourses
About their preparation and their forces,

XXV.

Approving everything that had been done—
  " It serves to put the giants off their guard,
Less hazard and less danger will be run ;
  I doubt not we shall find them unprepared—
The castle will more easily be won,
  And many valuable lives be spared ;
The ladies else, while we blockade and threaten,
Will most infallibly be killed and eaten."

XXVI.

Sir Tristram talked incomparably well ;
  His reasons were irrefragably strong.
As Tristram spoke Sir Gawain's spirits fell,
  For he discovered clearly before long
(What Tristram never would presume to tell),
  That his whole system was entirely wrong ;
In fact, his confidence had much diminished
Since all the preparations had been finished.

XXVII.

" Indeed !" Sir Tristram said, " for aught we know—
  For aught that we can tell—this very night
The valley's entrance may be closed with snow,
  And we may starve and perish here outright ;

'Tis better risking a decided blow—
    I own this weather puts me in a fright."
In fine, this tedious conference to shorten,
Sir Gawain trusted to Sir Tristram's fortune.

XXVIII.

'Twas twilight, ere the wintry dawn had kist
    With cold salute the mountain's chilly brow ;
The level lawns were dark, a lake of mist
    Inundated the vales and depths below,
When valiant Tristram, with a chosen list
    Of bold and hardy men, prepared to go,
Ascending through the vapours dim and hoar,
A secret track, which he descried before.

XXIX.

If ever you attempted, when a boy,
    To walk across the playground or the yard
Blindfolded, for an apple or a toy,
    Which, when you reached the spot, was your reward,
You may conceive the difficult employ
    Sir Tristram had, and that he found it hard,
Deprived of landmarks and the power of sight,
To steer their dark and doubtful course aright.

XXX.

They climbed an hour or more with hand and knee
    (The distance of a fathom or a rood
Was farther than the keenest eye could see) ;
    At last the very ground on which they stood,
The broken turf, and many a battered tree—
    The crushed and shattered shrubs and underwood—
Apprised them that they were arrived once more
Where they were overwhelmed the time before.

XXXI.

Sir Tristram saw the people in a fluster;
    He took them to a sheltered hollow place :
They crowded round like chickens in a cluster,
    And Tristram, with an unembarrassed face,
Proceeded quietly to take a muster,
    To take a muster, and to state the case—
" It was," he said, " an unexpected error,
Enough to strike inferior minds with terror;

XXXII.

" But since they were assembled and collected "
    (All were assembled except nine or ten),
" He thought that their design might be effected;
    All things were easy to determined men.
If they would take the track which he directed,
    And try their old adventure once again ; "
He slapped his breast, and swore within an hour
That they should have the castle in their power.

XXXIII.

This mountain was like others I have seen ;
    There was a stratum or a ridge of stone
Projecting high beyond the sloping green,
    From top to bottom, like a spinal bone,
Or flight of steps, with gaps and breaks between ;
    A copper-plate would make my meaning known
Better than words, and therefore, with permission,
I'll give a print of it the next edition.

XXXIV.

Thither Sir Tristram with his comrades went,
    For now the misty cloud was cleared away,
And they must risk the perilous ascent,
    Right in the giants' front, in open day :

They ran to reach the shelter which it lent,
  Before the battery should begin to play.
Their manner of ascending up that ridge
Was much like climbing by a broken bridge;

XXXV.

For there you scramble on from pier to pier,
  Always afraid to lose your hold half-way;
And as they clambered each successive tier
  Of rugged upright rocks, I dare to say,
It was not altogether without fear—
  Just fear enough to make brave people gay:
According to the words of Mr. Gray,
" They wound with toilsome march their long array."

XXXVI.

The more alert and active upward sprung,
  And let down ropes to drag their comrades after;
Those ropes were their own shirts together strung,
  Stript off and twisted with such mirth and laughter,
That with their jokes the rocky echoes rung:
  Like countrymen that on a beam or rafter
Attempt to pass a raging wintry flood,
Such was the situation where they stood:

XXXVII.

A wild tumultous torrent raged around,
  Of fragments tumbling from the mountain's height;
The whirling clouds of dust the deafening sound,
  The hurried motion that amazed the sight,
The constant quaking of the solid ground,
  Environed them with phantoms of affright;
Yet with heroic hearts they held right on,
Till the last point of their ascent was won.

XXXVIII.

The giants saw them on the topmost crown
    Of the last rock, and threatened and defied—
" Down with the mangy dwarfs there !   Dash them
        down !
    Down with the dirty pismires !"   Thus they cried.
Sir Tristram, with a sharp sarcastic frown,
    In their own giant jargon thus replied,
" Mullinger !—Cacamole !—and Mangonell !
You cursed cannibals, I know you well—

XXXIX.

" I'll see that pate of yours upon a post,
    And your left-handed squinting brother's too—
By Heaven and earth, within an hour at most,
    I'll give the crows a meal of him and you ;
The wolves shall have you, either raw or roast,
    I'll make an end of all your cursed crew."
These words he partly said, and partly sang,
As usual with the giants, in their slang.

XL.

He darted forward to the mountain's brow,
    The giants ran away, they knew not why,
Sir Tristram gained the point, he knew not how,
    He could account for it no more than I.
Such strange effects we witness often now ;
    Such strange experiments true Britons try
In sieges, and in skirmishes afloat,
In storming heights, and boarding from a boat.

XLI.

True courage bears about a charm or spell,
    It looks, I think, like an instinctive law
By which superior natures daunt and quell
    Frenchmen and foreigners with fear and awe.

I wonder if philosophers can tell—
  Can they explain the thing with all their jaw?
I can't explain it, but the fact is so,
  A fact which every midshipman must know.

XLII.

Then instantly the signal was held out,
  To show Sir Gawain that the coast was clear:
They heard his camp re-echo with a shout,
  In half an hour Sir Gawain will be here.
But still Sir Tristram was perplexed with doubt,
  The crisis of the ladies' fate drew near,
He dreaded what those poor defenceless creatures
Might suffer from such fierce and desperate natures.

XLIII.

The giants, with their brutal want of sense,
  In hurling stones to crush them with the fall,
And in their hurry taking them from thence,
  Had half dismantled all the new-built wall.
They left it here and there, a naked fence
  Of stakes and palisades, upright and tall.
Sir Tristram formed a sudden resolution,
And recommended it for execution.

XLIV.

" My lads," he cried, " an effort must be made
  To keep those monsters half an hour in play,
While Gawain is advancing to our aid,
  Or else the ladies will be made away.
By mounting close within the palisade,
  You'll parry their two-handed, dangerous sway—
Their clubs and maces : recollect my words,
And use your daggers rather than your swords."

XLV.

That service was most gallantly performed:
  The giants still endeavoured to repel
And drive them from the breach that they had stormed:
  The foremost of the crew was Mangonell.
At sight of him Sir Tristram's spirit warmed;
  With aim unerring Tristram's faulchion fell,
Lopt off his club and fingers at the knuckle,
And thus disabled that stupendous chuckle.

XLVI.

The giant ran, outrageous with the wound,
  Roaring and bleeding, to the palisade;
Sir Tristram swerved aside, and reaching round,
  Probed all his entrails with his poniard's blade:
His giant limbs fall thundering on the ground,
  His goggling eyes eternal slumbers shade;
Then by the head or heels, I know not which,
They dragged him forth, and tost him in the ditch.

XLVII.

Sir Tristram, in the warfare that he waged,
  Strove to attract the giants' whole attention;
To keep it undivided and engaged,
  He racked his fiery brain and his invention;
And taunted and reviled, and stormed and raged,
  In terms far worse, and more than I can mention.
In the meanwhile, in a more sober manner,
Sir Gawain was advancing with his banner.

XLVIII.

But first I must commemorate in rhyme
  Sir Tristram's dext'rous swordmanship and might
(This incident appears to me sublime),
  He struck a giant's head off in the fight:

The head fell down of course, but for some time
　The stupid, headless trunk remained upright;
For more than twenty seconds there it stood,
But ultimately fell from loss of blood.

XLIX.

Behold Sir Gawain with his valiant band;
　He enters on the work with warmth and haste,
And slays a brace of giants out of hand,
　Sliced downward from the shoulder to the waist.
But our ichnography must now be planned,
　The keep or inner castle must be traced.
I wish myself at the concluding distich,
Although I think the thing characteristic.

L.

Facing your entrance, just three yards behind,
　There was a mass of stone of moderate height,
It stood before you like a screen or blind;
　And there, on either hand to left and right,
Were sloping parapets or planes inclined,
　On which two massy stones were placed upright,
Secured by staples and by leathern ropes,
Which hindered them from sliding down the slopes.

LI.

"Cousin, those dogs have some device or gin!
　I'll run the gauntlet, and I'll stand a knock."
He dashed into the gate through thick and thin,
　He hewed away the bands which held the block,
It rushed along the slope with rumbling din,
　And closed the entrance with a thundering shock
(Just like those famous old Symplegades
Discovered by the Classics in their seas).

LII.

This was Sir Tristram (as you may suppose),
    He found some giants wounded, others dead,
He shortly equalizes these with those;
    But one poor devil there was sick in bed,
In whose behalf the ladies interpose;
    Sir Tristram spared his life, because they said
That he was more humane and mild and clever,
And all the time had had an ague-fever.

LIII.

The ladies?—They were tolerably well,
    At least as well as could have been expected:
Many details I must forbear to tell,
    Their toilet had been very much neglected;
But by supreme good luck it so befell
    That when the castle's capture was effected,
When those vile cannibals were overpowered,
Only two fat duennas were devoured.

LIV.

Sir Tristram having thus secured the fort,
    And seen all safe, was climbing to the wall
(Meaning to leap into the outer court);
    But when he came, he saved himself the fall,
Sir Gawain had been spoiling all the sport,
    The giants were demolished one and all:
He pulled them up the wall, they climb and enter—
Such was the winding up of this adventure.

LV.

The only real sufferer in the fight
    Was a poor neighbouring squire of little fame,
That came and joined the party overnight;
    He hobbled home, disabled with a maim

Which he received in tumbling from a height :
  The knights from Court had never heard his name,
Nor recollected seeing him before—
Two leopards' faces were the arms he bore.

LVI.

Thus Tristram, without loss of life or limb,
  Conquered the Giants' Castle in a day;
But whether it were accident or whim
  That kept him in the woods so long away,
In any other mortal except him
  I should not feel a doubt of what to say;
But he was wholly guided by his humour,
Indifferent to report and public rumour.

LVII.

It was besides imagined and suspected
  That he had missed his course by deep design,
To take the track which Gawain had neglected—
  I speak of others' notions, not of mine :
I question even if he recollected—
  He might have felt a moment's wish to shine;
I only know that he made nothing of it,
Either for reputation or for profit.

LVIII.

The ladies, by Sir Gawain's kind direction,
  Proceeded instantaneously to Court,
To thank their Majesties for their protection.
  Sir Gawain followed with a grand escort,
And was received with favour and affection.
  Sir Tristram remained loitering in the fort;
He thought the building and the scenery striking,
And that poor captive giant took his liking.

G

LIX.

And now the thread of our romance unravels,
   Presenting new performers on the stage;
A giant's education and his travels
   Will occupy the next succeeding page:
But I begin to tremble at the cavils
   Of this fastidious, supercilious age;
Reviews, and paragraphs in morning papers—
The prospect of them gives my Muse the vapours.

LX.

" My dear," says she, " I think it will be well
   To ascertain our losses or our gains:
If this first sample should succeed and sell,
   We can renew the same melodious strains."
Poor soul! she's had, I think, a tedious spell,
   And ought to be considered for her pains.
And keeping of my company so long—
A moderate compliment would not be wrong.

———

Canto III.

I.

" I've a proposal here from Mr. Murray,
   He offers handsomely—the money down;
My dear, you might recover from your flurry
   In a nice airy lodging out of town,
At Croydon, Epsom, anywhere in Surrey;
   If every stanza brings us in a crown,
I think that I might venture to bespeak
A bedroom and front parlour for next week.

II.

" Tell me, my dear Thalia, what you think ;
   Your nerves have undergone a sudden shock ;
Your poor dear spirits have begun to sink ;
   On Banstead Downs you'd muster a new stock,
And I'd be sure to keep away from drink,
   And always go to bed by twelve o'clock.
We'll travel down there in the morning stages ;
Our verses shall go down to distant ages.

III.

" And here in town we'll breakfast on hot rolls,
   And you shall have a better shawl to wear ;
These pantaloons of mine are chafed in holes ;
   By Monday next I'll compass a new pair :
Come, now, fling up the cinders, fetch the coals,
   And take away the things you hung to air,
Set out the tea-things, and bid Phœbe bring
The kettle up."—*Arms and the Monks I sing.*

IV.

Some ten miles off, an ancient abbey stood,
   Amidst the mountains, near a noble stream ;
A level eminence, enshrined with wood,
   Sloped to the river's bank and southern beam ;
Within were fifty friars fat and good,
   Of goodly persons, and of good esteem,
That passed an easy, exemplary life,
Remote from want and care, and worldly strife.

V.

Between the monks and giants there subsisted,
   In the first abbot's lifetime, much respect ;
The giants let them settle where they listed ;
   The giants were a tolerating sect.

A poor lame giant once the monks assisted,
  Old and abandoned, dying with neglect,
The prior found him, cured his broken bone,
And very kindly cut him for the stone.

VI.

This seemed a glorious, golden opportunity,
  To civilize the whole gigantic race;
To draw them to pay tithes, and dwell in unity;
  The giants' valley was a fertile place,
And might have much enriched the whole community,
  Had the old giant lived a longer space;
But he relapsed, and though all means were tried,
They could but just baptize him—when he died.

VII.

And, I believe, the giants never knew
  Of the kind treatment that befell their mate;
He broke down all at once, and all the crew
  Had taken leave, and left him to his fate;
And though the monks exposed him full in view,
  Propped on his crutches, at the garden gate,
To prove their cure, and show that all was right,
It happened that no giants came in sight:

VIII.

They never found another case to cure,
  But their demeanour calm and reverential,
Their gesture and their vesture grave and pure,
  Their conduct sober, cautious, and prudential,
Engaged respect, sufficient to secure
  Their properties and interests most essential;
They kept a distant, courteous intercourse;
Salutes and gestures were their sole discourse.

IX.

Music will civilize, the poets say,
  In time it might have civilized the giants;
The Jesuits found its use in Paraguay;
  Orpheus was famous for harmonic science,
And civilized the Thracians in that way;
  My judgment coincides with Mr. Bryant's;
He thinks that Orpheus meant a race of cloisterers,
Obnoxious to the Bacchanalian roysterers.

X.

Deciphering the symbols of mythology,
  He finds them monks, expert in their vocation;
Teachers of music, med'cine, and theology,
  The missionaries of the barbarous Thracian;
The poet's fable was a wild apology
  For an inhuman bloody reformation,
Which left those tribes uncivilized and rude,
Naked and fierce, and painted and tattooed.

XI.

It was a glorious Jacobinic job
  To pull down convents, to condemn for treason
Poor peeping Pentheus—to carouse and rob,
  With naked raving goddesses of reason,
The festivals and orgies of the mob
  That every twentieth century come in season.
Enough of Orpheus—the succeeding page
Relates to monks of a more recent age;

XII.

And oft that wild untutored race would draw,
  Led by the solemn sound and sacred light
Beyond the bank, beneath a lonely shaw,
  To listen all the livelong summer night,

Till deep, serene, and reverential awe
  Environed them with silent calm delight,
Contemplating the minster's midnight gleam,
Reflected from the clear and glassy stream;

XIII.

But chiefly, when the shadowy moon had shed
  O'er woods and waters her mysterious hue,
Their passive hearts and vacant fancies fed
  With thoughts and aspirations strange and new,
Till their brute souls with inward working bred
  Dark hints that in the depth of instinct grew
Subjective—not from Locke's associations,
Nor David Hartley's doctrine of vibrations.

XIV.

Each was ashamed to mention to the others
  One-half of all the feelings that he felt,
Yet thus far each could venture—"Listen, brothers,
  It seems as if one heard heaven's thunder melt
In music!—all at once it soothes—it smothers—
  It overpowers one—Pillicock, don't pelt!
It seems a kind of shame, a kind of sin,
To vex those harmless worthy souls within."

XV.

In castles and in courts Ambition dwells,
  But not in castles or in courts alone;
She breathed a wish, throughout those sacred cells,
  For bells of larger size, and louder tone;
Giants abominate the sound of bells,
  And soon the fierce antipathy was shown,
The tinkling and the jingling, and the clangour,
Roused their irrational gigantic anger.

XVI.

Unhappy mortals ! ever blind to fate !
    Unhappy monks ! you see no danger nigh ;
Exulting in their sound and size and weight,
    From morn till noon the merry peal you ply :
The belfry rocks, your bosoms are elate,
    Your spirits with the ropes and pulleys fly ;
Tired, but transported, panting, pulling, hauling,
Ramping and stamping, overjoyed and bawling.

XVII.

Meanwhile the solemn mountains that surrounded
    The silent valley where the convent lay,
With tintinnabular uproar were astounded,
    When the first peal burst forth at break of day :
Feeling their granite ears severely wounded,
    They scarce knew what to think, or what to say ;
And (though large mountains commonly conceal
Their sentiments, dissembling what they feel,

XVIII.

Yet) Cader-Gibbrish from his cloudy throne
    To huge Loblommon gave an intimation
Of this strange rumour, with an awful tone,
    Thund'ring his deep surprise and indignation ;
The lesser hills, in language of their own,
    Discussed the topic by reverberation ;
Discoursing with their echoes all day long,
Their only conversation was, " ding-dong."

XIX.

Those giant-mountains inwardly were moved,
    But never made an outward change of place :
Not so the mountain-giants—(as behoved
    A more alert and locomotive race),

Hearing a clatter which they disapproved,
　　They ran straight forward to besiege the place
With a discordant universal yell,
Like house-dogs howling at a dinner-bell.

XX.

Historians are extremely to be pitied,
　　Obliged to persevere in the narration
Of wrongs and horrid outrages committed,
　　Oppression, sacrilege, assassination ;
The following scenes I wished to have omitted,
　　But truth is an imperious obligation.
So—"my heart sickens, and I drop my pen,"
And am obliged to pick it up again,

XXI.

And, dipping it afresh, I must transcribe
　　An ancient monkish record, which displays
The savage acts of that gigantic tribe ;
　　I hope, that from the diction of those days,
This noble, national poem will imbibe
　　A something (in the old reviewing phrase)
" Of an original flavour, and a raciness ;"
I should not else transcribe it out of laziness.

XXII.

The writer first relates a dream, or vision,
　　Observed by Luke and Lawrence in their cells,
And a nocturnal hideous apparition
　　Of fiends and devils dancing round the bells :
This last event is stated with precision ;
　　Their persons he describes, their names he tells,
Klaproth, Tantallan, Barbanel, Belphegor,
Long-tailed, long-taloned, hairy, black and meagre.

XXIII.

He then rehearses sundry marvels more,
   Damping the mind with horror by degrees,
Of a prodigious birth a heifer bore,
   Of mermaids seen in the surrounding seas,
Of a sea-monster that was cast ashore ;
   Earthquakes and thunder-stones, events like these,
Which served to show the times were out of joint,
And then proceeds directly to the point.

XXIV.

   Erant rumores et timores varii ;
      Dies horroris et confusionis
   Evenit in calendis Januarii ;
      Gigantes, semen maledictionis
   Nostri potentes impii adversarii,
      Irascebantur campanarum sonis,
   Horâ secundâ centum tres gigantes
   Venerunt ante januam ululantes.

XXV.

   At fratres pleni desolationis,
      Stabant ad necessarium præsidium,
   Perterriti pro vitis et pro bonis,
      Et perduravit hoc crudele obsidium,
   Nostri claustralis pauperis Sionis,
      Ad primum diem proximorum Idium ;
   Tunc in triumpho fracto tintinnabulo,
   Gigantes ibant alibi pro pabulo.

XXVI.

   Sed frater Isidorus decumbebat
      In lecto per tres menses brachio fracto,
   Nam lapides Mangonellus jaciebat,
      Et fregit tintinnabulum lapide jacto ;

Et omne vicinagium destruebat,
   Et nihil relinquebat de intacto,
Ardens molinos, Casas, messuagia,
   Et alia multa damna atque outragia.

XXVII.

Those monks were poor proficients in divinity,
   And scarce knew more of Latin than myself ;
Compared with theirs they say that true Latinity
   Appears like porcelain compared with delf ;
As for the damage done in the vicinity,
   Those that have laid their Latin on the shelf
May like to read the subsequent narration
Done into metre from a friend's translation.

XXVIII.

Squire Humphry Bamberham, of Boozley Hall
   (Whose name I mention with deserved respect),
On market-days was often pleased to call,
   And to suggest improvements, or correct ;
I own the obligation once for all,
   Lest critics should imagine they detect
Traces of learning and superior reading,
Beyond, as they suppose, my birth and breeding.

XXIX.

Papers besides, and transcripts most material,
   He gave me when I went to him to dine ;
A trunk full, one coach-seat, and an imperial,
   One bandbox— But the work is wholly mine ;
The tone, the form, the colouring ethereal,
   " The vision and the faculty divine,"
The scenery, characters, and triple-rhymes,
I'll swear it—like old Walter of the *Times.*

XXX.

Long, long before, upon a point of weight,
　　Such as a ring of bells complete and new,
Chapters were summoned, frequent, full, and late ;
　　The point was viewed in every point of view,
Till, after fierce discussion and debate,
　　The wiser monks, the wise are always few,
That from the first opposed the plan *in toto*,
Were overborne, *canonicali voto.*

XXXI.

A prudent monk, their reader and librarian,
　　Observed a faction, angry, strong, and warm
(Himself an anti-tintinnabularian),
　　He saw, or thought he saw, a party form
To scout him as an alien and sectarian.
　　There was an undefined impending storm !
The opponents were united, bold, and hot;
They might degrade, imprison him—what not?

XXXII.

Now faction in a city, camp, or cloister,
　　While it is yet a tender raw beginner,
Is nourished by superfluous warmth and moisture,
　　Namely, by warmth and moisture after dinner;
And therefore, till the temper and the posture
　　Of things should alter—till a secret inner
Instinctive voice should whisper, all is right—
He deemed it safest to keep least in sight.

XXXIII.

He felt as if his neck were in a noose,
　　And evermore retired betimes from table,
For fear of altercation and abuse,
　　But made the best excuse that he was able ;

He never rose without a good excuse
  (Like Master Stork invited in the fable
To Mr. Fox's dinner); there he sat,
Impatient to retire and take his hat.

XXXIV.

For only once or twice that he remained
  To change this constant formal course, he found
His brethren awkward, sullen, and constrained;
  He caught the conversation at a bound,
And, with a hurried agitation, strained
  His wits to keep it up, and drive it round.
It saved him, but he felt the risk and danger,
Behaved-to like a pleasant utter stranger.

XXXV.

Wise people sometimes will pretend to sleep,
  And watch and listen while they droop and snore,
He felt himself a kind of a black sheep,
  But studied to be neither less nor more
Obliging than became him, but to keep
  His temper, style, and manner as before;
It seemed the best, the safest, only plan,
Never to seem to feel as a marked man.

XXXVI.

Wise curs, when canistered, refuse to run;
  They merely crawl and creep about, and whine,
And disappoint the boys, and spoil the fun,
  That picture is too mean, this monk of mine
Ennobled it, as others since have done,
  With grace and ease, and grandeur of design;
He neither ran nor howled, nor crept nor turned,
But wore it as he walked, quite unconcerned.

XXXVII.

To manifest the slightest want of nerve
   Was evidently perfect, utter ruin,
Therefore the seeming to recant or swerve,
   By meddling any way with what was doing,
He felt within himself would only serve
   To bring down all the mischief that was brewing;
" No duty binds me, no constraint compels
To bow before the Dagon of the Bells.

XXXVIII.

" To flatter this new foolery, to betray
   My vote, my conscience, and my better sense,
By bustling in the belfry day by day;
   But in the grange, the cellar, or the spence
(While all are otherwise employed), I may
   Deserve their thanks, at least avoid offence;
For (while this vile anticipated clatter
Fills all their hearts and senses), every matter

XXXIX.

" Behoveful for our maintenance and needs
   Is wholly disregarded, and the course
Of our conventual management proceeds
   At random, day by day, from bad to worse;
The larder dwindles and the cellar bleeds!
   Besides—besides the bells, we must disburse
For masonry, for framework, wheels and fliers;
Next winter we must fast like genuine friars."

XL.

As bees, that when the skies are calm and fair,
   In June, or the beginning of July,
Launch forth colonial settlers in the air,
   Round, round, and roundabout, they whiz, they fly

With eager worry whirling here and there,
  They know not whence, nor whither, where, nor why,
In utter hurry-scurry, going, coming,
Maddening the summer air with ceaseless humming;

XLI.

Till the strong frying-pan's energic jangle
  With thrilling thrum their feebler hum doth drown,
Then passive and appeased, they droop and dangle,
  Clinging together close, and clustering down,
Linked in a multitudinous living tangle
  Like an old tassel of a dingy brown;
The joyful farmer sees, and spreads his hay,
And reckons on a settled sultry day.

XLII.

E'en so the monks, as wild as sparks of fire
  (Or swarms unpacified by pan or kettle),
Ran restless round the cloisters and the choir,
  Till those huge masses of sonorous metal
Attracted them toward the tower and spire;
  There you might see them cluster, crowd, and settle,
Thronged in the hollow tintinnabular hive;
The belfry swarmed with monks; it seemed alive.

XLIII.

Then, while the cloisters, courts, and yards were still,
  Silent and empty, like a long vacation;
The friar prowled about, intent to fill
  Details of delegated occupation,
Which, with a ready frankness and goodwill,
  He undertook; he said, "the obligation
Was nothing, nothing, he could serve their turn
While they were busy with this new concern."

XLIV.

Combining prudence with a scholar's pride,
    Poor Tully, like a toad beneath a harrow,
Twitchéd, jerked, and hauled and mauled on every side,
    Tried to identify himself with Varro;
This course our cautious friar might have tried,
    But his poor convent was a field too narrow;
There was not, from the prior to the cook,
A single soul that cared about a book:

XLV.

Yet, sitting with his books, he felt unclogged,
    Unfettered; and for hours together tasted
The calm delight of being neither dogged,
    Nor watched, nor worried; he transcribed, he pasted,
Repaired old bindings, indexed, catalogued,
    Illuminated, mended clasps, and wasted
An hour or two sometimes in actual reading;
Meanwhile the belfry business was proceeding;

XLVI.

And the first opening peal, the grand display,
    In prospect ever present to his mind,
Was fast approaching, pregnant with dismay,
    With loathing and with horror undefined,
Like the expectation of an ague day;
    The day before he neither supped nor dined,
And felt beforehand, for a fortnight near,
A kind of deafness in his fancy's ear:

XLVII.

But most he feared his ill-digested spleen,
    Inflamed by gibes, might lead him on to wrangle,
Or discompose, at least, his looks and mien;
    So, with the belfry's first prelusive jangle,

He sallied from the garden-gate unseen,
  With his worst hat, his boots, his line and angle,
Meaning to pass away the time, and bring
Some fish for supper, as a civil thing.

XLVIII.

The prospect of their after-supper talk
  Employed his thoughts, forecasting many a scoff,
Which he with quick reply must damp and baulk,
  Parrying at once, without a hem or cough,
" Had not the bells annoyed him in his walk?
  No, faith ! he liked them best when farthest off."
Thus he prepared and practised many a sentence
Expressing ease, good-humour, independence.

XLIX.

His ground bait had been laid the night before,
  Most fortunately !—for he used to say,
" That more than once the belfry's bothering roar
  Almost induced him to remove away ;"
Had he so done, the gigantean corps
  Had sacked the convent on that very day,
But providentially the perch and dace
Bit freely, which detained him at the place.

L.

And here let us detain ourselves awhile,
  My dear Thalia ! party's angry frown
And petty malice in that monkish pile
  (The warfare of the cowl and of the gown),
Had almost dried my wits and drained my style ;
  Here, with our legs, then, idly dangling down,
We'll rest upon the bank, and dip our toes
In the poetic current as it flows.

LI.

Or in the narrow sunny plashes near,
  Observe the puny piscatory swarm,
That with their tiny squadrons tack and veer,
  Cruising amidst the shelves and shallows warm,
Chasing, or in retreat, with hope or fear
  Of petty plunder or minute alarm;
With clannish instinct how they wheel and face,
Inherited arts inherent in the race;

LII.

Or mark the jetty, glossy tribes that glance
  Upon the water's firm unruffled breast,
Tracing their ancient labyrinthic dance
  In mute mysterious cadence unexpressed;
Alas! that fresh disaster and mischance
  Again must drive us from our place of rest!
Grim Mangonell, with his outrageous crew,
Will scare us hence within an hour or two.

LIII.

Poets are privileged to run away—
  Alcæus and Archilochus could fling
Their shields behind them in a doubtful fray;
  And still sweet Horace may be heard to sing
His filthy fright upon Philippi's day
  (You can retire, too, for the Muse's wing
Is swift as Cupid's pinion when he flies,
Alarmed at periwigs and human ties).

LIV.

This practice was approved in times of yore,
  Though later bards behaved like gentlemen,
And Garcilasso, Camoens, many more,
  Disclaimed the privilege of book and pen;

And bold Aneurin, all bedripped with gore,
  Bursting by force from the beleaguered glen,
Arrogant, haughty, fierce, of fiery mood,
Not meek and mean, as Gray misunderstood.

LV.

But we, that write a mere campaigning tour,
  May choose a station for our point of view
That's picturesque and perfectly secure;
  Come, now we'll sketch the friar, that will do:
" Designs and etchings by an amateur;
  A frontispiece, and a vignette or two:"
But much I fear that aquatint and etching
Will scarce keep pace with true poetic sketching.

LVI.

Dogs that inhabit near the banks of Nile
  (As ancient authors or old proverbs say),
Dreading the cruel critic crocodile,
  Drink as they run, a mouthful and away;
'Tis a true model for descriptive style;
  " Keep moving " (as the man says in the play),
The power of motion is the poet's forte,
Therefore, again, " keep moving ! that's **your sort** !"

LVII.

For, otherwise, while you persist and paint,
  With your portfolio pinioned to a spot,
Half of your picture grows effaced and faint,
  Imperfectly remembered, or forgot;
Make sketch, then, upon sketch; and if they ain't
  Complete, it does not signify a jot;
Leave graphic illustrations of your work
To be devised by Westall or by Smirke.

LVIII.

I'll speak my mind at once, in spite of raillery;
   I've thought and thought again a thousand times,
What a magnificent poetic gallery
   Might be designed from my Stow Market rhymes;
I look for no reward, nor fee, nor salary,
   I look for England's fame in foreign climes
And future ages—*Honos alit Artes,*
And such a plan would reconcile all parties.

LIX.

I'm strongly for the present state of things;
   I look for no reform, nor innovation,
Because our present Parliaments and Kings
   Are competent to improve and rule the nation,
Provided projects that true genius brings
   Are held in due respect and estimation.
I've said enough—and now you must be wishing
To see the landscape, and the friar fishing.

Canto IV.

I.

A MIGHTY current, unconfined and free,
   Ran wheeling round beneath the mountain's shade,
Battering its wave-worn base; but you might see
   On the near margin many a watery glade,
Becalmed beneath some little island's lee
   All tranquil, and transparent, close embayed;
Reflecting in the deep, serene and even,
Each flower and herb, and every cloud of heaven;

II.

The painted kingfisher, the branch above her,
  Stands in the steadfast mirror fixed and true;
Anon the fitful breezes brood and hover,
  Fresh'ning the surface with a rougher hue;
Spreading, withdrawing, pausing, passing over,
  Again returning to retire anew:
So rest and motion, in a narrow range,
Feasted the sight with joyous interchange.

III.

The monk with handy jerk, and petty baits,
  Stands twitching out apace the perch and roach;
His mightier tackle, pitched apart, awaits
  The grovelling barbel's unobserved approach:
And soon his motley meal of homely cates
  Is spread, the leather bottle is a-broach;
Eggs, bacon, ale, a napkin, cheese and knife,
Forming a charming picture of still-life.

IV.

The friar fishing—a design for Cuyp,
  A cabinet jewel, "Pray remark the boot;
And, leading from the light, that shady stripe,
  With the dark bulrush-heads how well they suit;
And then, that mellow tint so warm and ripe,
  That falls upon the cassock and surtout:"
If it were fairly painted, puff'd and sold,
My gallery would be worth its weight in gold.

V.

But hark! the busy chimes fall fast and strong,
  Clattering and pealing in their full career;
Closely the thickening sounds together throng.
  No longer painful to the friar's ear,

They bind his fancy with illusion strong;
　While his rapt spirit hears, or seems to hear,
" *Turn, turn again—yen—yèn, thou noble friar,*
Eleele—lèele—lèele—lected prior."

VI.

Thus the mild monk, as he unhooked a gudgeon,
　Stood musing, when far other sounds arise,
Sounds of despite and ire, and direful dudgeon;
　And soon across the river he espies,
In wrathful act a hideous huge curmudgeon
　Calling his comrades on with shouts and cries—
" There ! there it is ! I told them so before;"
He left his line and hook and said no more;

VII.

But ran right forward (pelted all the way),
　And bolted breathless at the convent-gate,
The messenger and herald of dismay;
　But soon with conscious worth, and words of weight,
Gives orders which the ready monks obey:
　Doors, windows, wickets, are blockaded straight;
He reinspires the convent's drooping sons,
Is here and there, and everywhere, at once.

VIII.

" Friends ! fellow monks !" he cried ("for well you
　That mightiest giants must in vain essay　　[know
Across yon river's foaming gulf to go):
　The mountainous, obscure and winding way,
That guides their footsteps to the ford below,
　Affords a respite of desired delay,
Seize then the passing hour !" the monk kept bawling,
In terms to this effect, though not so drawling.

IX.

His words were these, "Before the ford is crost,
 We've a good hour, at least three-quarters good,
Bestir yourselves, my lads, or all is lost,   [wood;
 Drive down this staunchion, bring those spars of
This bench will serve; here, wedge it to the post;
 Come, Peter, quick! strip off your gown and hood,
Take up the mallet, man, and bang away!
Tighten these ropes, now lash them, and belay.

X.

"Finish the job while I return. I fear
 Yon postern-gate will prove the convent's ruin;
You, brother John, my namesake! stay you here,
 And give an eye to what these monks are doing;
Bring out the scalding sweet-wort, and the beer,
 Keep up the stoke-hole fire, where we were brewing:
And pull the gutters up, and melt the lead
(Before a dozen aves can be said),

XI.

"I shall be back amongst you." Forth he went,
 Secured the postern, and returned again,
Disposing all with high arbitrement,
 With earnest air, and visage on the main
Concern of public safety fixed and bent;
 For now the giants, stretching o'er the plain,
Are seen, presenting in the dim horizon
Tall awful forms, horrific and surprising.

XII.

I'd willingly walk barefoot fifty mile,
 To find a scholar, or divine, or squire,
That could assist me to devise a style
 Fit to describe the conduct of the friar;

I've tried three different ones within a while,
 The grave, the vulgar, and the grand high-flyer;
All are I think improper, more or less,
I'll take my chance amongst 'em, you shall guess.

XIII.

Intrepid, eager, ever prompt to fly
 Where danger and the convent's safety call;
Where doubtful points demand a judging eye,
 Where on the massy gates huge maces fall;
Where missile volleyed rocks are whirled on high,
 Pre-eminent upon the embattled wall,
In gesture and in voice he stands confest;
Exhorting all the monks to do their best.

XIV.

We redescend to phrase of low degree,
 For there's a point which you must wish to know,
The real ruling abbot, where was he?
 For (since we make so classical a show,
Our convent's mighty structure, as you see,
 Like Thebes or Troy beleaguered by the foe:
Our friar scuffling like a kind of Cocles),
You'll figure him perhaps like Eteocles

XV.

In Æschylus, with sentries, guards and watches,
 Ready for all contingencies arising,
Pitting his chosen chiefs in equal matches
 Against the foe, anon soliloquizing;
Then occupied anew with fresh dispatches—
 Nothing like this!—but something more surprising,
Was he like Priam then, that's stranger far,
That in the ninth year of his Trojan war,

XVI.

Knew not the names or persons of his foes,
    But merely points them out as stout or tall,
While (as no Trojan knew them, I suppose),
    Helen attends her father to the wall,
To tell him long details of these and those?
    'Twas not like this, but strange and odd withal;
" Nobody knows it—nothing need be said,
Our poor dear abbot is this instant dead.

XVII.

" They wheeled him out, you know, to take the air—
    It must have been an apoplectic fit—
He tumbled forward from his garden-chair—
    He seemed completely gone, but warm as yet:
I wonder how they came to leave him there;
    Poor soul! he wanted courage, heart, and wit
For times like these—the shock and the surprise!
'Twas very natural the gout should rise.

XVIII.

" But such a sudden end was scarce expected;
    Our parties will be puzzled to proceed;
The belfry set divided and dejected: ·
    The crisis is a strange one, strange indeed;
I'll bet you fighting friar is elected;
    It often happens in the hour of need,
From popular ideas of utility,
People are pitched upon for mere ability.

XIX.

" I'll hint the subject, and communicate
    The sad event—he's standing there apart;
Our offer, to be sure, comes somewhat late,
    But then, we never thought he meant to start,

And if he gains his end, at any rate,
   He has an understanding and a heart;
He'll serve or he'll protect his friends, at least,
With better spirit than the poor deceased;

XX.

" The convent was all going to the devil
   While he, poor creature, thought himself beloved
For saying handsome things, and being civil,
   Wheeling about as he was pulled and shoved,
By way of leaving things to find their level."
   The funeral sermon ended, both approved,
And went to Friar John, who merely doubted
The fact, and wished them to inquire about it ;

XXI.

Then left them, and returned to the attack :
   They found their abbot in his former place ;
They took him up and turned him on his back ;
   At first (you know) he tumbled on his face :
They found him fairly stiff and cold and black ;
   They then unloosed each ligature and lace,
His neckcloth and his girdle, hose and garters,
And took him up, and lodged him in his quarters.

XXII.

Bees served me for a simile before,
   And bees again—" Bees that have lost their king,"
Would seem a repetition and a bore;
   Besides, in fact, I never saw the thing;
And though those phrases from the good old store
   Of " feebler hummings and a flagging wing,"
Perhaps may be descriptive and exact ;
I doubt it ; I confine myself to fact.

XXIII.

Thus much is certain, that a mighty pother
  Arises; that the frame and the condition
Of things is altered, they combine and bother,
  And every winged insect politician
Is warm and eager till they choose another.
  In our monastic hive the same ambition
Was active and alert; but angry fortune
Constrained them to contract the long, importune,

XXIV.

Tedious, obscure, inexplicable train,
  Qualification, form, and oath and test,
Ballots on ballots, balloted again;
  Accessits, scrutinies, and all the rest;
Theirs was the good old method, short and plain;
  Per acclamationem they invest
Their fighting Friar John with robes and ring,
Crozier and mitre, seals, and everything.

XXV.

With a new warlike active chief elected,
  Almost at once, it scarce can be conceived
What a new spirit, real or affected,   [grieved
  Prevailed throughout; the monks complained and
That nothing was attempted or projected;
  While choristers and novices believed
That their new fighting abbot, Friar John,
Would sally forth at once, and lead them on.

XXVI.

I pass such gossip, and devote my cares
  By diligent inquiry to detect
The genuine state and posture of affairs:
  Unmannered, uninformed, and incorrect,

Falsehood and malice hold alternate chairs,
   And lecture and preside in envy's sect;
The fortunate and great she never spares,
Sowing the soil of history with tares.

XXVII.

Thus, jealous of the truth, and feeling loth
   That Sir Nathaniel henceforth should accuse
Our noble monk of cowardice and sloth,
   I'll print the affidavit of the Muse,
And state the facts as ascertained on oath,
   Corroborated by surveys and views,
When good King Arthur granted them a brief,
And ninety groats were raised for their relief.

XXVIII.

Their arbours, walks, and alleys were defaced,
   Riven and uprooted, and with ruin strown,
And the fair dial in their garden placed
   Battered by barbarous hands, and overthrown;
The deer with wild pursuit dispersed and chased,
   The dove-house ransacked, and the pigeons flown;
The cows all killed in one promiscuous slaughter,
The sheep all drowned, and floating in the water.

XXIX.

The mill was burned down to the water wheels;
   The giants broke away the dam and sluice,
Dragged up and emptied all the fishing-reels;
   Drained and destroyed the reservoir and stews,
Wading about, and groping carp and eels;
   In short, no single earthly thing of use
Remained untouched beyond the convent's wall:
The friars from their windows viewed it all.

XXX.

But the bare hope of personal defence,
　　The church, the convent's, and their own protection,
Absorbed their thoughts, and silenced every sense
　　Of present loss, till Friar John's election ;
Then other schemes arose, I know not whence,
　　Whether from flattery, zeal, or disaffection,
But the brave monk, like Fabius with Hannibal,
Against internal faction, and the cannibal

XXXI.

Inhuman foe, that threatened from without,
　　Stood firmly, with a self-sufficing mind,
Impregnable to rumour, fear, or doubt,
　　Determined that the casual, idle, blind
Event of battle with that barbarous rout,
　　Flushed with success and garbage, should not bind
Their future destinies, or fix the seal
Of ruin on the claustral commonweal.

XXXII.

He checked the rash, the boisterous, and the proud,
　　By speech and action, manly but discreet ;
During the siege he never once allowed
　　Of chapters, or convoked the monks to meet,
Dreading the consultations of a crowd.
　　Historic parallels we sometimes meet—
I think I could contrive one—if you please,
I shall compare our monk to Pericles.

XXXIII.

In former times, amongst the Athenians bold,
　　This Pericles was placed in high command,
Heading their troops (as statesmen used of old),
　　In all their wars and fights by sea and land ;

Besides, in Langhorne's Plutarch we are told
   How many fine ingenious things he planned;
For Phidias was an architect and builder,
Jeweller and engraver, carver, gilder;

XXXIV.

But altogether quite expert and clever;
   Pericles took him up and stood his friend,
Persuading these Athenians to endeavour
   To raise a work to last to the world's end,
By means of which their fame should last for ever;
   Likewise an image (which, you comprehend,
They meant to pray to, for the country's good):
They had before an old one made of wood,

XXXV.

But being partly rotten and decayed,
   They wished to have a new one spick and span,
So Pericles advised it should be made
   According to this Phidias's plan,
Of ivory, with gold all overlaid,
   Of the height of twenty cubits and a span,
Making eleven yards of English measure,
All to be paid for from the public treasure.

XXXVI.

So Phidias's talents were requited
   With talents that were spent upon the work,
And everybody busied and delighted,
   Building a temple—this was their next quirk—
Lest it should think itself ill-used and slighted.
   This temple now belongs to the Grand Turk,
The finest in the world allowed to be,
That people go five hundred miles to see.

XXXVII.

Its ancient carvings are safe here at home,
  Brought round by shipping from as far as Greece,
Finer, they say, than all the things at Rome;
  But here you need not pay a penny-piece;
But curious people, if they like to come,
  May look at them as often as they please—
I've left my subject, but I was not sorry
To mention things that raise the country's glory.

XXXVIII.

Well, Pericles made everything complete,
  Their town, their harbour, and their city wall;
When their allies rebelled, he made them treat
  And pay for peace, and taxed and fined them all,
By which means Pericles maintained a fleet,
  And kept three hundred galleys at his call:
Pericles was a man for everything:
Pericles was a kind of petty king.

XXXIX.

It happened Sparta was another State;   [bear
  They thought themselves as good; they could not
To see the Athenians grown so proud and great,
  Ruling and domineering everywhere,
And so resolved, before it grew too late,
  To fight it out and settle the affair;
Then, being quite determined to proceed,
They mustered an amazing force indeed;

XL.

And (after praying to their idol Mars)
  Marched on, with all the allies that chose to join,
As was the practice in old heathen wars,
  Destroying all the fruit trees, every vine,

And smashing and demolishing the jars
   In which those classic ancients kept their wine ;
The Athenians ran within the city wall
To save themselves, their children, wives, and all.

XLI

Then Pericles (whom they compared to Jove,
   As being apt to storm and play the deuce),
Kept quiet, and forbad the troops to move,
   Because a battle was no kind of use ;
The more they mutinied, the more he strove
   To keep them safe in spite of their abuse,
For while the farms were ransacked round the town,
This was the people's language up and down :

XLII.

" 'Tis better to die once than live to see
   Such an abomination, such a waste."
" No ! no ! " says Pericles, " that must not be,
   You're too much in a hurry, too much haste—
Learned Athenians, leave the thing to me ;
   You think of being bullied and disgraced ;
Don't think of that, nor answer their defiance ;
We'll gain the day by our superior science."

XLIII.

Pericles led the people as he pleased,
   But in most cases something is forgot :
What with the crowd and heat they grew diseased,
   And died in heaps like wethers with the rot ;
And, at the last, the same distemper seized
   Poor Pericles himself, he went to pot.
It answered badly ; therefore I admire
So much the more the conduct of the friar,

XLIV.

For in the garrison where he presided
   Neither distress, nor famine, nor disease
Were felt, nor accident nor harm betided
   The happy monks; but plenteous, and with ease,
All needful monkish viands were provided;
   Bacon and pickled-herring, pork and peas;
And when the table-beer began to fail,
They found resources in the bottled ale.

XLV.

Dinner and supper kept their usual hours;
   Breakfast and luncheon never were delayed,
While to the sentries on the walls and towers
   Between two plates hot messes were conveyed.
At the departure of the invading powers,
   It was a boast the noble abbot made,
None of his monks were weaker, paler, thinner,
Or, during all the siege, had lost a dinner.

XLVI.

This was the common course of their hostility;
   The giant forces being foiled at first,
Had felt the manifest impossibility
   Of carrying things before them at a burst,
But still, without a prospect of utility,
   At stated hours they pelted, howled, and cursed;
And sometimes, at the peril of their pates,
Would bang with clubs and maces at the gates;

XLVII.

Them the brave monkish legions, unappalled,
   With stones that served before to pave the court
(Heaped and prepared at hand), repelled and mauled,
   Without an effort, smiling as in sport,

With many a broken head, and many a scald
  From stones and molten lead and boiling wort;
Thus little Pillicock was left for dead,
And old Loblolly forced to keep his bed.

XLVIII.

The giant troops invariably withdrew
  (Like mobs in Naples, Portugal, and Spain),
To dine at twelve o'clock, and sleep till two,
  And afterwards (except in case of rain),
Returned to clamour, hoot, and pelt anew.
  The scene was every day the same again;
Thus the blockade grew tedious: I intended
A week ago, myself, to raise and end it.

XLIX.

One morn the drowsy sentry rubbed his eyes,
  Foiled by the scanty, baffling, early light;
It seemed a figure of inferior size
  Was traversing the giants' camp outright;
And soon a monkish form they recognize,
  And now their brother Martin stands in sight,
That on that morning of alarm and fear
Had rambled out to see the salmon-weir;

L.

Passing the ford, the giants' first attack
  Left brother Martin's station in their rear,
And thus prevented him from falling back
  But during all the siege he watched them near,
Saw them returning by their former track
  The night before, and found the camp was clear;
And so returned in safety with delight
And rapture, and a ravenous appetite.

LI.

"Weil! welcome, welcome, brother! brother Martin!
　Why, Martin! we could scarce believe our eyes:
Ah, brother! strange events here since our parting—"
　And Martin dined (dispensing brief replies
To all the questions that the monks were starting,
　Betwixt his mouthfuls), while each friar vies
In filling, helping, carving, questioning;
So Martin dined in public like a king.

LII.

And now the gates are opened, and the throng
　Forth issuing, the deserted camp survey;
"Here Murdomack, and Mangonell the strong,
　And Gorboduc were lodged," and "here," they say,
"This pigsty to Poldavy did belong;
　Here Brindleback, and here Phagander lay."
They view the deep indentures, broad and round,
Which mark their posture squatting on the ground.

LIII.

Then to the traces of gigantic feet,
　Huge, wide apart, with half a dozen toes;
They track them on, till they converge and meet
　(An earnest and assurance of repose),
Close at the ford; the cause of this retreat
　They all conjecture, but no creature knows;
It was ascribed to causes multifarious,
To saints, as Jerome, George, and Januarius,

LIV.

To their own pious founder's intercession,
　To Ave-Maries, and our Lady's Psalter;
To news that Friar John was in possession,
　To new wax candles placed upon the altar,

To their own prudence, valour, and discretion ;
.   To reliques, rosaries, and holy water ;
To beads and psalms, and feats of arms—in short,
There was no end of their accounting for't.

LV.

But though they could not, you, perhaps, may guess ;
  They went, in short, upon their last adventure :
After the ladies—neither more nor less—
  Our story now revolves upon its centre,
And I'm rejoiced myself, I must confess,
  To find it tally like an old indenture ;
They drove off mules and horses half a score,
The same that you saw roasted heretofore.

LVI.

Our giants' memoirs still remain on hand,
  For all my notions, being genuine gold,
Beat out beneath the hammer and expand,
  And multiply themselves a thousandfold
Beyond the first idea that I planned ;
  Besides—this present copy must be sold :
Besides—I promised Murray t'other day,
To let him have it by the tenth of May.

THE CYPRESS CROWN.

A TALE.

BY

Mr. DE LA MOTTE-FOUQUET.

[*Translated out of German into English by a Dutchman.*]

THE CYPRESS CROWN.

WHAT the peace promised was to be accomplished. The regiments returned ; they gravely and solemnly entered the released, miraculously delivered city. It was on a Sunday morning ; young and old pressed from daybreak through the streets towards the gate. The guards with difficulty checked the impetuosity of their immoderate joy ; all stood expecting, pressing, pinching, interlacing and winding about each other, but became more calm and mentally affected as the moment approached. There was scarcely a sound to be heard, when the trumpet rejoicingly and dolefully saluted hitherward. Tears of anguish flowed from a thousand eyes ; many a beating heart was swelled to bursting ; the lips trembled when the glittering arms first entered through the open gate. Flowers and crowns flew to meet them, all trees had given their tribute, the gardens had bestowed their variegated splendour of colours. A most charming child, standing in a high arched window, raised his round white arms towards heaven and threw a crown of leaves (given him by his weeping, face-averted mother) down among the soldiers. A lancer caught it upon his lance, kindly winking at the little white angel above him, towards whom his eyes were still turned when his officer galloping by, cried out, "Heigh, Wolf! A cypress crown! How came it to you ?—'tis a bad omen."

Wolf placed the crown upon his right arm and rode onwards somewhat affected.

The billets for quartering were finally distributed after a long and tiresome delay ; the horses were put into their stables, fed and watered. Wolf received a billet upon a known rich butcher ; his comrades congratulated him, and rallied him upon the tit-bits he would find there ; they prelusively invited themselves to dine or sup with him. In the meanwhile Wolf took off his cap, put the billet between the gold leashes, passed his hand softly over his forehead (covered with rich hairs), and said, half angrily : " I fear you are much mistaken, I know these rich fellows well, and I know their covetousness. I wished to lodge elsewhere." " Fool !" cried one of his friends, " what is it to you whether your host be a miser or a liberal man ? It is always good for the soldier when the host is rich, but it is necessary that the guest be well behaved, that is a thing of course." " Politeness has nothing to do in this case," answered Wolf (taking his baggage upon his shoulders and hanging the cypress crown upon his lance), "they are brutal, rude, uncivil men, they neither feel for man nor beast ; I always shudder and can with difficulty forbear beating such fellows. When I see a waggon-load of calves tied together, pressing each other, their heads hanging danglingly, and such a clown walking slowly after them, void of feeling, perhaps singing or whistling, callous and totally insensible to the poor animals' cries, I am cut to the heart. Besides, I am weary of slaughter and blood ; I am disgusted, satiated ; they are my abhorrence." " Oh ! oh !" cried they, laughing, " Wolf can't see blood! Dove's heart! since when came it ? " " Speak not so foolishly," cried Wolf angrily, " when my duty calls, or that I wish to augment my honour (beating his iron cross), then you will not find me backward ; but I will not deny that my nerves seem to contract when I reflect that I am brought to this pass—to be exalted to a butchery, to see the bloody cleaver, and hear the pitiable and lamentable roaring; can you then wonder that I should wish for another quarter?" They continued laughing when he was gone away. He looked back threateningly; half jocosely, half angrily he swung the lance towards them who remained behind sporting about, till they lost sight of him.

He soon found the street and the number of the directed house, at the gateway of which he saw a gigantic man, standing and strutting with spread legs; his yellowish brown face was much covered with black, bushy, hanging eyebrows. His small pink eyes seemed to follow, without soul, the thick cloud of smoke which issued from a small tobacco-pipe. One of his hands played in the pocket of his scarlet waistcoat, the other buttoned and unbuttoned its silver buttons over a considerable paunch.

Wolf made his obeisance and showed him, with much civility, his quartering billet; the other looked anew at him, and, without taking any notice of his guest, pointed with his thumb bent backwards towards the house, peevishly and coolly saying, " Thither, my servants know already." Wolf gnashed his teeth, and went quickly forward, whereby his dragging sabre rudely touched Mr. John's leg. " Devil!" cried he, stamping his foot. Wolf remained unmoved by it and stepped into the foreyard, where a very pale, sickly-looking girl was carrying, with difficulty, two pails of water from the pump. Wolf, inclining towards her, asked her if she was the butcher's servant; she stopped short, speechless and perplexed; she put the pails down upon the ground, and directing her fire-extinguished eyes towards him, she stared fixedly, her face and cheeks became more deadly pale, and her whole frame appeared inanimate. Wolf asked again, a little impatiently; she took up her pails, bowed her head upon her breast, and looking at a steep staircase in the back part of the house, she said, " That way; when up, the first door on the right hand is your room."

Wolf stood buried in thought, followed her with his eyes a long time before he ascended the stairs. He found all as she had intimated ; the room was obscure, close and confined; the air thick and damp; a great deal of the plastering had fallen off the walls, which were blackened with smoke, and here and there were characters, numbers, human faces, and heads of beasts painted on the wall with coals. A miserable, mean bed was opposite to the smoke-clouded, almost blind-grown window. A very rusty long nail was in the wall near the bed, upon which Wolf hung the crown, put his lance and sabre into a corner and his baggage upon the old table. occasionally muttering betwixt his teeth, "The rich are worthless, are rascals !" He pushed two fragile chairs aside, leaned on the opened window, and whistled until his anger was suppressed.

He saw over the courtyard and penthouse, in a fine and spacious garden, which was shining and odoriferous compared to the cloudy appearance and damp unwholesome air of the city, the trees of dark shady walks, vaulted high, and as holy, over the solitary places, the golden sunflowers also waggled on their flexible stalks over long windings of white and red roses, which bordered the alleys and hedges. There all was silent, and seemed to be a sacred thicket, unbeaten by human feet. Wolf looked thitherward and wished much to be walking there, but desisted, and repressed that wish; his room became more comfortable, however, in consequence of this charming prospect.

During the day he remained very quiet, not troubling himself with what passed in the house. His duty obliged him to go out towards the evening, and it became somewhat dark when he returned. The window was always open : he took a chair near it, sat down, and filled his pipe with tobacco, then blowing the smoke into the air, he indulged his thoughts, and many things flashed across his mind.

The salubrity of the garden, the black tops of the trees, the fiery disc of the moon, which emitted its flaming rays over him, melted his very soul. He remembered his home, his old mother, and grew very tender and sorrowful. The

thought that in that place there was no one solicitous
or concerned about him presented itself to his mind; he felt
an anxious and ardent desire to hear about his brother, who
had been abroad a long time without it being known where
he was. At first he was a miller's man, then he engaged
himself as a carrier's man, since when they had lost his
track.

"Perhaps he went for a soldier," said Wolf. "Now that
it is peace all over the world, I think at home they know
where he is." It seemed to him not only probable but sure,
and he determined upon instantly writing to inquire. The
remembrance of his brother came upon him so suddenly
and so forcibly that the anguish it excited nearly suffocated
him.

He but just now discovered, with much vexation, that they
had not left him a candle—that, at least, he would call for; he
stepped (with a rude oath) out of the door clothed in a small
linen waistcoat, without a neckcloth, and just as he then
was; resentment was painted in his face, he had stroked his
hair upwards, as he was accustomed to do when he was angry,
so that it stood an end; thus he groped along in the dark,
and descended the stairs. A small lamp burnt faintly on the
floor of the house; Wolf stepped near it, to see where he
was to go, and stood inclining and feeling about with his
hands for the iron wire to ring the bell, when Mr. John
returned home from his merry bout at the tavern, with his
face all on fire, and his eyes sparkling; he gave his usual
signal with his thick stick full of knots at the door without perceiving his guest. Wolf drew near him; his face
shone by the light of the lamp; he said with a loud imperious voice: "Am I to remain in darkness all the night?"
Mr. John was as much terrified as if thunderstruck, the stick
fell from his hand, he wildly stared at him, then with a
hollow howl he violently rushed through the partly opened
door.

"Is he a fool, mad, or drunk?" thought Wolf. More irritated by this strange conduct he rudely pulled the bell, and began to make a great noise and bustle, when Louisa, the pale girl, came shyly out, made an excuse for her carelessness, and hastened before him with a candle in consequence of his demand. She put the candle upon the table in his chamber, shut the window, wiped the dust off the chairs, and occupied herself some time in her usual soft and gentle manner. Wolf was always very modest and cautious with women, he hated and feared ill renown ; and as he had no very good opinion of this house, the neatness of the girl tormented and perplexed him ; he turned aside and beat the panes of glass with his fingers, whilst Louisa stood at the bedside flattening the blanket with the palm of her hand. Wolf heard her sigh deeply, and looked about; she walked out of the chamber sobbing, and with her head sunk upon her breast; this touched him to the quick. "Why does she weep?" thought he ; "has my rudeness frightened her, or have I uttered in my hurry and vexation any unpleasant words?" He took the candle, and hastily and attentively following her, he cried out : "Pray, miss, stop a little ; it is very dark and you may hurt yourself." She was only at the first step. Wolf leaned upon the low rails of the stairs, and carried the candle towards her ; she thanked him with affection, and cast her tearful eyes seemingly with pain upon him. Wolf looked upon her with much pleasure; she was truly beautiful. A fine, somewhat languishing redness changed playing and shining over her cheeks. He took her hand modestly and said, "Dear miss, you are much afflicted. Have I offended you?" "Oh God! no sir," answered she, weeping again. "Or has some other done you any harm?" asked he more earnestly. She joined her hands, pressed them against her eyes, and gently shook her head ; at last she exclaimed : "God wills it so! Even you are sent by Him ; just heavens ! All was already well and quiet, now it is again as before." She then by a sign begged him to remain behind, wiped the tears from her cheeks with her apron, and descended slowly and silently. Wolf sat a long time facing the lighted candle, his head on his hands, his elbows resting upon the table, without knowing what to do with himself. His soul was as heavy and oppressed as if he was upon the brink of a great misfortune ; he was void of a single rational thought. The weeping voice of Louisa struck melancholy through his heart, and resounded in it as with a thousand-fold echo. With difficulty he had refrained from tears in her presence ; her deep-rooted, tender affliction made his heart bleed within him, and he felt as if he partook of her sorrow and disease.

Thus affected and absent he carved and cut in the old table before him different lines and figures with a little knife which he used as pipe-cleaner, and which lay at hand with the tobacco purse.

Unwittingly and unknown he had engraven the name of Louisa (which he had heard called more than once in the house) on the old scratched and hacked table board. He was quite astonished at it, and would have effaced it by crosswise lines with the knife, but as he looked more attentively he discovered the same name all over the table and in his own characters.

Wolf rubbed his forehead and gazed with surprise at the great L, and the other characters which he had learned with much difficulty, and compared them.

"Am I bewitched!" cried he, considering whether he had not written them all himself; but he could not reach so far and had not removed the table, moreover the characters were not new. "Nonsense," murmured he, and looked about his gloomy chamber, somewhat distrustful. The cracks in the walls, the places over the bed where the lime had fallen off, the coal-sketched black faces, the melancholy devastation of the room (which seemed to have been uninhabited a long time) combined, had a terrible and dreadful appearance in the dim, shallow, and wavering light.

Wolf thought at times that he knew the faces ; he shud-

dered involuntarily, and hastily blew out the candle, in order
to avoid the illusion of his senses; besides, it was too late to
write the proposed letters. He wished to take fresh air for
an instant and opened the window. The lukewarm night
air softly blew upon him as if saluting him; all seemed to
repose and to sleep, save that a faint ray of light shone out
of a cave of the penthouse; and soon he heard a hammering
upon an avil. "Poor devil!" said he to himself, "already
thou employest the midnight hour which should lead only
to the new toilsome week." The red-hot iron emitted its
flakes as out of the grave, sparkling upwards in the still
night. "Probably," thought Wolf to himself, "it is a cutler
who forges cleavers and knives for the butcher; it must be
convenient to him, and advantageous and useful to both.
See how all link, conjoin, and hang together in this world."
He became quiet and calm, and looked a long while
into the fine garden, which seemed to be inhabited
during the night only; for Wolf plainly saw somebody
walking slowly in the dark alleys, sometimes standing,
sometimes raising his arm and moving it, as if beckoning
for a companion.

Wolf could not clearly discern the figure because the
rising fog began to cover it as with long white veils, and
the more his sight was fixed upon it the more loose and
duskish it swam and melted before him. Wolf stepped
at last away from the window, which he left open,
and threw himself upon the bed. The dried leaves
of the cypress crown over him moved by the entering air,
rustled and whispered as it were many weak, low murmur-
ing human voices. Wolf started, rose up; the crown was
agitated and waggled against the wall. "It is but that,"
said Wolf, and recollected, although half drowned with
sleep, where he was. His eyes glanced towards the window;
it appeared to him that the figure looked out of the garden
into the room. "Tush!" cried Wolf, irritated at his fears,
and, putting his head between the blankets, he fell asleep,

with so loud a palpitation of the heart that it might have been heard at a distance.

It might be an hour or more that he was sunk in a world of dreams, when a voice suddenly awoke him. The moon struggled still against the beginning break of day, faintly dawning through the window. Wolf heard a plaintive voice near him, he rashly threw the blankets off his face and breast, and disengaged both his arms; thus, with one hand leaning on the bed, the other grasping at his sword for defence, he wildly and with widely opened eyes stared about him.

He was somewhat afraid when a large white dog put his fore-paw upon the bed, stretched his head towards him, and cast his round eyes (which shined in the dark) upon him. The dog wagged his tail and licked the hand raised to repulse and punish him. Wolf was not able to beat him, but suffered him to crawl and crouch nearer and nearer till his head reposed on Wolf's breast, where it remained as if it were his usual custom.

Wolf thought probably this was his home, and fondled and caressed him. "Perhaps he takes me for his master, perhaps he takes me for the person who quitted this room for me, but whom I do not know." He had scarcely said so, when he remembered the surprising dream he was awaked out of, and his seeing somebody in the room; but he would not dwell upon this remembrance, or recall any part of it to his mind; he therefore rose, and as the day broke, put his baggage into order and prepared to go to the stable, whilst the dog was fawning about him and following him step by step. Wolf sometimes showed him the door, which the impetuous beast had most probably bounced open with his snout during the night, and which still remained so, but he moved not from his side. Now they began to awake in the house, and the journeymen butchers were busy in it and the court, whistling and singing, now religious, then riotous songs. Wolf leaned upon the window, brushed the dust from off his cap, looking about upon the wrangling rude manners and sports of these sturdy stout fellows; one of them, older and with a peevish-looking face, led a meagre animal out of the stable, put an old faded and scabbled surtout on, and hanging his thick whip over his shoulder, he twisted the mane and bridle on his hand, put one leg in the stirrup, and raised the other with a mighty jerk over the horse's back; but the poor tired jade (not being recovered from the fatigue of her last journey) pranced and kicked, and would not let him mount. The awkward rider, transported with rage, pulled the bridle, kicked and thrust the poor animal's flank, and beat and cuffed it upon the head. "Infamous dog!" murmured Wolf, whose blood began to boil; "the slouch knows not how to manage a horse, why does he undertake it? These fellows who never were soldiers are poor devils; they know not how to extricate themselves out of trouble." At length the poor sad rider sat upon the saddle, slouched his white felt cap over his ears, and jogged along through the gate.

Wolf's heart was very much eased after his departure, but it was not of long duration; he soon after heard the long-legged jade trample on the planks—the rider had forgotten something. He called, whistled, and blasphemed alternately, and without intermission, and finally bawled in at an open window, "Has anybody seen my Lux?" The dog lay snarling at Wolf's feet, and showed his teeth as often as the rude voice called him. Wolf was not willing to bring himself into trouble for his sake, and gently scratching the head of the good animal, he said: "If you call for the large white dog, he is here; I do not detain him, but he will not leave me, and I cannot drive him out of the door."

The blustering fellow stared at him with large opened mouth, pulled the cap off, and rode on without uttering a word. "Well," said Wolf, and smoothing the bristled hair of Lux; "stay here, my old dog, and keep a good guard over my baggage whilst I am out." Lux looked at him as if he understood his words, extended his hind legs under his breast, stretched his fore-feet out and remained on the doorsill, watching with elevated head.

Wolf went to his business, and did all he could to forget the disgusting night. He therefore appeared more merry than he was wont to be, more merry than he really was, and sung one song after another, during the carrying and cleaning, while his companions related and complained much of their reception and entertainment in the city, and wished for the past good days back again. "That one," said they, pointing at the trilling Wolf, "is happy; but an old proverb says, 'birds which sing so early in the morning will be taken by the vulture in the evening.'" "It is possible," answered Wolf seriously, his heart presaging no good, but threatening him with a great quarrel with the butcher, upon which his every thought was occupied. One of his comrades said, "Heh! you tell us nothing about your reception—say then, how are you?" Wolf replied, "Why should I speak of it? It will make things no better. I knew it before; the people here spoke too much, showed themselves too eager, too impetuous for us to expect much good treatment. They think it flatters the quartered soldiers, who must be satisfied privately with little. Nobody knows of it, nobody then speaks of it, and nobody would believe it, were the poor fellows to tell of it, because they are supposed to be never satisfied." "Upon conscience!" cried they all, laughing, "you have hit the right nail upon the head; it is just so. They were very generous with their grass and leaves which they threw upon us at our entrance: neither horse nor man will eat them; but surely they must know that nobody can live upon air."

"Desist from that," said Wolf; "do not quarrel about bits of bread, they are forgotten as soon as swallowed." "But it is of honour we speak," said an under-officer; "due respect is wanting, the soldier is not sufficiently esteemed." "Respect!" repeated Wolf over again; "it is what they cannot comprehend; they are ashamed, they spit poison and gall, and wish to dishonour the soldier in their own proper eyes, such a sabre seems to them an executioner's axe. Fear renders them insolent." "Companions," said the under-officer, "it will soon be over, we shall be quartered otherwise, we shall then live at our own cost." "God be thanked!" said Wolf; "I wish heartily to have done with these peevish, morose faces, although I have not much money." One of his companions sung a gay air which made them all laugh; Wolf laughed also, because he was now eased of a great load; he thought that for a few days all might remain tranquil and quiet. He avoided being much in his quarters during the day; besides, Louisa was not to be seen, and he wished not to see any other person in the house. Late in the evening he stood at the gate, and as he was looking into the street, the rider, who in the morning rode away, returned back in a jog-trot; probably he did not perceive Wolf, because he rode directly to the stable, towards which the puffing, blowing jade impetuously steered her course. After a while he came out of the stable, bent his knees stiffened by the short riding, beat his dangling jack-boots together so that the dust and dirt flew off, and then entered to Mr. John. Wolf walked in the street before the house, and soon heard a great noise in it; he looked involuntarily in at an open window, the old journeyman seemed to quarrel with his master; he had in his hand an empty money pouch, and sometimes beat the table before him with it. Mr. John walked about the room and scratched himself behind his ears, greatly embarrassed, when the other cried out: "You do not bring into account what you lose at cards and dice, but will make me suffer for it; you mistake, upon my soul! I neither can nor will support it."

The butcher became appeased, but the journeyman continued, his face quite inflamed: "Devil!—why should I endure to be chided for so small a sum, who helped you to

so much more." " Well," said Mr. John, " let us think no
more about it ; " but the other, stepping nearer him, raised
his closed hand towards him and cried, " Recollect that
I can destroy your good name, that I can bring you to
ruin."

At these words Wolf was seized with a deadly fear ; he
ran to his room and shut the door. He thought himself in
a cut-throat house. Lux, the faithful dog, crept towards
him ; he pressed him to his heart as a friend, as a companion,
and looked in his cheerful eyes. The roof of the house
seemed to cover him as with an extremely great weight, he
could take no refreshment, neither think nor do anything.
He mechanically measured the room by steps more than a
hundred times, and went to sleep very late. With a feverish
shivering, Wolf awoke suddenly out of a most frightful
dream, which had kept his soul in a half-senseless suspension
for some hours, when a trumpeter sounded for feeding in
the morning. He leaped out of bed in a most agitated and
disordered state. A small piece of mirror he had in his
baggage reflected his pale, wan countenance, and the sad-
dened features thereof, in which the marks of a dreadful
unhappy struggling were visible. He was cheerless and
discomposed the whole day, although he did all he could
to dissipate his sorrow and disquiet of mind. His companions were all astonished at his appearance, asked, insisted,
and pressed him to explain ; but he kept his secret, and
entered into no conversation. He walked as if dreaming,
did his business in a most abstracted manner, and evinced
neither shame nor sensibility when reprimanded for it
The whole day wasted thus away. He sat in the evening
with some of his companions on a bench before the main
guard ; it was sultry weather, the sky over them was lower-
ing, gloomy, and overcast. All were quiet, singing only
some good old songs in chorus. Wolf neither heard nor
saw, his heart was oppressed, and his knees trembled so
that he could not stand, when one of them said, " Now,

companions, it is time we should go to our quarters." He
who spoke had observed Wolf a long while, and as he
thought him sick, he took his arm and walked with him.
Wolf stopped short when they approached the butcher's
house, and, inwardly shrinking, breathed with difficulty.
"No!" said he, recovering himself; "no, I will no longer
bear about the phantoms, which, if continued hidden in my
heart, will fester and waste it to death." "Well," said the
other, "go on boldly; courage! tell me freely what affects
you." "Do not laugh," said Wolf seriously, "it is a dream
of so horrific a nature that the description alone will harrow
up your soul to madness." The other was greatly surprised
and alarmed at Wolf's fixed look and weak unsteady voice.
They looked at each other with pale and ruffled countenances
when they entered into Wolf's room. At length Wolf
began, " Look about you! It is here! These two last nights
methought I saw a grey white figure withered and gnawed,
by the vapour of the grave! Its haggard look and tattered
garb seemed to bespeak variety of wretchedness. It sat
upon the chair at my bedside, put its head upon its hands,
and looked upon me in a most pitiable, beseeching manner.
I was neither asleep nor awake. I felt and saw, but my
senses were so overwhelmed and agonized that I was inca-
pable of moving a single limb. After remaining some time,
it rose, and pointed towards the garden you see there. It
spoke not; but a secret voice seemed to say: 'Go there, see
you not that sunken ice-house; the linden-tree, whose
double branches spring from the same trunk, search there!'
and ceased not entreatingly to urge me on by signs and
gestures till break of day, and till I, half dead with terror
and dismay, roused and collected myself." Both looked
on the ground sometime silent and thoughtful; but Wolf
felt much easier for having divulged his painful secret, and
having freely given words to his gloomy dismal thoughts.

Growing bolder he said: "If it comes this night I will
speak to it, I will follow it; I must, at one blow, undo this

Gordian knot; otherwise I shall for ever remain bodily and mentally tormented."

" Will you do so?" asked his companion.

" Why should I not?" said Wolf.

" I would advise you not to do it," continued the other; "you do not know what you may see there."

" That is what I must know," replied Wolf, "to recover my quiet and peace of mind."

The lancer played with the tufts of his cordon and said no more. It lightened at a distance, and began to rain. Wolf stood at the window, and looking at his companion said, " You must now go home ; besides, you cannot help me ; a second person is unnecessary in this affair." The undetermined position and appearance of his friend raised his courage.

He tendered his hand to him ; and leading him out, whispered as they proceeded, " God Almighty will bless and help me." He had scarcely spoken these words when the recollection of his Creator's kindness and nearness to him upon many occasions, and particularly in the last war, presented itself to his mind. How a short and pious prayer offered to his God in misery and danger had relieved and pacified his troubled spirit ! Therefore, as soon as he had led his companion beyond the stairs, had ordered Lux to be at rest, and had sufficiently recollected himself, he blew out the candle, knelt in a corner, joined his hands and raising them upwards, prayed heartily, Our Father, &c.

After which he became composed and quiet, and for a while took delight in the awful thunder which passed high and majestically over the city, and its thousands and thousands of high and low inhabitants, and which at times sent forth its lightning, closing all eyes by dazzling them. Wolf, exhausted and enfeebled by the sluggish, half dreaming passed day, soon closed his eyes in sleep, when his nightly vision again appeared to him, and seemed, by its gesture and emotion, to be more disturbed and anxious than before.

Wolf thought Lux yelped loudly, and pulled him violently by the arm ; but his internal anguish and the total suspension of his mental powers rendered his efforts and struggling to awake vain and abortive.

At length a most terrible peal of thunder and vivid flash of lightning roused him out of his lethargic agony. He started, and at one leap was out of his bed. The wind and rain rattled at the window. The garden appeared but a single sheet of fire, and Wolf saw nought but flame and lightning. Heaven's loud acclamation swelled and increased his courage. He put on his cloak, put his sabre under his arm, called Lux, who, affrighted by the roaring of the tempest, was running about howling in a most hideous manner, and left the room praying to his God. All were awake in the house ; he found the folding-gate half open, and entered the court. The clouds over him rushed and roared like as a whirlwind, the rain streamed down so that he could scarcely advance, the dog jumped before him in short heavy skips, and with fiery sparkling eyes, he sometimes bayed with a mighty noise. Thus Lux showed him the way towards the wall ; Wolf groped on it with his hands until he found a small door ; he pressed and pushed back the bolt, and soon found himself in the entrance of the fine garden he was in quest of. The trees shook their watered heads and saluted him with hollow plaintive soundings. He advanced rashly, and always more rashly, beyond their rustling tops. His breast was oppressed, labouring, full, and it was with difficulty he breathed. The hurricane whipped the flowers vehemently together, pressed their tender heads down upon the ground, and drove whirls of leaves of white and red roses upwards through the rebelling night. A dreadful flash of lightning broke through the black veil of clouds just as Wolf stood before the destroyed, moss-overgrown ice-house. The linden-tree, exactly as his dream had showed him, extended its branches over it, and pointed with the dry ends, as if with long black fingers, towards its entrance. Wolf burst the little door open with his foot : he experienced not the smallest emotion of fear, and all inquietude was supplanted by the growing propensity to discover something in this place. It became so violent a passion that, notwithstanding the hindrance of the weather, following the direction he had received in his dream, he raked the out-dug rubbish and rottenness with an almost incredible infatuated rage. Lux stood snivelling and scratching, and threw earth away archwise over him with his snout; on a sudden he yelped in a frightful manner, and stood staring wildly as if bewitched. Wolf inclined towards him, the tempest passed roaring over him, a single star shone pale through the deep blue cloak of night. Wolf tremblingly started back with horror. A cleaver, a bright cleaver, lay at his feet. "To what purport, to what does this tend?" said he, taking it, and stepping from under the shade of the trees into the open air. The little star sparkled on the polished steel. Wolf saw with terror two enrusted spots of blood hard by its edge. His blood compressed his heart. "A murder!" cried he in uncertain guessing, "an execrable murder!" He trembled through fury, and putting the cleaver under his cloak, involuntarily, and without knowing what to wish or how to act, directed his steps towards his lodging. In the meanwhile it became calm, the black mount of clouds sunk down in the north seeming an outburnt volcano. Already the day dawned. The wind drove only red-grey, forky clouds from the east. Wolf moved with long wide step stowards the back-door, his white cloak flew in the wind, his hair stood an end, stiff and wild over his forehead, his eyes were all on fire, and his whole frame was dreadfully agitated. Thus he went to Mr. John, who, quietly looking at the clouds, was smoking his morning pipe under the gateway. "See here, master," cried Wolf, taking the cleaver from under his cloak, and pointing it towards him; "see what I found last night." The butcher's pipe fell from his hand, his eyes turned and broke, and he exclaimed with a hollow groaning, "God himself has judged!" then fell headlong on the ground and expired.

Wolf stood as if rooted to the spot, and the cleaver still grasped in his fast joined fingers, when Louisa, looking over his shoulder, cried out with a most penetrating voice: "O Lord! it is Andrew's cleaver: there is his name, 'Andrew Wolf;'" and, like lightning recalling the connecting circumstances, she suddenly exclaimed, half choked with grief, and clapping her hands lamentably together, "'Tis Andrew's blood! they have murdered him!" The noise attracted all the inhabitants of the house, who impetuously insisted upon Wolf's disclosing the frightful secret. He was as if his head and breast were bound with cramp irons. His mind was void of thought. His tongue was speechless. He stared at the characters on the cleaver, and felt as if a wheel was turning in his head.

Suddenly a torrent of hot tears burst from his eyes, and grinding his teeth, he threw himself in a fury upon the fallen butcher, raised him up, and cried in a frightful manner, "Hast thou, infernal bloodhound, murdered him?" But the cold lips opened no more, death had sealed them. Wolf drew back, let fall the stiff corpse, and looking wildly about him, ran from the gate towards the garden and ice-house. The others followed him, shovels and ladders were brought, they trenched and raked up the ground, and at last drew out of the deep grave a mouldered body. Nothing remained of it, by which it could be known, except a silver ring, which was still in a preserved state on his nibbled finger-bone.

Wolf fell on the ground in a swoon, when Louisa whispered with trembling lips: "It is he!" They carried Wolf, who was seized with violent convulsions, to the hospital, where a mortal fever detained him. In the meantime the court inquired and collected several depositions, compared them with undeniable facts, and found that eleven years before, a young, brisk, and active fellow, by name Andrew Wolf, had engaged himself in Mr. John's service. He was nimble and hasty, exercised in writing and casting accompts, and soon rendered himself very necessary to Mr. John, whose affairs succeeded well after Andrew became his servant. Therefore Mr. John softened in some degree his haughty, surly humour; and Andrew commanded his temper and submitted, somewhat in regard of the secret, cordial love he felt for Louisa.

Louisa and Andrew agreed together, and as he had gained a small capital by his industry and activity, he intended to settle himself and render his faithful girl happy. He was upon the point of breaking the matter to his master, when the malicious Martin, the infamous fellow he never trusted in, entangled him one evening at dice. Mr John was there also, and both pressed the poor youth very much; but he won from both and ceased playing, because it was very late, and because Louisa, walking about, made him a sign to do so. He went to his chamber, having kissed her in haste, and whispering her secretly, that to-morrow he would tell her all, and soften and make her happy for the future. Late in the same evening some of the people of the house heard Mr. John and Martin whispering on the staircase, and saw them afterwards ascend towards Andrew's room. On the following day he was missing, and nobody knew how or for what reason. Mr. John reported that he had sided with the French and had gone with them.

During the examination of Louisa and some other witnesses they perceived that Martin was absent; they searched and inquired after him, and discovered that he had rode out at daybreak on the old jade, assured that God's judgment would overtake him sooner or later.

After this time Louisa took a calm resigning care of poor Wolf, who, in the clear moments of his sickness, made her relate everything, and often said with joined, upraised hands: "God has judged, let us forgive the guilty!" Death soon closed his upright, guiltless eyes. Louisa put the Cypress Crown upon his coffin, and followed with Lux at a distance when his comrades buried him by his murdered brother's side!

She often weeps still over both graves, but her heart is more quiet and reconciled, as Andrew was not faithless, and God had judged. That poor white rose piously looks forward to that period when the storm of life will pluck her off entirely, and sink her into the dead night of the grave.

THE LIBRARY.

THE LIBRARY.

WHEN the sad soul, by care and grief oppressed,
Looks round the world, but looks in vain for rest ;
When every object that appears in view,
Partakes her gloom and seems dejected too ;
Where shall affliction from itself retire ?
Where fade away and placidly expire ?
Alas ! we fly to silent scenes in vain ;
Care blasts the honours of the flowery plain :
Care veils in clouds the sun's meridian beam,
Sighs through the grove, and murmurs in the stream ;
For when the soul is labouring in despair,
In vain the body breathes a purer air :
No storm-tossed sailor sighs for slumbering seas—
He dreads the tempest, but invokes the breeze ;
On the smooth mirror of the deep resides
Reflected woe, and o'er unruffled tides
The ghost of every former danger glides.
Thus, in the calms of life, we only see
A steadier image of our misery ;
But lively gales and gently clouded skies
Disperse the sad reflections as they rise ;
And busy thoughts and little cares avail
To ease the mind, when rest and reason fail.
When the dull thought, by no designs employed,

Dwells on the past, or suffered or enjoyed,
We bleed anew in every former grief,
And joys departed furnish no relief.

Not Hope herself, with all her flattering art,
Can cure this stubborn sickness of the heart:
The soul disdains each comfort she prepares,
And anxious searches for congenial cares;
Those lenient cares, which with our own combined,
By mixed sensations ease th' afflicted mind,
And steal our grief away, and leave their own behind;
A lighter grief! which feeling hearts endure
Without regret, nor e'en demand a cure.

But what strange art, what magic can dispose
The troubled mind to change its native woes?
Or lead us willing from ourselves, to see
Others more wretched, more undone than we?
This Books can do; nor this alone; they give
New views to life, and teach us how to live;
They soothe the grieved, the stubborn they chastise,
Fools they admonish, and confirm the wise:
Their aid they yield to all: they never shun
The man of sorrow, nor the wretch undone:
Unlike the hard, the selfish, and the proud,
They fly not sullen from the suppliant crowd;
Nor tell to various people various things,
But show to subjects what they show to kings.

Come, Child of Care! to make thy soul serene,
Approach the treasures of this tranquil scene;
Survey the dome, and, as the doors unfold,
The soul's best cure, in all her cares, behold!
Where mental wealth the poor in thought may find,
And mental physic the diseased in mind;
See here the balms that passion's wounds assuage;
See coolers here, that damp the fire of rage;
Here alt'ratives., by slow degrees control
The chronic habits of the sickly soul;

And round the heart and o'er the aching head,
Mild opiates here their sober influence shed.
Now bid thy soul man's busy scenes exclude,
And view composed this silent multitude:
Silent they are—but, though deprived of sound,
Here all the living languages abound;
Here all that live no more; preserved they lie,
In tombs that open to the curious eye.

 Blest be the gracious Power, who taught mankind
To stamp a lasting image of the mind!
Beasts may convey, and tuneful birds may sing,
Their mutual feelings, in the opening spring;
But man alone has skill and power to send
The heart's warm dictates to the distant friend;
'Tis his alone to please, instruct, advise
Ages remote, and nations yet to rise.

 In sweet repose, when Labour's children sleep,
When Joy forgets to smile and Care to weep,
When passion slumbers in the lover's breast,
And Fear and Guilt partake the balm of rest,
Why then denies the studious man to share
Man's common good, who feels his common care?

 Because the hope is his, that bids him fly
Night's soft repose, and sleep's mild power defy;
That after-ages may repeat his praise,
And fame's fair meed be his, for length of days.
Delightful prospect! when we leave behind
A worthy offspring of the fruitful mind!
Which, born and nursed through many an anxious day,
Shall all our labour, all our care repay.

 Yet all are not these births of noble kind,
Not all the children of a vigorous mind;
But where the wisest should alone preside,
The weak would rule us, and the blind would guide;
Nay, man's best efforts taste of man, and show
The poor and troubled source from which they flow;

Where most he triumphs, we his wants perceive,
And for his weakness in his wisdom grieve.
But though imperfect all ; yet wisdom loves
This seat serene, and virtue's self approves :
Here come the grieved, a change of thought to
    find ;
The curious here to feed a craving mind ;
Here the devout their peaceful temple choose ;
And here the poet meets his favouring Muse.

    With awe, around these silent walks I tread ;
These are the lasting mansions of the dead :
"The dead !" methinks a thousand tongues reply ;
"These are the tombs of such as cannot die !
Crowned with eternal fame, they sit sublime,
And laugh at all the little strife of time."

    Hail, then, immortals ! ye who shine above,
Each, in his sphere, the literary Jove ;
And ye the common people of these skies,
A humbler crowd of nameless deities ;
Whether 'tis yours to lead the willing mind
Through history's mazes, and the turnings find ;
Or, whether led by science, ye retire,
Lost and bewildered in the vast desire :
Whether the Muse invites you to her bowers,
And crowns your placid brows with living flowers ;
Or godlike wisdom teaches you to show
The noblest road to happiness below ;
Or men and manners prompt the easy page
To mark the flying follies of the age :
Whatever good ye boast, that good impart ;
Inform the head and rectify the heart.

    Lo, all in silence, all in order stand,
And mighty folios first, a lordly band ;
Then quartos their well-ordered ranks maintain,
And light octavos fill a spacious plain :

See yonder, ranged in more frequented rows,
A humbler band of duodecimos ;
While undistinguished trifles swell the scene,
The last new plain and frittered magazine.
Thus 'tis in life, where first the proud, the great,
In leagued assembly keep their cumbrous state ;
Heavy and huge, they fill the world with dread,
Are much admired, and are but little read :
The commons next, a middle rank, are found ;
Professions fruitful pour their offspring round ;
Reasoners and wits are next their place allowed,
And last, of vulgar tribes a countless crowd.

First, let us view the form, the size, the dress ;
For these the manners, nay the mind express :
That weight of wood, with leathern coat o'erlaid ;
Those ample clasps, of solid metal made ;
The close-pressed leaves, unclosed for many an age ;
The dull red edging of the well-filled page ;
On the broad back the stubborn ridges rolled,
Where yet the title stands in tarnished gold ;
These all a sage and laboured work proclaim,
A painful candidate for lasting fame :
No idle wit, no trifling verse can lurk
In the deep bosom of that weighty work ;
No playful thoughts degrade the solemn style,
Nor one light sentence claims a transient smile.

Hence, in these times, untouched the pages lie,
And slumber out their immortality :
They had their day, when, after all his toil,
His morning study, and his midnight oil,
At length an author's *one* great work appeared,
By patient hope, and length of days, endeared :
Expecting nations hailed it from the press ;
Poetic friends prefixed each kind address ;
Princes and kings received the pond'rous gift,
And ladies read the work they could not lift.

I

Fashion, though Folly's child, and guide of fools,
Rules e'en the wisest, and in learning rules ;
From crowds and courts to Wisdom's seat she goes
And reigns triumphant o'er her mother's foes.
For lo ! these fav'rites of the ancient mode
Lie all neglected like the Birthday Ode.

Ah ! needless now this weight of massy chain ;
Safe in themselves, the once-loved works remain :
No readers now invade their still retreat,
None try to steal them from their parent-seat ;
Like ancient beauties, they may now discard
Chains, bolts, and locks, and lie without a guard.

Our patient fathers trifling themes laid by,
And rolled, o'er laboured works, th' attentive eye :
Page after page, the much-enduring men
Explored the deeps and shallows of the pen ;
Till, every former note and comment known,
They marked the spacious margin with their own ;
Minute corrections proved their studious care ;
The little index, pointing, told us where ;
And many an emendation showed the age
Looked far beyond the rubric title-page.

Our nicer palates lighter labours seek,
Cloyed with a folio-Number once a week ;
Bibles, with cuts and comments, thus go down :
E'en light Voltaire is numbered through the town :
Thus physic flies abroad, and thus the law,
From men of study, and from men of straw ;
Abstracts, abridgments, please the fickle times,
Pamphlets and plays, and politics and rhymes :
But though to write be now a task of ease,
The task is hard by manly arts to please,
When all our weakness is exposed to view
And half our judges are our rivals too.

Amid these works, on which the eager eye
Delights to fix, or glides reluctant by,

When all combined, their decent pomp display,
Where shall we first our early offering pay?

　To thee Divinity! to thee, the light
And guide of mortals, through their mental night;
By whom we learn our hopes and fears to guide;
To bear with pain, and to contend with pride;
When grieved, to pray; when injured to forgive;
And with the world in charity to live.
　Not truths like these inspired that numerous
　　race,
Whose pious labours fill this ample space;
But questions nice, where doubt on doubt arose,
Awaked to war the long-contending foes.
For dubious meanings, learned polemics strove,
And wars on faith prevented works of love;
The brands of discord far around were hurled,
And holy wrath inflamed a sinful world:
Dull though impatient, peevish though devout,
With wit disgusting, and despised without;
Saints in design, in execution men,
Peace in their looks, and vengeance in their pen.
　Methinks I see, and sicken at the sight,
Spirits of spleen from yonder pile alight;
Spirits who prompted every damning page,
With pontiff pride and still-increasing rage:
Lo! how they stretch their gloomy wings around,
And lash with furious strokes the trembling ground!
They pray, they fight, they murder, and they weep,—
Wolves in their vengeance, in their manners sheep;
Too well they act the prophet's fatal part,
Denouncing evil with a zealous heart;
And each, like Jonah, is displeased if God
Repent His anger, or withhold His rod.
　But here the dormant fury rests unsought,
And Zeal sleeps soundly by the foes she fought;

Here all the rage of controversy ends,
And rival zealots rest like bosom-friends:
An Athanasian here, in deep repose,
Sleeps with the fiercest of his Arian foes;
Socinians here with Calvinists abide,
And thin partitions angry chiefs divide;
Here wily Jesuists simple Quakers meet,
And Bellarmine has rest at Luther's feet.
Great authors, for the Church's glory fired,
Are for the Church's peace to rest retired;
And close beside, a mystic, maudlin race,
Lie " Crumbs of Comfort for the Babes of Grace."

   Against her foes Religion well defends
Her sacred truths, but often fears her friends;
If learned, their pride, if weak, their zeal she dreads,
And their hearts' weakness, who have soundest heads:
But most she fears the controversial pen,
The holy strife of disputatious men;
Who the blest Gospel's peaceful page explore,
Only to fight against its precepts more.

   Near to these seats behold yon slender frames,
All closely filled and marked with modern names;
Where no fair science ever shows her face,
Few sparks of genius, and no spark of grace;
There sceptics rest, a still-increasing throng,
And stretch their widening wings ten thousand strong,
Some in close fight their dubious claims maintain:
Some skirmish lightly, fly, and fight again;
Coldly profane, and impiously gay,
Their end the same, though various in their way,

   When first Religion came to bless the land,
Her friends were then a firm believing band;
To doubt was then to plunge in guilt extreme,
And all was gospel that a monk could dream;
Insulted Reason fled the grov'ling soul,
For fear to guide, and visions to control:

But now, when Reason has assumed her throne,
She, in her turn, demands to reign alone ;
Rejecting all that lies beyond her view,
And, being judge, will be a witness too :
Insulted Faith then leaves the doubtful mind,
To seek for truth, without a power to find :
Ah ! when will both in friendly beams unite,
And pour on erring man resistless light ?

Next to the seats, well stored with works divine,
An ample space, Philosophy ! is thine ;
Our reason's guide, by whose assisting light
We trace the moral bounds of wrong and right ;
Our guide through Nature, from the sterile clay,
To the bright orbs of yon celestial way !
'Tis thine, the great, the golden chain to trace,
Which runs through all, connecting race with
        race ;
Save where those puzzling, stubborn links remain,
Which thy inferior light pursues in vain :
    How vice and virtue in the soul contend ;
How widely differ, yet how nearly blend ;
What various passions war on either part,
And now confirm, now melt the yielding heart :
How Fancy loves around the world to stray,
While Judgment slowly picks his sober way ;
The stores of memory, and the flights sublime
Of genius, bound by neither space nor time ;
All these divine Philosophy explores,
Till, lost in awe, she wonders and adores,
    From these, descending to the earth, she turns,
And matter, in its various form, discerns ;
She parts the beamy light with skill profound,
Metes the thin air, and weighs the flying sound ;
'Tis hers the lightning from the clouds to call,
And teach the fiery mischief where to fall.

Yet more her volumes teach—on these we look
As abstracts drawn from Nature's larger book:
Here, first described, the torpid earth appears,
And next, the vegetable robe it wears;
Where flowery tribes, in valleys, fields, and groves,
Nurse the still flame, and feed the silent loves;
Loves, where no grief, nor joy, nor bliss, nor pain,
Warm the glad heart or vex the labouring brain;
But as the green blood moves along the blade,
The bed of Flora on the branch is made;
Where, without passion, love instinctive lives,
And gives new life, unconscious that it gives.
Advancing still in Nature's maze, we trace,
In dens and burning plains, her savage race;
With those tame tribes who on their lord attend,
And find, in man, a master and a friend;
Man crowns the scene, a world of wonders new,
A moral world, that well demands our view.

This world is here; for, of more lofty kind,
These neighbouring volumes reason on the mind;
They paint the state of man ere yet endued
With knowledge;—man, poor, ignorant, and rude;
Then, as his state improves, their pages swell,
And all its cares, and all its comforts, tell:
Here we behold our inexperience buys,
At little price, the wisdom of the wise;
Without the troubles of an active state,
Without the cares and dangers of the great,
Without the miseries of the poor, we know
What wisdom, wealth, and poverty bestow;
We see how reason calms the raging mind,
And how contending passions urge mankind:
Some, won by virtue, glow with sacred fire;
Some, lured by vice, indulge the low desire;
Whilst others, won by either, now pursue
The guilty chase, now keep the good in view;

For ever wretched, with themselves at strife,
They lead a puzzled, vexed, uncertain life;
For transient vice bequeaths a lingering pain,
Which transient virtue seeks to cure in vain.
    Whilst thus engaged, high views enlarge the
      soul,
New interests draw, new principles control:
Nor thus the soul alone resigns her grief;
But here the tortured body finds relief;
For see where yonder sage Arachnè shapes
Her subtile gin, that not a fly escapes!
There Physic fills the space, and far around,
Pile above pile her learned works abound:
Glorious their aim—to ease the labouring heart;
To war with death, and stop his flying dart;
To trace the source whence the fierce contest grew,
And life's short lease on easier terms renew;
To calm the frenzy of the burning brain;
To heal the tortures of imploring pain;
Or, when more powerful ills all efforts brave,
To ease the victim no device can save,
And smooth the stormy passage to the grave.
    But man, who knows no good unmixed and pure,
Oft finds a poison where he sought a cure;
For grave deceivers lodge their labours here,
And cloud the science they pretend to clear;
Scourges for sin, the solemn tribe are sent;
Like fire and storms, they call us to repent;
But storms subside, and fires forget to rage.
These are eternal scourges of the age:
'Tis not enough that each terrific hand
Spreads desolation round a guilty land;
But trained to ill, and hardened by its crimes,
Their pen relentless kills through future times.
    Say, ye, who search these records of the dead—
Who read huge works, to boast what ye have read;

Can all the real knowledge ye possess,
Or those—if such there are—who more than guess,
Atone for each impostor's wild mistakes,
And mend the blunders pride or folly makes?
   What thought so wild, what airy dream so light,
That will not prompt a theorist to write?
What art so prevalent, what proof so strong,
That will convince him his attempt is wrong?
One in the solids finds each lurking ill,
Nor grants the passive fluids power to kill;
A learned friend some subtler reason brings,
Absolves the channels, but condemns their springs;
The subtile nerves, that shun the doctor's eye,
Escape no more his subtler theory;
The vital heat, that warms the labouring heart,
Lends a fair system to these sons of art;
The vital air, a pure and subtile stream,
Serves a foundation for an airy scheme,
Assists the doctor, and supports his dream.
Some have their favourite ills, and each disease
Is but a younger branch that kills from these;
One to the gout contracts all human pain;
He views it raging in the frantic brain;
Finds it in fevers all his efforts mar,
And sees it lurking in the cold catarrh:
Bilious by some, by others nervous seen,
Rage the fantastic demons of the spleen;
And every symptom of the strange disease
With every system of the sage agrees.
   Ye frigid tribe, on whom I wasted long
The tedious hours, and ne'er indulged in song;
Ye first seducers of my easy heart,
Who promised knowledge ye could not impart;
Ye dull deluders, truth's destructive foes;
Ye sons of fiction, clad in stupid prose;
Ye treacherous leaders, who, yourselves in doubt,
Light up false fires, and send us far about;

Still may yon spider round your pages spin,
Subtile and slow, her emblematic gin !
Buried in dust and lost in silence, dwell,
Most potent, grave, and reverend friends—farewell !

Near these, and where the setting sun displays,
Through the dim window, his departing rays,
And gilds yon columns, there, on either side,
The huge abridgments of the Law abide ;
Fruitful as vice the dread correctors stand,
And spread their guardian terrors round the land ;
Yet, as the best that human care can do,
Is mixed with error, oft with evil too,
Skilled in deceit, and practised to evade,
Knaves stand secure, for whom these laws were made,
And justice vainly each expedient tries,
While art eludes it, or while power defies.
" Ah ! happy age," the youthful poet sings,
" When the free nations knew not laws nor kings ;
When all were blest to share a common store,
And none were proud of wealth, for none were poor ;
No wars nor tumults vexed each still domain,
No thirst of empire, no desire of gain :
No proud great man, nor one who would be great,
Drove modest merit from its proper state ;
Nor into distant climes would Avarice roam,
To fetch delights for Luxury at home :
Bound by no ties which kept the soul in awe,
They dwelt at liberty, and love was law !"
" Mistaken youth ! each nation first was rude,
Each man a cheerless son of solitude,
To whom no joys of social life were known,
None felt a care that was not all his own ;
Or in some languid clime his abject soul
Bowed to a little tyrant's stern control ;
A slave, with slaves his monarch's throne he raised,
And in rude song his ruder idol praised :

The meaner cares of life were all he knew ;
Bounded his pleasures, and his wishes few ;
But when by slow degrees the Arts arose,
And Science wakened from her long repose ;
When Commerce, rising from the bed of ease,
Ran round the land, and pointed to the seas :
When Emulation, born with jealous eye,
And Avarice, lent their spurs to industry ;
Then one by one the numerous laws were made,
Those to control, and these to succour trade ;
To curb the insolence of rude command,
To snatch the victim from the usurer's hand ;
To awe the bold, to yield the wronged redress,
And feed the poor with Luxury's excess."
Like some vast flood, unbounded, fierce, and strong,
His nature leads ungoverned man along ;
Like mighty bulwarks made to stem that tide,
The laws are formed, and placed on every side ;
Whene'er it breaks the bounds by these decreed,
New statutes rise, and stronger laws succeed ;
More and more gentle grows the dying stream,
More and more strong the rising bulwarks seem ;
Till, like a miner working sure and slow,
Luxury creeps on, and ruins all below ;
The basis sinks, the ample piles decay ;
The stately fabric shakes and falls away ;
Primeval want and ignorance come on,
But Freedom, that exalts the savage state, is gone.

Next, History ranks :—there full in front she lies,
And every nation her dread tale supplies ;
Yet History has her doubts, and every age
With sceptic queries marks the passing page ;
Records of old nor later date are clear,
Too distant those, and these are placed too near ;
There time conceals the objects from our view,
Here our own passions and a writer's too :

Yet, in these volumes, see how states arose!
Guarded by virtue from surrounding foes;
Their virtue lost, and of their triumphs vain,
Lo! how they sunk to slavery again!
Satiate with power, of fame and wealth possessed,
A nation grows too glorious to be blest;
Conspicious made, she stands the mark of all,
And foes join foes to triumph in her fall.

Thus speaks the page that paints ambition's race,
The monarch's pride, his glory, his disgrace;
The headlong course, that madd'ning heroes run,
How soon triumphant, and how soon undone;
How slaves, turned tyrants, offer crowns to sale,
And each fall'n nation's melancholy tale.

Lo! where of late the Book of Martyrs stood,
Old pious tracts, and Bibles bound in wood;
There, such the taste of our degenerate age,
Stand the profane delusions of the Stage:
Yet virtue owns the Tragic Muse a friend,
Fable her means, morality her end;
For this she rules all passions in their turns,
And now the bosom bleeds, and now it burns;
Pity with weeping eye surveys her bowl,
Her anger swells, her terror chills the soul:
She makes the vile to virtue yield applause,
And own her sceptre while they break her laws;
For vice in others is abhorred of all,
And villains triumph when the worthless fall.

Not thus her sister Comedy prevails,
Who shoots at Folly, for her arrow fails;
Folly, by Dulness armed, eludes the wound,
And harmless sees the feathered shafts rebound;
Unhurt she stands, applauds the archer's skill,
Laughs at her malice, and is Folly still.
Yet well the Muse portrays, in fancied scenes,
What pride will stoop to, what profession means;

How formal fools the farce of state applaud,
How caution watches at the lips of fraud ;
The wordy variance of domestic life ;
The tyrant husband, the retorting wife ;
The snares for innocence, the lie of trade,
And the smooth tongue's habitual masquerade.
 With her the Virtues too obtain a place,
Each gentle passion, each becoming grace ;
The social joy in life's securer road,
Its easy pleasure, its substantial good ;
The happy thought that conscious virtue gives,
And all that ought to live, and all that lives.

 But who are these ? Methinks a noble mien
And awful grandeur in their form are seen,
Now in disgrace : what though by time is spread
Polluting dust o'er every reverend head :
What though beneath yon gilded tribe they lie,
And dull observers pass insulting by :
Forbid it shame, forbid it decent awe,
What seems so grave, should no attention draw !
Come, let us then with reverend step advance,
And greet—the ancient worthies of Romance.
 Hence, ye profane ! I feel a former dread,
A thousand visions float around my head :
Hark ! hollow blasts through empty courts resound,
And shadowy forms with staring eyes stalk round :
See ! moats and bridges, walls and castles rise,
Ghosts, fairies, demons, dance before our eyes :
Lo ! magic verse inscribed on golden gate,
And bloody hand that beckons on to fate !
" And who art thou, thou little page, unfold ?
Say, doth thy lord my Claribel withhold ?
Go, tell him straight, Sir Knight, thou must resign
The captive queen ; for Claribel is mine."
Away he flies ; and now for bloody deeds,
Black suits of armour, masks, and foaming steeds :

The giant falls; his recreant throat I seize,
And from his corslet take the massy keys:
Dukes, lords, and knights in long procession move,
Released from bondage with my virgin love:
She comes! she comes! in all the charms of youth,
Unequalled love, and unsuspected truth!
    Ah! happy he who thus, in magic themes,
O'er worlds bewitched, in early rapture dreams,
Where wild Enchantment waves her potent wand,
And Fancy's beauties fill her fairy land;
Where doubtful objects strange desires excite,
And Fear and Ignorance afford delight!
    But lost, for ever lost, to me these joys,
Which Reason scatters, and which Time destroys;
Too dearly bought: maturer judgment calls
My busied mind from tales and madrigals;
My doughty giants all are slain or fled,
And all my knights—blue, green, and yellow—
    dead!
No more the midnight fairy tribe I view,
All in the merry moonshine tippling dew;
E'en the last lingering fiction of the brain,
The churchyard ghost, is now at rest again;
And all these wayward wanderings of my youth
Fly Reason's power, and shun the light of Truth.
    With Fiction then does real joy reside,
And is our reason the delusive guide?
Is it then right to dream the syrens sing?
Or mount enraptured on the dragon's wing?
No; 'tis the infant mind, to care unknown,
That makes th' imagined paradise its own;
Soon as reflections in the bosom rise,
Light slumbers vanish from the clouded eyes:
The tear and smile, that once together rose,
Are then divorced: the head and heart are foes:
Enchantment bows to Wisdom's serious plan,
And Pain and Prudence make and mar the man.

While thus, of power and fancied empire vain,
With various thoughts my mind I entertain;
While books, my slaves, with tyrant hand I seize,
Pleased with the pride that will not let them please,
Sudden I find terrific thoughts arise,
And sympathetic sorrow fills my eyes;
For, lo! while yet my heart admits the wound,
I see the Critic army ranged around.

 Foes to our race! if ever ye have known
A father's fears for offspring of your own;
If ever, smiling o'er a lucky line,
Ye thought the sudden sentiment divine,
Then paused and doubted, and then, tired of doubt,
With rage as sudden dashed the stanza out;—
If, after fearing much and pausing long,
Ye ventured on the world your laboured song,
And from the crusty critics of those days
Implored the feeble tribute of their praise;
Remember now the fears that moved you then,
And, spite of truth, let mercy guide your pen.

 What vent'rous race are ours! what mighty foes
Lie waiting all around them to oppose!
What treacherous friends betray them to the fight!
What dangers threaten them!— yet still they write:
A hapless tribe! to every evil born,
Whom villains hate, and fools affect to scorn:
Strangers they come, amid a world of woe,
And taste the largest portion ere they go.

 Pensive I spoke, and cast mine eyes around;
The roof, methought, returned a solemn sound;
Each column seemed to shake, and clouds, like smoke,
From dusty piles and ancient volumes broke;
Gathering above, like mists condensed they seem,
Exhaled in summer from the rushy stream;
Like flowing robes they now appear, and twine
Round the large members of a form divine;

His silver beard, that swept his aged breast,
His piercing eye, that inward light expressed,
Were seen—but clouds and darkness veiled the rest.
Fear chilled my heart: to one of mortal race,
How awful seemed the genius of the place!
So in Cimmerian shores, Ulysses saw
His parent-shade, and shrunk in pious awe;
Like him I stood, and wrapt in thought profound,
When from the pitying power broke forth a solemn
    sound:—

  " Care lives with all; no rules, no precepts save
The wise from woe, no fortitude the brave;
Grief is to man as certain as the grave:
Tempests and storms in life's whole progress rise,
And hope shines dimly through o'erclouded skies;
Some drops of comfort on the favoured fall,
But showers of sorrow are the lot of all:
Partial to talents, then, shall Heaven withdraw
Th' afflicting rod, or break the general law?
Shall he who soars, inspired by loftier views,
Life's little cares and little pains refuse?
Shall he not rather feel a double share
Of mortal woe, when doubly armed to bear?
  " Hard is his fate who builds his peace of mind
On the precarious mercy of mankind;
Who hopes for wild and visionary things,
And mounts o'er unknown seas with vent'rous wings:
But as, of various evils that befall
The human race, some portion goes to all;
To him perhaps the milder lot's assigned,
Who feels his consolation in his mind;
And, locked within his bosom, bears about
A mental charm for every care without.
E'en in the pangs of each domestic grief,
Or health or vigorous hope affords relief;

And every wound the tortured bosom feels,
Or virtue bears, or some preserver heals;
Some generous friend of ample power possessed;
Some feeling heart, that bleeds for the distressed;
Some breast that glows with virtues all divine;
Some noble Rutland, misery's friend and thine.
   " Nor say, the Muse's song, the Poet's pen,
Merit the scorn they meet from little men.
With cautious freedom if the numbers flow,
Not wildly high, nor pitifully low;
If vice alone their honest aims oppose,
Why so ashamed their friends, so loud their foes?
Happy for men in every age and clime,
If all the sons of vision dealt in rhyme.
Go on, then, Son of Vision! still pursue
Thy airy dreams; the world is dreaming too.
Ambition's lofty views, the pomp of state,
The pride of wealth, the splendour of the great,
Stripped of their mask, their cares and troubles known,
Are visions far less happy than thy own:
Go on! and, while the sons of care complain,
Be wisely gay and innocently vain;
While serious souls are by their fears undone,
Blow sportive bladders in the beamy sun,
And call them worlds! and bid the greatest show
More radiant colours in their worlds below:
Then, as they break, the slaves of care reprove,
And tell them, such are all the toys they love."

PRINTED BY BALLANTYNE, HANSON AND CO.
LONDON AND EDINBURGH

HOMER'S ILIAD

WITH THE PLAYS OF

ÆSCHYLUS AND SOPHOCLES

[B.C. . . . 800 . . . TO B.C. 405]

WITH INTRODUCTIONS BY HENRY MORLEY

LL.D., PROFESSOR OF ENGLISH LITERATURE AT
UNIVERSITY COLLEGE, LONDON

LONDON
GEORGE ROUTLEDGE AND SONS
BROADWAY, LUDGATE HILL
GLASGOW AND NEW YORK
1888

THE PLAYS

OF

EURIPIDES

[B.C. 455 TO B.C. 408]

WITH INTRODUCTIONS BY HENRY MORLEY

LL.D., PROFESSOR OF ENGLISH LITERATURE AT
UNIVERSITY COLLEGE, LONDON

LONDON

GEORGE ROUTLEDGE AND SONS

BROADWAY, LUDGATE HILL

GLASGOW AND NEW YORK

1888

THREE PLAYS OF

ARISTOPHANES

THE POLITICS OF ARISTOTLE

VIRGIL'S ÆNEID

[B.C. 425 TO B.C. 19]

WITH INTRODUCTIONS BY HENRY MORLEY
LL.D., PROFESSOR OF ENGLISH LITERATURE AT
UNIVERSITY COLLEGE, LONDON

LONDON
GEORGE ROUTLEDGE AND SONS
BROADWAY, LUDGATE HILL
GLASGOW AND NEW YORK
1888

HITOPADESA

MEDIÆVAL TALES

THE CHRONICLE OF THE CID

[A.D. . . . 1100 TO A.D. 1473]

WITH INTRODUCTIONS BY HENRY MORLEY
LL.D., PROFESSOR OF ENGLISH LITERATURE AT
UNIVERSITY COLLEGE, LONDON

LONDON
GEORGE ROUTLEDGE AND SONS
BROADWAY, LUDGATE HILL
GLASGOW AND NEW YORK
1888

THE DIVINE COMEDY AND THE BANQUET

OF

DANTE

BOCCACCIO'S DECAMERON

[A.D. 1300 TO A.D. 1350]

WITH INTRODUCTIONS BY HENRY MORLEY
LL.D., PROFESSOR OF ENGLISH LITERATURE AT
UNIVERSITY COLLEGE, LONDON

LONDON
GEORGE ROUTLEDGE AND SONS
BROADWAY, LUDGATE HILL
GLASGOW AND NEW YORK
1888

THOMAS À KEMPIS

CAVENDISH'S
LIFE OF WOLSEY

AND

IDEAL COMMONWEALTHS

[A.D. 1425 TO A.D. 1630]

WITH INTRODUCTIONS BY HENRY MORLEY

LL.D., PROFESSOR OF ENGLISH LITERATURE AT
UNIVERSITY COLLEGE, LONDON

LONDON
GEORGE ROUTLEDGE AND SONS
BROADWAY, LUDGATE HILL
GLASGOW AND NEW YORK
1888

CONTENTS.

THE PRINCE

GARGANTUA AND PANTAGRUEL

MACHIAVELLI

RABELAIS

[A.D. 1513 TO A.D. 1553]

WITH INTRODUCTIONS BY HENRY MORLEY

LL.D , PROFESSOR OF ENGLISH LITERATURE AT
UNIVERSITY COLLEGE, LONDON

LONDON
GEORGE ROUTLEDGE AND SONS
BROADWAY, LUDGATE HILL
GLASGOW AND NEW YORK
1888

THE TWO PARTS OF

GOETHE'S FAUST

(WITH MARLOWE'S FAUSTUS)

SCHILLER'S

POEMS AND BALLADS

[A.D. 1780 TO A.D. 1831]

WITH INTRODUCTIONS BY HENRY MORLEY
LL.D., PROFESSOR OF ENGLISH LITERATURE AT
UNIVERSITY COLLEGE, LONDON

LONDON
GEORGE ROUTLEDGE AND SONS
BROADWAY, LUDGATE HILL
GLASGOW AND NEW YORK
1888

TALES OF TERROR AND WONDER
M. G. LEWIS

CONFESSIONS
OF AN
ENGLISH OPIUM-EATER
THOMAS DE QUINCEY

ESSAYS OF ELIA
CHARLES LAMB

[A.D. 1800 TO A.D. 1824]

WITH INTRODUCTIONS BY HENRY MORLEY

LL.D., PROFESSOR OF ENGLISH LITERATURE AT
UNIVERSITY COLLEGE, LONDON

LONDON
GEORGE ROUTLEDGE AND SONS
BROADWAY, LUDGATE HILL
GLASGOW AND NEW YORK
1888